JEREMY CATTO

A Portrait of the
Quintessential Oxford Don

JEREMY CATTO

A Portrait of the Quintessential Oxford Don

DAVID VAIANI

with a Foreword by
Sir Alan Duncan

UNICORN

Published in 2024 by Unicorn,
an imprint of Unicorn Publishing Group
Charleston Studio
Meadow Business Centre
Lewes BN8 5RW
www.unicornpublishing.org

Every effort has been made to trace copyright holders
and to obtain their permission for the use of copyrighted
material. The publisher apologises for any errors or
omissions and would be grateful to be notified of any
corrections that should be incorporated in future reprints
or editions of this book.

ISBN 978-1-916846-41-8

10 9 8 7 6 5 4 3 2 1

Typeset by Matthew Wilson

Printed in Malta by Gutenberg Press

Contents

Foreword

by Sir Alan Duncan

(First produced in The Spectator, *June 2006)*

SIR JOHN BETJEMAN GRIPPED THE SWORD AND, WITH GREAT GUSTO, sliced through the marzipan towers of Battersea power station. The party, nearly 50 years ago, was for the launch of 'Temples of Power', Glynn Boyd Harte's delicious compendium of unusual industrial paintings.

Such memorable occasions were not so unusual in the life of Jeremy Catto. He was the quintessential Oxford don – his portrait by Boyd Harte shows him in black tie and plimsolls,[i] with his left foot shooting out of the frame. I couldn't detect Jeremy anywhere in his friend Alan Hollinghurst's novels, but if one were to devour C.P. Snow, Goodbye Mr Chips and Porterhouse Blue, there was a smattering of Catto in each.

In 2006 the cruel dictates of age forced him to retire from Oriel College. Oxford undergraduates, past and present, wanted to storm the Bodleian to prevent it. With university lecturers having so recently threatened to strike ('Not so much red brick as breeze block', some might say) and with even Oxbridge becoming more uniform and systematised, the example of Jeremy Catto remains as a powerful antidote to the modern transformation of our universities. Some dons become pundits and take to television; others forsake collegiate life and bicycle home

---

i These were in fact brown and white shoes, owned by John Wolfe, which were once popular in Chicago.

every evening to north Oxford. Jeremy Catto, in contrast, was the focal point of college life and devoted everything to the pastoral care of his charges. Rather like Fagin to the Artful Dodger, a tutorial might have ended with 'Now shut up and drink your gin.'

'Uncle Thomas' was governor of the Bank of England and 'Cousin Stephen' was a scion of Morgan Grenfell. Jeremy, on the other hand, enjoyed no such riches. His father had for a time managed a rubber plantation in Malaya, and his schooling in Newcastle, where he befriended the young Bryan Ferry, took him by sheer merit to Balliol. His contemporaries included Chris Patten, now Oxford's Chancellor, whose time in the Cabinet prompted many a Cattoesque quip about the lack of spine around the Great Lady.

Anyone wanting to read mediaeval history naturally gravitated to Oriel. The subject came alive in Catto's tutorials and no undergraduate emerged from three years there unappreciative of what it means to know how to think. The first two volumes of the mammoth History of the University of Oxford bear his name, and his lasting friendship with the late Hugh Trevor-Roper saw a powerful, sometimes hilarious axis in the incessant scheming of university politics.

Jeremy embodied the best virtues of the best teacher. He delighted in quoting Harold Macmillan, who said, 'All Oxford need teach you is to know when someone is talking rot'. His approach was one of profound intellectual rigour combined with a broader appreciation of society, conversation and personality. 'The best bankers are historians, not economists. They know how to think strategically.'

Thus Jeremy Catto was always a constant influence in other parts of university life. As a senior officer of the Oxford Union for 30 years he steered countless ambitious students to greater things. 'Well, Alan. I've pointed out to William Hague here that Pitt was already prime minister by 21.' 'Thank you — and bugger Pitt.'

Those who enjoyed drinking claret and hearing a weekly paper from one of their number would be invited to join the Canning. It was entirely natural that it would continue in Jeremy's rooms late into the evening, rarely without some former student, now a figure of great influence somewhere, phoning for a chat above the din.

His network of friends was unbeatable, both for its variety and for its affectionate loyalty. One such was Sir David Manning, our man in Washington, a former pupil whose career Jeremy followed with growing delight. 'I've stayed in every embassy he's ever been posted to.

I like it when my pupils run the world.' Twenty years ago, on a flight to Singapore to visit another, he caused consternation by changing into his pyjamas. 'But it's bedtime....'

Never censorious of anyone's politics, he took pleasure in everyone's success. Where so many of the Left will sneeringly put down a youngster whose politics they don't share, such an attitude was unthinkable to Catto. 'Now, I hope you're never rude across the Chamber to that nice Paul Murphy.' A Labour MP he may be, but no one may insult an Oriel man.

There were limits to his talents. He couldn't sing, and if 'donnish' can mean 'erratic', then it accurately described his driving. Only through Jeremy could one make a new friend while suppressing giggles in chapel during his rendition of 'O God, our help in ages past'.

Whether he was at high table, in the Garrick or in the Greek taverna in Summertown, he was a master of conversation. 'Remember — all white wine is non-alcoholic.' His private language was like a passport to humour for all who now adopt it. 'Ah! You wicked old thing. What deep gigglette and shriekino.'

If there are no more dons like Jeremy Catto, where are our universities heading? The insatiable thirst for firsts risks narrowing the purpose and benefits of a university education. Too many professors and tutors look on extracurricular activity with undisguised scorn. But a university education should be the most potent of all civilising experiences. Library slaves who know little else of the world will not make their best contribution to its improvement. University life is not just a knowledge machine: it should build characters and confident opinions.

If any university, especially Oxford, intends to draw on the financial generosity of its alumni, it will need to pay careful attention to what they think of the institution they once attended. Oriel's successful endowments over the last few years were in no small part down to the admiration donors had for Catto.

Jeremy Catto embodied the true idea of a university. His retirement in 2006 marked the end of one of the most constant influences in Oxford life. It should also have marked the start of some serious questioning about what an Oxford education — or one at any university — should entail. His many admirers are a worldly bunch. When they gathered in college to honour him at the end of June 2006, I would not have liked to have been the Dean who had to contain their unrestrained cheers for this don of all dons.

Preface

'Just be aware that the old man will fall asleep during your interview. He may remain asleep for quite some time, but don't let that put you off. His questions, when he wakes up, will be razor sharp, and you'd better be ready for them. Good luck!' It was unclear to the nervous young man, who had barely slept a wink the night before, whether these hurriedly delivered words of advice were meant to help or hinder his chances of success. But before he even had time to consider this thought, he was ushered into a warm and dimly lit, book-lined study for an interview that would determine whether he was going to secure a place at Oxford University. It was the autumn of the year 2000, and the interview took place in an ancient quadrangle tucked alongside the High Street in the very heart of the city. The nervous young man, as you will have guessed by now, dear reader, was the author of this book. The man who was about to interview my younger self for a place to read modern history at Oriel College, and who would go on to change my life in ways that I would not fully appreciate until many years later, was Jeremy Catto, the subject of this book.

The genesis of this book can be found in my desire to celebrate the remarkable life of a fascinating, generous, paradoxical, witty and eccentric man, whose story, I felt, deserved exposure to a wider audience. Catto was a history don at Oriel College, Oxford for the best part of forty years until his retirement in 2006. A noted scholar and a very fine teacher, he was the quintessential Oxford don, who also seemed to know everyone and cultivated an extraordinary network that included politicians, diplomats, judges, spies, artists, writers, members of the royal family, and even a few rock stars. As a character, he provided a seemingly direct link to legendary Oxford figures of the past, such as John Sparrow, Hugh Trevor-Roper, and Maurice Bowra, the don friend of Evelyn Waugh who, according to some, provided the inspiration for Mr Samgrass, the fictional country house don in Waugh's *Brideshead Revisited*. But Catto was no mere caricature. His influence on the people he met throughout his life was profound and, without perhaps realising it at the time, hundreds of men and women over the course of four decades had their minds and characters shaped by him. His death in the summer of 2018 marked the end of an era in British academic life.

The backdrop to the book is the University of Oxford, with all the long history and rich tradition commonly associated with that ancient seat of learning. Catto's time at the university saw some very significant changes – from the expansion of student numbers and the admission of women to his own college, to changes to funding and teaching and, of course, growing pressure from beyond the university's walls to make Oxford more socially inclusive by admitting more candidates from state-school backgrounds. As well as being a portrait of the quintessential Oxford don, therefore, the book also tells the story of an Oxford that, even if it does still exist in some form, has largely vanished to become little more than a distant memory. What makes Catto a central character in this story of change is that, far from being a reactionary, he in fact sought to accommodate changes that were in many ways inevitable, whilst continuing to represent the values, attitudes and traditions that had held sway when he himself had been an undergraduate at Balliol College in the late 1950s. In that sense, as well as being a conventional biography, the book is also intended to provide a vivid insight into a fascinating slice of cultural history without, I hope, descending into too much nostalgia for the past.

Finally, by paying tribute to a truly inspirational teacher, this book attempts to examine many modern educational orthodoxies and seeks to record how the world of education has changed over the past fifty years. And there is much that has changed: Teachers and lecturers operate today in a depressing world of spreadsheets, assessment data and safeguarding guidelines, and they often find themselves drowning in a sea of impenetrable jargon. The guiding principle is often a rigidly utilitarian one, based on the idea that everything that has some value must be measured in a numerical and pseudo-scientific manner. As a consequence, there is a sense that schools and universities are factories

whose sole purpose, in the immediate term, is to prepare students for
their exams and, in the longer term, to produce men and women who,
like cogs in a machine, will slot neatly into the country's economic
system. The result of this rather arid approach is that, all too often, we
lose sight of what really matters in education. Catto, by contrast, had
no time for jargon, never thought of his students as data points, and
is unlikely ever to have gone near a spreadsheet. His goal instead was
to teach undergraduates how to think, rather than what to think. He
believed that it was his role to cultivate the minds of his students in the
broadest possible sense, and to prepare them not merely for their exams,
but for life itself.

Writing this book has, for so many reasons, been a genuine pleasure,
even though there have also been moments that I have found daunting.
In the end, however, despite wishing to provide a balanced and fair
assessment of his life, I cannot deny that it has been a genuine labour of
love. I both admired and adored Jeremy Catto in equal measure, as did
the vast majority of people who were lucky enough to have known him,
many of whom appear in this book. When I emerged from that interview
in the autumn of the year 2000, I could not have imagined that I would
one day end up as Catto's biographer. After having to endure teaching
me for three years, I suspect that the thought would not have crossed
his mind either. But in any case, even though I have enjoyed the process
tremendously, I have also felt a certain weight of responsibility on my
shoulders, and I can only hope that in laying out his life in this manner I
have done justice to his life and legacy.

One final thought occurs. Catto was, in many ways, a very private
man, and he was adept at compartmentalising his life. Part of me has
wondered, therefore, whether he would have been horrified at the
thought of someone opening up every aspect of his life in such a public
way. On the other hand, in the course of my conversations with his many
friends, colleagues and former students, I have also been reassured that
he would, in all probability, have been tickled by the prospect of someone
writing his biography. If he were still with us today, I can only hope that
he would not be too disappointed with the result.

Introduction

THE TERM 'DON' IS A PECULIAR ONE. ALTHOUGH STILL COMMONLY used for Roman Catholic priests, its origins are ancient, deriving from the Latin term *dominus*, meaning 'master' or 'owner'. At the universities of Oxford and Cambridge, the term is an historical remnant, which reminds its users that both universities were founded as medieval ecclesiastical institutions. In his introductory chapter to *The Dons*, Noel Annan digs a bit deeper to explain what the term actually meant in practical terms:

> Essentially he was a teacher and a fellow of an Oxford or Cambridge college; a teacher who stood in peculiar relation to his pupils in that they came to his rooms individually each week and were taught by him personally. And since these pupils were men of his own college, his first allegiance was not to the university but to his college – to the close-knit society whose members had elected him. To the other fellows he was bound by ties of special loyalty and affection – sometimes, of course, by the no less binding ties of enmity and loathing which led to feuds and vendettas within the society.[1]

In other words, a don was quite simply a teacher who formed part of an academic community, and played an active and indeed leading role within that community. As will be seen in this book, Jeremy Catto came to embody this ideal during his four decades at Oriel College.

How does a person become a don? Annan covers the history of this process in meticulous detail, but suffice it to say that until the early part of the nineteenth century, becoming a don was largely the result of good old-fashioned patronage. As Canon Barnes of Christ Church, Oxford, put it in the 1830s: 'I don't know what we're coming to. I've given studentships to my sons, and to my nephews, and to my nephew's children, and there are no more of my family left. I shall have to give them by merit one of these days.'[2] As the tone of this extract implies, the idea of handing out studentships (i.e. fellowships) on the basis of merit horrified some leading members of the university. But attitudes tend to change, even at Oxford, and by the time Catto arrived back at the university in 1969 to take up a fellowship at Oriel College, positions were being awarded on academic merit rather than family connections. And as a Brackenbury scholar with a formal first-class degree from Balliol and a five-year spell as a lecturer at Durham University, Catto was undoubtedly eminently qualified to secure such a position.

Aside from academic credentials, Catto also possessed those qualities that had characterised dons of an earlier age: he was clubbable, civilised, devoted to his college and, most important of all, he was dedicated to teaching his undergraduates. While more ambitious modern dons periodically appeared on television or wrote scholarly but impenetrable books to cement their reputations as learned men, dons like Catto focused their energies on teaching. This, of course, was the original purpose of these establishments. In the thirteenth century, the term 'universitas' meant the total number of those entitled to teach in the first medieval colleges. In that sense, the first universities were essentially teachers' guilds. Catto understood all of this and was devoted to both his college and to his undergraduates. Moreover, because he was a bachelor don, who had no children of his own, he was able to give a huge amount of time to the undergraduates in his care, often at the expense of writing great books and scholarly articles.

In an attempt to provide a vivid portrait of Catto's life and times, this book consists of three main parts, and follows along both chronological and thematic lines. The first part of the book contains a remarkable array of experiences, and is dedicated to Catto's birth, early life and upbringing in the North East of England. As well as his schooling at the Royal Grammar School in Newcastle, it touches upon his time as an undergraduate at Balliol College, Oxford in the late 1950s, where he came under the influence of the great medievalist scholar Maurice Keen, and developed many of the habits and attitudes that he would carry with him into later life. Included here is an unlikely but highly formative dabbling in student politics, including with the Campaign for Nuclear Disarmament. From there, the story moves on to more personal matters. It was in 1961 that Catto met John Wolfe, an American, studying Philosophy at UCL, and a graduate of Hunter College in New York City, with whom he would be associated for the next fifty-seven years of his life, culminating in a civil partnership. Then, in 1964, he returned to his native North East to take up a lectureship at Durham University. It was here, at a student party, that the future Oxford don would meet a young Bryan Ferry, the future lead vocalist and principal songwriter of the English rock band Roxy Music. On the face of it, these two men had little in common, but they became firm and lifelong friends, another example of the eclectic and wide-ranging group of friends that Catto cultivated throughout his life. The first part ends in Czechoslovakia at the height of the Cold War. The year was 1968 and Catto found himself in the thick of the action during the so-called Prague Spring, when Soviet tanks rolled into the capital to crush the popular uprising of that year.

The second part of the book covers the four decades he spent at Oriel College, Oxford. From 1969 to 2006, Catto was an unmistakable figure at Oriel, and his influence spread far beyond the college's walls and, indeed, beyond the university itself. Whilst this part will follow along broadly chronological lines, it will also run thematically. Specifically, his teaching style and scholarship are covered, as well as his pastoral responsibilities, his attitude towards discipline, and his broader activities across college life, including the thorny questions of admissions and the admission of women to Oriel in 1985. Beyond Oriel, Catto was an active faculty man and served for thirty years as senior librarian at the Oxford Union. He also presided for many years over the Canning Club, a Conservative debating society and breeding ground for future government ministers, senior lawyers and academics. Finally, readers will be provided with a vivid insight into the extraordinary network of contacts he developed across the worlds of academia, politics, diplomacy, the law and royalty. This network was a central part of his persona, and not only was its breadth and quality unmatched in his own time, but it is hard if not impossible to imagine any academic in today's world putting together a similar network.

The third part of the book deals with his retirement, final years and death at the age of seventy-nine. As a devoted college man, there is no doubt that Catto found it hard to sever his ties with Oriel. But he would ultimately find a profound form of domestic contentment at the cottage in Northamptonshire he shared with John Wolfe for the remaining years of his life. In addition, no book of this kind would be complete without casting at least a glance at the subject's private and domestic life. As will become clear, Catto's private life was in many ways a simple extension of his public persona and played an important part in his appeal to a very broad range of people. Finally, an attempt is made at the end to weigh up his overall legacy. When Catto died, his funeral at the Oratory and memorial service at St Mary's Church in Oxford were attended by a host of famous names, as well as many distinguished men and women who had been fortunate enough to have been taught by him. Much like this book, the mood was celebratory in the sense that those gathered at the memorial service were there to commemorate the life and legacy of a remarkable and much-loved man. This book aims to honour that legacy and to share it with a wider audience.

1

Early Life

It's cold up there in Summer,
It's like sitting inside a fridge,
But ah wish ah was on the Quayside,
Looking at the auld Tyne Bridge...
> – 'Home Newcastle', Ronnie Lambert, 1981

'As for the curve of Grey Street, I shall never forget seeing it to perfection,
traffic-less on a misty Sunday morning. Not even Regent Street, even old
Regent Street London, can compare with that descending subtle curve.'
> – Sir John Betjeman

THE CITY OF NEWCASTLE, IN THE COUNTY OF TYNE AND WEAR, SITS
proudly on the northern bank of the River Tyne. It is situated between
Northumberland in the north and County Durham in the south. Today,
some of its streets look tired and dilapidated, but many grand buildings and
monumental thoroughfares indicate that this was once a thriving part of
the country. In its heyday during the late nineteenth century, the city, with
its dominant port, was at the very heart of the Industrial Revolution, and
hosted a series of maritime trades, notably shipbuilding and ship-repair.
Coal was another lucrative source of income for the city, and it was coal
from Newcastle that powered London throughout the period, leading the
capital to become known as the 'Big Smoke'. Not only did coal make many
families in the North East very rich indeed, but it also played a vital role in

Britain's war effort during both world wars. Harold Macmillan, who was the MP for neighbouring Stockton-on-Tees for many years, understood this all too well. In his maiden speech to the House of Lords during the 1984 miners' strike, he argued that the miners were 'the best men in the world, who beat the Kaiser and Hitler's armies and never gave in'.[3] Nothing lasts forever, however, and thanks to those two world wars, as well as the Great Depression, Newcastle specifically – and North East England more broadly – endured a difficult and at times precarious first half of the twentieth century. A disproportionately high number of men from this corner of the country were killed in the First World War and, more significantly for the region's long-term economic prospects, the decline of heavy industries hit this part of the country particularly hard. The town of Jarrow, which lies just across the river from Newcastle, became the symbol of the so-called 'Hungry 30s', when around 200 men marched to London to demonstrate against the devastatingly high levels of poverty and unemployment in the region. Whilst other parts of the country emerged from the Depression and recovered relatively quickly towards the end of the 1930s, the North East was not so fortunate. Indeed, it could be argued that the region has yet to recover fully from this period and is still struggling with its legacy.

It was into this world that Robert Jeremy Adam Inch Catto was born on 27 July 1939. As the son of Archibald Inch Catto, a sometime prosperous businessman who had run a rubber plantation in Malaya for a number of years, the young Jeremy was left relatively untouched by the region's gradual economic decline. Archie, as he was always known to family and friends, was the son of John Catto, a native of Peterhead in Aberdeenshire. Born in 1867, John was the second of six children to Isabella (née Yule), who was widowed in 1879. With six children to support, the family moved to North Shields, where they struggled through difficult and uncertain times. After leaving school, John was apprenticed to the ship-repair company Wallsend Slipway and Engineering Company. He then worked for Cowlairs in Glasgow and spent some time at Anderson's College, which had merged with other institutions in 1887 to become the main component in the Glasgow and West of Scotland Technical College. After that, he went to sea, obtained his first-class Board of Trade certificate, and from 1892 served as a chief engineer for around fifteen years on various vessels, including work with Captain Archibald Inch. Over time, John would mix business with family life, and in 1903 he married Archibald's daughter, Harriet Inch. (That explains the 'Inch' in Jeremy's full name, which was chosen as per the

Scottish tradition of taking a grandmother's maiden name. 'Jeremy' was his mother's choice, 'Robert' was a great-grandfather, and 'Adam' was a great-uncle on his father's side.) After 1907, John went into business as a consulting engineer and ship surveyor, served with the Ministry of Shipping during the First World War, before resuming his practice on the Tyne, where he supervised vessel construction for Silverline and was one of the founders of the Society of Consulting Marine Engineers and Ship Surveyors. The shipping industry had been kind to the family, and as they became increasingly prosperous, they moved from North Shields to a large house in Jesmond, a leafy and comfortable suburb of Newcastle.

Despite having been dealt a reasonably strong hand in life, and notwithstanding some successes along the way, Jeremy's father Archie never fully lived up to his own father's career, and endured something of a chequered life. Born in North Shields in 1905, he was the eldest of three boys, and attended the Royal Grammar School in Newcastle during the First World War. After that, he briefly went to Durham School, but was asked to leave after little more than a year. The circumstances of his enforced departure from Durham were never made entirely clear at the time, but years later it emerged that the young Archie had got himself entangled with the headmaster's daughter. After leaving school, he was employed by the Tyneside shipbuilding firm Swan Hunter as an apprentice engineer, followed by a stint as fourth engineer on two ships until 1927. However, he did not enjoy this line of work and was possibly not ideally suited to it. As a result, he changed career, becoming a rubber planter for Dunlop Plantations Ltd in Malaya. Things initially went well in Malaya, where Archie learnt Malay, derived considerable satisfaction from his work, and was eventually given sole responsibility for the management of a plantation. In 1929, however, disaster struck when the Wall Street Crash caused the company's fortunes to nose-dive, with the result that Archie lost his job. The inevitable slump in rubber sales following the crash proved fatal for the company,[ii] but the fact that Archie also caught a bad case of malaria at the time clearly did not help his cause either. Left with no other choice, he returned home to England and to Newcastle.[iii] After a brief stint selling toffee, he began work for

ii The invention of synthetic rubber around this time also proved fateful.

iii Many years later, and not long before Archie died, Jeremy visited Malaya to see where his father had worked, and took photos to show him back at home. It is not known how Archie reacted to this gesture, but it is reasonable to assume that he must have been touched by his son's sense of fealty.

F. Turnbull and Co. as a sales engineer. It was at this point in his life that his luck finally changed. Fred Turnbull not only provided Archie with some much-needed financial stability, but Archie, like his father before him, also found love in the shape of his employer's daughter.

The Turnbulls were, by all accounts, a lively and very sociable clan. Picnics and tennis parties, with everyone dressed in boaters and immaculate whites, were regular features of life in Monkseaton, where the family lived in a large and very pleasant house for many years. Born in 1868, Frederick Turnbull was the second of four children and was originally from Darlington, but the family eventually moved to Spennymoor near Bishop Auckland in County Durham. His father was a blacksmith, and Frederick followed in his father's footsteps and served his time at Coulson's Engineering Works in Spennymoor, before working for the Weardale Iron and Steel Company as a draughtsman engineer. He met Annie Charlton, daughter of Robert Charlton, who also worked for Weardale, and they married in 1901. Soon after their first child was born, they moved to Newcastle, where Frederick established himself as a consulting mining engineer, before setting up F. Turnbull & Co. in Heaton in 1910. The company specialised in making castings as well as mining machinery, and became so successful that drain covers with the inscription F. Turnbull & Co Heaton Junction can still be seen on the streets of Newcastle to this day. Inevitably, the young Jeremy and his sisters called them 'grandpa's drains'. As a result of this success, the family moved to a larger property near the coast and, in 1933, to an even more impressive house in Jesmond. Sadly for Jeremy, he never really knew his grandfather, as Frederick died of a heart attack in December 1939.

Frederick Turnbull's daughter, who would go on to marry Archie Catto, was called Kathleen Grace Turnbull. Known as Gracie to her friends and family, she was a warm, loving and highly intelligent but also very private woman. She went to Newcastle Central High School for Girls, where she won several prizes, but eventually left school to attend domestic science college instead because she had not achieved the distinction she had hoped to get in her higher certificate. She briefly worked as a teacher, but did not enjoy the work, so with a view to starting a family, the young couple married in 1931. The family then lived in various rented flats until 1937, at which point they moved to a pleasant semi-detached house in Jesmond, near Gracie's sister May and her family. Their first child was born in 1936, a girl by the name of Jane. Then, in 1939, Jeremy came along, followed in 1951 by their last child, Annabel.

A few months after Jeremy was born, Britain found herself at war with Germany. With the outbreak of the Second World War, Archie was called up and served very briefly in the Durham Light Infantry, followed by a spell in the Tyneside Scottish Battalion in Newcastle. However, after no more than a year, he was invalided out from active service due to a suspected bad heart. It is safe to assume that Gracie and the rest of the family were relieved by this development.

Throughout the period of the Second World War, Jeremy enjoyed a happy country life at Barcombe House, Thorngrafton, which he never forgot. He was devoted to his sisters and was, according to them, great fun as a child. The family were joined by the legendary Dora, who had worked as a housekeeper for the Turnbulls for many years. She was adored by the children, who always enjoyed being in her company. Dora loved them in return and always referred playfully to Jeremy as 'little hateful'. In 1945 there was a big change when the family moved to Tynemouth, to a terraced house in Hotspur Street. Jeremy's sister Jane, by now nine years of age, was sent away to Polam Hall, a boarding school in Darlington, before returning for the Christmas holidays to the new house in Tynemouth. Jeremy, meanwhile, was enrolled at Hillbrow preparatory school, which had relocated from Rugby to Featherstone Castle near Haltwhistle in Northumberland in 1940. He was happy there, but life in general was not easy at this time. Like all other families during the war, the Cattos did everything they could to maintain a semblance of normal family life, but it was a struggle. Despite his best efforts, Archie was not the most reliable father or husband, with the result that Gracie was not altogether happy during this period.

The strain of the war and the setbacks Archie had experienced during his career proved to be too much to bear, and he and Gracie divorced in 1953. To the family's surprise, Archie married a much younger woman not long after the divorce but, sadly, that marriage did not last either. Gracie and the children, meanwhile, moved to a semi-detached house in Jesmond, which allowed them to be nearer the rest of her family, including Archie's mother, Harriet. Following the end of his second marriage, Archie's finances went from bad to worse and he could do nothing to stop his various businesses from failing. He lived something of a peripatetic life at this time and moved through a series of addresses in Newcastle. What little money he had left was administered from a trust run by Catto family members, including his brother Bill Catto, a state of affairs which must have been a humiliating experience for him. Archie was, in many ways, a genuinely kind man who meant well, but felt misjudged by others. He was, somewhat paradoxically, a man who could be very generous, but also had traces of selfishness in his character. There is no question that he was devoted to his family, but it is probably also true to say that he married too young and in too much haste, and never really found what he wanted to do with his life. Although he could not be described as a successful businessman, he was proud of some of the mining machinery developments with which he was associated. In later life, he became widely admired for his representation of disabled war pensioners in his work for the British Legion, which was a role he would successfully carry on until he finally retired in his late sixties.

Overall, then, and despite Archie's difficulties, the Cattos were a pretty conventional and relatively prosperous middle-class family. This was to change with the actions of Jeremy's uncle Thomas Catto, who succeeded in elevating the family's fortunes. He had enjoyed what used to be called 'a good war' during the First World War, being involved in purchasing munitions and food in the United States. For this he was appointed Commander of the Order of the British Empire (CBE) in 1918, before being created a baronet in the 1921 Birthday Honours List. By 1936, he was raised to the peerage and became Baron Catto of Cairncatto. His crowning glory, however, would come in 1944. After spending the war years advising the Treasury and thereby recommending himself as a man of genuine ability, he was appointed as Governor of the Bank of England. At the general election in 1945, Clement Attlee and his Labour Party secured a landslide victory over Winston Churchill's exhausted Conservatives. As a result, a large part of Thomas Catto's brief was to oversee the nationalisation of the bank as part of the new Attlee government's socialist agenda.

Although Thomas Catto is scarcely known these days beyond the narrow confines of the world of finance and the Bank of England, it is worth noting that he was viewed as a man of very considerable weight and achievement in his day. When he became Governor in the aftermath of the Second World War, the country's economy was bankrupt. As Clement Attlee said at the time of Catto's retirement, 'no governor has had to face such a difficult world situation',[4] and in the judgment of the historian E.H.H. Green, who wrote Catto's entry for the *Oxford Dictionary of National Biography*, Thomas Catto 'played a significant part in calming some of the turbulence which characterized post-war economic and financial reconstruction'.[5] As for Catto's broader significance, his biographer notes that his career 'formed a bridge between the pre-1914 world, in which informal business contacts and the

JEREMY CATTO: A PORTRAIT OF THE QUINTESSENTIAL OXFORD DON

presence of individual merchant companies, especially from Britain, were responsible for much of the world's commerce, and the post-1945 world, in which international financial institutions and conglomerates, and the emergence of world trading blocs, had become the engine of increasingly complex capital and trade flows and relationships'.[6] His greatest achievement was without question the manner in which he piloted the Labour government's programme for nationalising the Bank of England. As Green notes: 'In the short term his adroit management of bank and City opinion indeed helped to ensure a minimum of public controversy. In the long term, however, his successful attempt to preserve much of the bank's independence was to prove crucial in shaping the future role of the financial sector and the governance of the post-war economy.'[7]

Although he did not know his uncle very well, Jeremy was clearly proud of his achievements and, in later years, a portrait of him would be prominently displayed in his rooms when Jeremy became an Oxford don. It is also apparent that Jeremy inherited some of his uncle's best attributes. In Thomas Catto's entry in the *Oxford Dictionary of National Biography*, he is described in the following manner:

> In appearance Catto was short of stature, with a fresh complexion and clear blue eyes. His open countenance and quiet manner perhaps tended to conceal his shrewdness and skill as a negotiator, so well displayed while he was governor of the bank. If there was occasion for controversy, he avoided a head-on collision, and used his judgement to carry his objective without sacrificing any point of importance. As the head of a large organization, he imposed his will with courtesy and with sensitivity towards his subordinates.[8]

Like his uncle, Jeremy would in later life be known as a shrewd and astute operator in the murky world of Oxford college and university politics; he too was skilled at avoiding 'head-on collisions' and preferred to deploy a more subtle and nuanced approach to achieve his objectives. One of Jeremy's future undergraduates, David Manning, who would go on to reach the pinnacle of the diplomatic profession as Britain's ambassador to the United States, once remarked that in a different life Jeremy would have made an exceptional diplomat himself.[iv]

---

iv Given his connections, Catto could have enjoyed a career in the world of finance, but chose instead to go his own way in the world of ideas.

Having served a full term as governor, Thomas Catto retired from
the post in 1949 (it was customary at the time for governors to retire
once they reached the age of seventy). Sadly, towards the end of his life
he suffered from Parkinson's disease and died in Holmbury St Mary, in
Surrey, in 1959. His only son, Stephen, succeeded to the title. Stephen, or
'Cousin Stephen', as Jeremy always called him in later life, was educated
at Eton and Trinity College, Cambridge, serving in the RAF from
1944–7. Like his father, he worked for Morgan Grenfell and enjoyed
a stellar banking career. The bank was widely viewed at the time as the
most blue-blooded and establishment-minded of the big three firms in
British merchant banking, and Stephen Catto was the very model of
an old-fashioned City banker. One observer described him as a 'gentle,
straightforward and approachable grandee of the old school' – hence the
legendary headline, 'Catto lies doggo',[9] which was frequently used by the
financial newsrooms of the time. But there was an element of dynamism
too, as he was largely responsible for turning the firm from something of
a sleepy giant into a leaner and more competitive outfit. In his obituary,
he was even described as 'one of the great contributors to globalization'.[10]
What was meant by this was that he used his banking skills to enable
the British *News of the World* and *Sun* newspapers to pass into the hands
of the Australian–American Rupert Murdoch, rather than those of
the Czech–British Robert Maxwell. At the time, this was considered a
quite daring and, indeed, controversial move in certain more traditional
quarters. Murdoch, for his part, subsequently said that he would 'always
remember with gratitude and affection what an indispensable guide
he was as we took our first steps into the British market'.[11] He also
described Stephen Catto as 'a good friend and a wise adviser both to me
and to News International over more than 30 years'.[12] Following this
early success, Morgan Grenfell became involved as advisers to Ernest
Saunders of Guinness during its bid for the Scottish Distillers Company.
The dubious shenanigans involved in this led to what became known as
the 'Guinness affair' and the imprisonment of four of those embroiled.
Although Stephen Catto was not personally implicated, the bank had
lost very considerable sums as a result of the affair and, on the strict
advice of the then Chancellor of the Exchequer, Nigel Lawson, he was
elevated to the honorary role of president. The final result of this affair
was the sale of Morgan Grenfell to Deutsche Bank in 1989, which meant
that Catto's bank had the dubious honour of becoming the first major
British merchant bank to lose its independence.

Stephen Catto's parting shot before he would leave the stage came in the House of Lords in October 1999. The issue at stake was the Blair government's plan to expel hereditary peers from the upper house. Having taken his seat for the first time since his father's death in 1959, Lord Catto addressed his fellow peers and initially appeared to back the Blair government's reforms: 'For the last 40 years since my father died, I have considered it morally wrong, purely from accident or birth, to presume to become a member of a legislative body...' However, he then quickly changed tack and declared: 'On the other hand, I strongly support a bicameral system with a small number of representative peers included to maintain and support the monarchy and the great traditions of our country.'[13] Not surprisingly, perhaps, when Lord Catto then put himself up for election as a crossbench representative peer, he failed to convince enough of their lordships and finished seventy-ninth. Stephen Catto married three times and had six children. When he died at his home in London on 3 September 2001, he left an estate valued at over £13 million and was succeeded as third baron by his eldest son, Innes Gordon Catto.[14]

By the time Jeremy had become a don at Oxford, he would rarely refer at any length to his family background, but there were occasional references to 'Uncle Tom' or 'Cousin Stephen', and it is clear that he had fond memories of his upbringing in the North East. Perhaps his reticence was yet another example of his instinctive desire to keep the different strands of his life separate and distinct from one another. Or perhaps he simply came to believe that his earlier life had no great bearing on the person he had become. Whatever the truth of the matter, it is certainly reasonable to say that, despite the kind of difficulties and setbacks that afflict all families at some stage, Jeremy had been afforded a loving and supportive family life, which had provided him with a solid start in life. By the early 1950s, it was time for Jeremy to attend senior school. According to one account, he had tried for a scholarship to Fettes College, the so-called 'Eton of the north', but had deliberately failed it as he did not wish to stray far from home. In any case, Jeremy's time in Newcastle would extend into his adolescent years with his attendance at the city's Royal Grammar School.

2

Novocastrian

'I forgot. He was one of Moises' boys.'
      – George III about Hugh Moises, Headmaster of RGS Newcastle,
1805

'He is utterly reliable of character, of complete integrity and, indeed, is an unusual boy with great charm.'
      – Mr Mitchell, Catto's headmaster at RGS Newcastle, 1957

When Jeremy was getting himself ready to start at the Royal Grammar School (RGS) in Newcastle as a fourteen-year-old boy in September 1953, Britain was standing at a crossroads. King George VI had died on 6 February of the previous year, and was succeeded by his daughter Elizabeth, who would go on to become the country's longest-serving monarch. The news was announced to the boys at the school during a sombre assembly that very morning. But despite the widespread sense of loss experienced by millions up and down the country and around the empire at the time of the king's death, there was also a sense of optimism in the air. Much of this positive mood was the result of the young and beautiful new queen who, even before she ascended to the throne, had pledged to devote her 'whole life whether it be long or short' to the nation's 'service and the service of our great imperial family to which we all belong'.[15] Not long before the coronation in 1953, James Watson and Francis Crick had discovered the structure of the DNA molecule,

25

and this was quickly followed by the exhilarating news of the conquest of Everest by a British expedition. On the sporting front, although the young Jeremy was not a football fan, tens of thousands across the North East would have rejoiced as Newcastle United lifted two of their six FA Cups in this period. In August, the England cricket team defeated Australia to win the Ashes for the first time in nineteen years. The following year, Roger Bannister became the first man to break the four-minute mile during an epoch-defining race at Oxford. A month earlier, wartime rationing came to an end, with meat freely available after fifteen long and hard years. Perhaps not surprisingly, commentators at the time remarked that Britain had entered a great new Elizabethan Age.

RGS Newcastle was founded in 1525 by Thomas Horsley, the Mayor of Newcastle-upon-Tyne, and received its royal foundation by Queen Elizabeth I. Today, it has the distinction of being the city's oldest institution of learning, and although it is now a co-educational school, it was an all-boys school when Jeremy was there as a pupil. For centuries, the school enjoyed a reputation for academic excellence. George III, on reading one of Admiral Collingwood's despatches after the Battle of Trafalgar in 1805, asked how the seaman had learned to write such splendid English. The king answered himself, recalling that, along with Eldon and Stowell, he had been a pupil of Hugh Moises, the headmaster of RGS: 'I forgot. He was one of Moises' boys.'[16]

That tradition of producing bright and articulate young men was still a noted feature of the school by the time Jeremy arrived there in 1953. The school had the status of being a fee-paying direct grant school that offered generous scholarships, which resulted in an intake of bright boys from a diverse set of backgrounds. But however bright they may have been, and despite the opportunities that the school afforded them, it was, in many ways, a difficult and uncertain time for the generation of boys that enrolled at the RGS in the early 1950s. Despite the war having ended in 1945, the legacy of that conflict cast a long shadow. All the boys knew family members who had fought in the war, and a number of the masters had also served their country. As a result, pupils arrived at the school full of the usual mix of excitement and trepidation, but with the added burden of expecting to have to do military service themselves at some stage. In addition, with the Cold War now in full swing, boys at the RGS had to learn to live in a world that was coming to terms with the existence of the atomic bomb. And although it was certainly a more prosperous time than the interwar years, the so-called 'Hungry 30s' were still a topic of conversation at the time. As one contemporary of Jeremy's at school summed up the mood of the time, 'there was a general feeling that the trials of that period had been successfully overcome, but that the new prosperity still felt somewhat precarious'.

By 1956 that sense of precarity came into sharper focus with the Suez Crisis. The event, which saw Britain forced into a humiliating withdrawal from Egypt following considerable diplomatic pressure from the United States, was a formative one for boys of Jeremy's generation. It led to many heated arguments at the RGS and may even have influenced the students' future voting tendencies. As Anthony Tuck, an old boy of the school, who was an almost exact contemporary of Jeremy's and would go on to co-edit the school's history, explained:

> The Suez episode of November 1956…provided those of us who had entered the School in the late 1940s and early 1950s with our first significant political memory…Opinion among both the boys and the staff was bitterly divided, mirroring the division in the nation at large, though I recall that the majority sense amongst the fifth- and sixth-formers was that the whole operation was a mistake. This view brought fierce argument with some members of staff and with the Headmaster. Lesson time was spent discussing the rights and wrongs of the action, and there was an undercurrent of fear that a much wider conflict might result. It also had a long-term effect on the political opinions of that generation: few of them were voters in the 1959 general election, for the age of majority was still 21, but all of them had the vote in 1964, and the sense of outrage and dismay at what had happened in 1956 had its effect in the ballot box then and not at the time of Macmillan's triumph in 1959.[17]

At this uncertain time in the nation's history, the boys at the RGS were very fortunate that their school was led by a thoroughly impressive headmaster. Oliver Mitchell, who had been decorated for courage during the First World War, was by all accounts an admirable and inspirational character. Like many headmasters then and now, he was also a somewhat distant and remote figure, but it was clear to everyone who met him that he had the school's best interests at heart. In the RGS's official history, Mitchell is described in the following terms: 'He was quick, excitable and adventurous, and sometimes shocked his colleagues and friends; but under him the School was alive with ideas and novelties of all kinds. He had great enthusiasm, sympathy for others, and loyalty to a wide range of causes. He was available to everyone, boys, staff, parents, Governors and friends of the School.'[18] Although he had no direct ties to the school himself, he was nevertheless focused on 'preserving the traditions of the School, and was keenly interested in its history'.[19] One of the ways in which he did this was to continue his predecessor's charming custom of presenting boys who had just arrived at the school with a copy of the *Story of the Royal Grammar School*. Under his leadership, the school enjoyed a strong academic atmosphere, and the boys were encouraged to pursue their interests in a wide range of fields, including music and the arts. In his own words, and in language that echoed the best of Victorian values, Mitchell wished to foster 'vigour, variety and vitality, and to combine boldness with caution'.[20] Overall, it seems that Mitchell succeeded in achieving his aims. When he retired in 1960, the following moving words were written in *The Novo*, the school's magazine:

> He has shown us the way to keep up with the quickening rhythm of life and yet maintain our stability. He has remained enviably young in spirit and outlook…We shall remember him for his broad humanity: his concern for the happiness and welfare of the individual; his compassion for those in difficulty or afflicted by misfortune; for the help and comfort so readily extended…He leaves us now, after being our Headmaster, our guide, our friend for close on twelve years, a period in which he has achieved much, and done it all with the quiet undramatic inevitability which is so typical of him. As for judging his achievement impartially, no-one can judge Mr Mitchell impartially – the affection in which he has been held is too real and insistent for that.[21]

As important as the headmaster undoubtedly was, Jeremy and his peers were also fortunate to have been taught by a group of exceptional schoolmasters. All of them were men, and most, if not all, of them had been to either Oxford or Cambridge. Many were dedicated to the school, and it was clear that the majority of them were on the side of the boys and wanted them to succeed. There was, for example, William Thornton, who penned frequent pieces for *Punch* and even published a novel, *Possit*, in 1962, which was described by contemporaries as 'the *Lucky Jim* of the provincial grammar school'. Anthony Tomkins was another brilliant schoolmaster, who was described in the school's history as being 'that rarity in the 1950s, a schoolmaster with a Ph.D.', while John Elders, who would go on to be appointed as coach to the England rugby team, 'brought a much more professional approach to Rugby Football training'.[22] Music, however, was taught in quite a traditional manner by the denizens of the music department, with Beethoven and Britten held up as unchallenged paragons of excellence to the virtual exclusion of more modern or less orthodox composers. Jeremy, always ready to display his mischievous sense of humour, enjoyed outraging some of the masters in the department by encouraging the other boys to ignore them and to listen instead to early English and Baroque music.

In history, Jeremy was especially lucky as he was taught by the incomparable Sidney Middlebrook, who would eventually help him towards winning a place at Oxford. A much-admired schoolmaster at the school, Middlebrook was described by one contemporary of Jeremy's as 'a very spare figure, but you always enjoyed his lessons, as he used to just talk without any notes'. This ability also appealed to Jeremy, who excelled at history and won several prizes, as well as a scholarship during his time at the school. To schoolfriends like Paddy Page, Jeremy was 'so absorbed in and enthusiastic about his academic work' that he seemed eminently suited to, possibly even destined for, an academic career, even though, in common with most of the other boys, 'he never really talked about his future in that way'. Jeremy's passion for history even extended to sharing with others his knowledge of the subject. His younger sister benefitted from this generosity and was grateful to receive his essays (always written in green ink), which were a huge help to her when she studied the subject at A Level, as they gave her, 'a very different and much more interesting perspective on 1485–1715' than she had learned at school.

In addition to inspiring his own love of history, Middlebrook's teaching methods also had a profound impact on Jeremy's future teaching style. In fact, it is striking that many of the qualities Jeremy attributed to his old schoolmaster were almost precisely the same ones which Jeremy's own students would associate with him half a century later when he was at Oxford. In a glowing tribute to Middlebrook published in the school magazine in 1958, Jeremy wrote the following:

> I remember in particular his effortless way of making his points with an extraordinary order and clarity. There is more than intensity of thought in this. Perhaps it is due just as much to the fact that he

treats his pupils not merely as pupils, but as persons. He teaches by courtesy, and I know how much it is appreciated. The trouble and the flattering attention which he devotes to his pupils teach them more than just history. And this quality merges into another, one which we had no right to expect: the quality of wisdom which pervades not only his own department but all his activities at school.[23]

Middlebrook was equally effusive about his young charge. In a letter to Richard Southern, a modern history tutor at Balliol, and himself a former pupil of Middlebrook's at the RGS, the old schoolmaster described Jeremy as 'a very able boy with an uncommonly good brain'. He went on to say that Jeremy was 'widely read in history, has real penetration and understanding…and a capacity for analysis that can be most impressive', and concluded by noting that he could 'warmly recommend him as the most promising boy I have had…for a considerable time'.[24]

Beyond the classroom, a big strength of the school at that time was its extracurricular activities, which included a seemingly endless list of clubs and societies, including the Debating Society, the XXI Club (devoted to play reading and an annual major dramatic production), the Science Society, the Linguists (a club which often produced plays in French or German), an astronomical society, an entomological society, a Scottish dancing club, a model railway club, and even a Gilbert and Sullivan society.[25] In addition, the Plender Library was run by boys who from time to time tried to improve the cataloguing and issuing system, and who sometimes published lists of acquisitions, even with reviews, especially of gifts from benefactors.[26] According to the school's official history, all this activity reflected very well on those who ran the school at that time: 'Thus life at the Royal Grammar School in those days was busy, exciting, various and exacting. The amount of thought and care which went into the organization which the staff shared amongst themselves was enormous, and boys were encouraged to take responsibility and use their initiative as soon as they were able.'[27] Games and sport were also a large, albeit not dominant, part of the school day. At a time when Newcastle United were at the peak of their powers, many of the boys dreamed of emulating their great hero, Jackie Milburn, when playing football for the school. Tennis was also played, and although it was not a major sport at the school, a group of boys enjoyed such a good run in the Glanvill Cup and the Youll Cup in 1958 that a correspondent from *The Times* felt compelled to refer to the team from the RGS as the 'Dark Horses of the North'.[28] In the same year, a group of three Old Novos carried off boxing blues at Oxford and Cambridge, prompting a delighted Mr Mitchell to declare boxing to be 'the cleanest English sport in the world'.[29] Rowing was also popular, but in the days when the shipping routes along the Tyne were much busier than they are today, the boys always ran the risk of coming across either the *Hexamshire Lass* or *Bobby Shaftoe* barges carrying ash out to sea from one of the local power stations.

It would be no exaggeration to say that sport was not one of Jeremy's key areas of interest at school. As an added aside in that same letter quoted above, Sidney Middlebrook commented on Jeremy's lack of sporting prowess and remarked drily that he 'of course…plays no games'.[30] Like at most schools, participation in games and sport was technically compulsory at the RGS, but for the more ingenuous boys there were usually ways of getting out of them. In the time-honoured tradition, some boys would skip games by feigning illness whereas others would simply disappear for the afternoon by jumping over the school's fence. Despite his slender physique at the time, Jeremy was not known as an inveterate player of games and was much more enterprising when it came to getting out of having to endure any form of physical exercise. Spotting that the rugby pitches were often covered in leaves during the autumn term, he managed to negotiate an agreement with a number of other boys which saw him convince the school that, instead of taking part in the games session, he should instead be allowed to lead an official 'leaf-sweeping' team that would render the pitches playable for the more athletic boys. His skills of diplomacy were clearly honed at an early stage during his time at school, and they would not only get him out of playing sport but would also serve him well as a wily committee man at Oxford many years later.

Overall, Jeremy's time at the RGS was a very happy one for him. The school was thriving under the leadership of Mitchell, and as the official history of the school makes clear, Jeremy and his peers were very fortunate to be there: 'If, as one may assume, the aim of a school is to offer stimulus and opportunity to boys to develop their individual capacities and enthusiasms, to work hard and seriously at their studies, and to reach high standards of performance in other enterprising activities, then the Royal Grammar School was outstandingly successful in these years.'[31] But although he was happy at the school, he was certainly viewed by many of his peers as a distinctive and indeed unusual character. One contemporary recalls that Jeremy was 'always seen as a little eccentric', adding that 'he was not viewed as a local, even though this was not held against him'. Paddy Page remembers him as 'a leading member' of a very lively group of boys, with Catto in particular being 'a very slender boy, who had intelligence, charm, and great wit'. However, to the surprise of some, Jeremy failed to become a prefect, possibly because, according to Page, 'he was seen as a bit too unconventional to be entrusted with the task of disciplining the other boys'.

That unconventional side of his character also manifested itself in the field of religion, and it was towards the end of his time at school that another important and formative moment in Jeremy's life took place. His decision, at the age of seventeen, to convert to Roman Catholicism was one that he did not take lightly, but once he had made up his mind, he was received at St Dominic's Priory in Newcastle, which was then a Dominican church. For this conversion to take place whilst he was still at the RGS was perhaps somewhat surprising given that the school was not especially noted for its religious character at the time. As the school's official history put it: 'Religious education was scarcely conducted at all, and there was considerable feeling that it need not be taken seriously. Although Mr Mitchell himself was a sincere and committed Christian, the ethos of the RGS in the 1950s remained strongly secular.'[32] According to his sister, the family became aware of Jeremy's conversion, and although they did not approve of the decision, they did not interfere either. The Cattos were not an especially church-going family, so the young Jeremy's decision certainly surprised the rest of them, but it was never discussed from that moment on. A contemporary at RGS claims his conversion also 'caused consternation at school', but Jeremy was never put off by this and remained committed to his new faith for the rest of his life.

The actual reason for his conversion is not easy to establish. His faith was a very private matter for him, and he did not discuss it with many people, even those who were closest to him. However, Dominique Dubois, a friend who knew him well later in life, and who had many conversations with him over the years about religion and faith, is able to shed some light on the motives behind his conversion:

The Catholic Church at that time celebrated Mass in a similar way to that of Jeremy's requiem: in Latin with little participation from the laity. The Second Vatican Council, held from 1962 to

1965, introduced many changes, including mass in the vernacular and participation by the laity. I believe that Jeremy was drawn to worship of the Catholic Church in the 1950s, after being drawn to a 'High' Anglican form of worship found within the Church of England. To me, he seems to have had a deeply private, intimate faith, which waxed and waned throughout his life, and gained a central place in his life in his last years.

Whatever the truth behind his conversion, it was a commitment that would help shape the rest of his life.[v]

But beyond excelling in the classroom and devoting himself to serious matters of religion, Jeremy also showed early on that he had a more playful side to his character. Later in life, and certainly by the time he was a don at Oxford, Catto was known to enjoy a drink. He rarely if ever drank to excess, but tutorials would sometimes begin or end with a glass of sherry, and guests to his rooms late at night would be asked whether they wanted 'whisk or bran', and the 'river whisk', as he liked to call it, flowed pretty steadily throughout the course of his life. It would appear that his fondness for alcohol developed early, probably whilst he was still at school. In a piece commissioned by his younger sister in 2012 for a publication entitled *That'll be the Day! 1950s Newcastle*, Catto recalled his days as a youthful drinker at school: 'The discipline in both school and pub was lax enough to allow us a pleasant lunchtime pint, albeit we were (I would have thought obviously, and in the case of some of us blatantly) under 18.' The pubs Jeremy and his friends frequented included the Brandling Arms, the Collingwood, and the Baltic. 'These were agreeable pubs where our fathers might have drunk on a Saturday lunchtime. (We were always there on a weekday, so avoided the ghastly experience of meeting an ancestor at the bar).' But best of all was the Royal Court. It was located in the Bigg Market and down a flight of stairs which, according to Catto, was 'always a hopeful outward sign of seedy decadence'. Once inside, Jeremy and his friends found the following: 'The decor was a faded sub-Mark Gertler mural of circus horses and gaudy carriages. The bar was a long loop, without much depth, so most people crowded up to the bar, where there was usually room; the effect was like being on stage.' As for the drinks chosen, Newcastle Brown Ale was, naturally, a regular favourite. 'That

---

v According to John Wolfe, Jeremy was successful in converting a few of his friends at school to Catholicism.

sweet, strong liquid, had prestige. Perhaps points were scored in proportion to the pain of drinking it.' The alternative beers from the Vaux Breweries were 'easier to get down, but duller in their effects'. And Merrydown Cider was also consumed, but was seen as 'rather girly', even though Jeremy and his friends 'secretly liked it better, though not, of course, its inevitable consequence'. Finally, on the Scotswood Road there were many pubs, and regulars used to play a game which involved drinking a pint in each, but with the added penalty of having to go back to a pub if you had to use the facilities. According to Catto, 'nobody ever got to the end', and even though he and his friends did not compete, they were grateful for the pubs they did visit and 'for the lax regime which allowed us, quite illegally, though nobody seemed to mind, to get used to the Demon Drink'.[33]

In common with at least some other young men at the time, Jeremy had one of his first sexual encounters at this time. The formative experience did not happen whilst he was at RGS, but took place towards the end of his time at Hillbrow prep. It was, however, as he explained to a friend many decades later, an experience which left him somewhat disappointed. The other boy, who was of a similar age to Jeremy and was also still at school, was the son of a local greengrocer. Following on from whatever happened between the two boys, the grocer's son whispered into Jeremy's ear that he had a secret to share with him. Naturally, Jeremy's curiosity was pricked, but his initial excitement vanished almost as quickly as it had appeared, when the boy whispered the words 'tea bags' into his ear. Of course, tea bags had existed since about the first decade of the twentieth century, but the take-up of this new invention in Britain was relatively slow and, as with so many things in Britain, there were class distinctions involved. In the end, Jeremy, who was from a more elevated social class than the grocer's boy, was so horrified at the use of tea bags, rather than the more traditional method of loose-leaf tea, that the incident, as he admitted to his friend many years after the event, 'rather made me lose my...interest'. Thankfully, there would be happier days ahead on the romantic front.

In many ways, the adolescent Jeremy was probably not that different to many young people at the time. In other ways, however, he was clearly carving out a distinctive image for himself from a relatively young age. Years after he left Balliol and went to Durham to work as a lecturer, his younger sister's future husband, Anthony Flowers, remembers that he used to sleep in what had been Jeremy's childhood bedroom when he stayed over at her house. What he recalls provides an interesting snapshot of the adolescent Jeremy, as well as a few glimpses into his future:

> His bedroom still had reminders of his teenage years: a bookcase
> full of largely Penguin paperbacks on a multitude of subjects, a
> walk-in cupboard that contained more books and pamphlets on
> Catholicism and politics and exploring sexuality; some items of
> clothing that he had left behind; and some early paintings by Bryan
> Ferry and Stephen Buckley. Hung on the back of the door was
> a red, white and blue striped jacket from Lord John in Carnaby
> Street that I coveted. Like much clothing from that period, it was
> impossibly close fitting, which shows what a slight frame Jeremy
> had then. Physically he reminded me of a young David Hockney,
> with his heavy-framed glasses, blonde hair and stylish clothes,
> though the years in halls later added bulk to his slim figure.

This vivid account tallies with what those who knew Jeremy best at
that stage of his life have said about him. As he left behind his early
adolescence, a picture begins to emerge of a young man who was clearly
very academically able, unusually charming, knew his own mind, and
had a distinctive style all his own. As his conversion to Catholicism
demonstrated, however, he was also not afraid to break with convention.
He had a mischievous streak to his character right from an early age,
and he was determined to enjoy life. In short, he was unusual and he
stood out.

One other important aspect of his character becomes apparent in
this period. Although Jeremy was a very caring son and brother, he also
showed from a relatively early age that he was determined to guard his
own independence as well as his private life. In later life, he kept the
Newcastle family well apart from his Oxford life, but that tendency to
compartmentalise was already evident during his time at school. Indeed,
so ruthlessly did he separate the different parts of his life in this period
that his mother and his sisters would often joke about the following and
all too frequent line of conversation when Jeremy was home after school:

> 'Where are you going, Jeremy?'
> 'Out', came the enigmatic reply.
> 'When will you be back?'
> 'Later', came the vague response.
> 'Who are you going to see?'

'Oh nobody you know... bye, must fly!'

And with that, he would disappear. His multifaceted private life was his own business and nobody else's, and he saw no reason to share it with others, even his closest family members. It was a character trait he would hold on to for the rest of his life.

When the time finally came to apply to university, Jeremy chose to apply to Oxford, and specifically to Balliol College. With the help of Sidney Middlebrook, as well as a glowing reference from Oliver Mitchell, the school's headmaster, Jeremy was able to secure a place there. Indeed, not only did he win a place at Balliol, but he also won the coveted Brackenbury scholarship, which, according to a contemporary of Jeremy's at the RGS, was seen as 'a bit of a triumph for the school' and was inscribed on the wooden honours board in the school hall for all to see. In fact, according to the school's official history, the RGS had a very proud record of sending boys to the two ancient universities: in the period 1949–61, there were forty-five awards at Cambridge and twenty-eight at Oxford, giving an average of six per year. The period would contain three so-called 'vintage years', with eight in 1957, eleven in 1958, and nine in 1959.[34] To his own sense of delight and pride, no doubt, Jeremy was part of one of those 'vintage years'. On his application form, he had stated that he would like to read either politics, philosophy and economics (PPE) or modern history. In the end, however, he chose the latter and was awarded a place to read the subject at Balliol. In his reference for Jeremy, Mitchell had written the following tribute: 'It is certain that he has a real flair for History, he has a very compendious knowledge of the subject, and has originality, penetration, and judgment. His essays are particularly good. He is utterly reliable of character, of complete integrity and, indeed, is an unusual boy with great charm.'[35]

3

Balliol

Here come I, my name is Jowett.
All there is to know I know it.
I am Master of this College,
What I don't know isn't knowledge.

— A Balliol rhyme about Benjamin Jowett,
Master of Balliol, from *The Balliol Masque*, 1880

'…the most distinguished historian in an exceptionally good year…'
— In a note about Catto's academic progress, March 1961

'…Mr Catto, it should be explained, spends so much time wondering whether to wear his spats over or under his jeans and rushing with glee from one library to another, signing enrolment forms, that the days are just too, too short…'
— From 'Oxford Letters', *The Novocastrian*, March 1959

DURING THE YEARS IN WHICH CATTO READ MODERN HISTORY AT Balliol, Britain was a country adjusting itself to the new postwar world. In 1957, Prime Minister Harold Macmillan, in a speech to his fellow Conservative Party members, told them triumphantly that 'most of our people have never had it so good'.[36] The so-called 'affluent society' had arrived, and the horrors of the Second World War were beginning to fade. A few years later, in January 1960, Macmillan made his famous 'Wind of Change' speech, indicating for the first time that his party had no desire to block independence for those territories of the British Empire that wished to carve out for themselves a new and independent future. There was also great change in the air on the cultural front. A few months after Macmillan's speech, a band from Liverpool calling themselves The Beatles, performed their first ever concert under that name in Hamburg. In November of that year, Penguin Books was found not guilty of obscenity in the *Lady Chatterley's Lover* trial, a verdict which delighted liberals across the country and would result in far greater freedoms to publish explicit material. In a memorable moment, the case's prosecutor, Mervyn Griffith-Jones, was ridiculed for being hopelessly out of touch with changing social norms, when he famously asked the jury if it was the kind of book 'you would wish your wife or servants to read'.[37]

For those who had been educated at a public school, going up to Oxford in the 1950s was, in many ways, a familiar experience. The *History of the University* paints the following vivid picture: 'In the 1950s undergraduates came up to Oxford by train, their trunks sent on ahead and piled high in the college lodge, awaiting their arrival. Once installed, they did not normally leave Oxford or see their parents until term was over. For those accustomed to boarding school or life in the army, the transition was easy. College was a continuation of public school existence, though with much greater freedom.'[38] Oxford in the late 1950s and early 1960s, then, was both an unusual and an exciting place to be for undergraduates. Robin Milner-Gulland, who was a near contemporary of Catto's, albeit at New College, and would go on to become a scholar of Russian and Byzantine literature, recalls that it was unusual in the sense that 'a majority of undergraduates had done national service, and people were very conscious of that'. The result was that undergraduates did not see Oxford merely as an extension of school life: 'We perhaps did not take things that seriously, and in the first instance we were there to enjoy ourselves'. Nevertheless, volatile world events gave the city an air of excitement. The Suez Crisis and the Hungarian Uprising were hot topics of conversation among undergraduates and dons alike in 1956. Milner-Gulland reflects that 'it was an exciting time and although we always felt like we might be recalled for war at some point in the future, there seemed to be many opportunities' and perhaps most importantly, 'we felt we could change the world'.

Beneath the surface, however, this heady sense of excitement was also accompanied by a certain amount of anxiety about the future, which was reflected in the debates at the Oxford Union during this time. Then

as now, the Union, which remains perhaps the world's pre-eminent
undergraduate debating society, would host a series of both serious and
humorous debates, with the more earnest ones in the late 1950s and
early 1960s undoubtedly reflecting a preoccupation with foreign affairs
and with Britain's changing role in the world. In 1957, for example, a
debate was held on the Cold War arms race, and the motion was that
'This House deplores the decision of Her Majesty's Government to
continue tests of the Hydrogen Bomb'. In a debate in 1959, the desire
of undergraduates at the time to avoid another conflict could be seen
in the motion which declared that 'The Anglo-American alliance is the
Western world's best instrument for ensuring peace'. A couple of years
later, in 1961, a similar motion before the house held that 'This country
should unilaterally renounce any policy based on Nuclear Weapons'.[39]
There is sadly no record of Catto attending these debates at the time,
and he certainly does not appear to have spoken in any of them, but
extracts from the 'Oxford Letters', written by anonymous former pupils
from the RGS who had gone up to Oxford, and published in *The
Novocastrian*, the school's magazine, show that his contemporaries from
school certainly shared these concerns about the future, even if they
used an element of humour to distract themselves from their worries.
In a letter dated 1 April 1958, the authors note that 'undergraduates
can be seen earnestly discussing their future annihilation' by the atomic
bomb and attending meetings addressed by leaders of the Campaign
for Nuclear Disarmament.[40] According to Paddy Page, one of Catto's
friends from RGS, there is no question that, in common with most of his
contemporaries, 'Jeremy shared these anxieties and interests'.

If you were fortunate enough to be an Oxford undergraduate at
Balliol College, then ideas about changing the world or discussing
Britain's role within it would not have seemed out of place, especially
given the college's illustrious pedigree. Balliol's origins are cloaked in
uncertainty, but the college certainly has a strong claim, along with
University College, to be Oxford's oldest college, and therefore the most
ancient in the English-speaking world. It has existed as a community of
scholars on its present Broad Street site without interruption since about
1263. Aptly enough, given Catto's roots in the North East, the college
came into being following a dispute between John de Balliol and the
Bishop of Durham, which erupted into violence. The Bishop had Balliol
whipped, and forced upon him a penance, consisting of a significant
act of charity. This he did by renting a property and creating a house

of scholars, which was soon known by his name. A few centuries later, the intellectual malaise which affected eighteenth-century Oxford also touched Balliol, but by the late nineteenth century, under the leadership of Master Jowett, the college enjoyed something of a rejuvenation. Academic brilliance was encouraged, but so too was originality, and there was a heavy emphasis on character, leadership, duty and public service. At the height of the British Empire, Balliol boasted three successive Viceroys of India between 1888 and 1905, and it has also produced four British prime ministers to date. Finally, it is perhaps appropriate that the end of the British Empire was supervised by a Balliol man, in the shape of Chris Patten, who was a near contemporary of Catto's and would go on to become the last Governor of Hong Kong, presiding over its handover to China in 1997.

During Catto's time as an undergraduate at Balliol, the college was led by the formidable Sir David Lindsay Keir. Like Catto, the Master hailed from the North East, but owing to his father being a Scotsman, he eventually arrived at Oxford via the Glasgow Academy and Glasgow University. The outbreak of the First World War cut short his studies, and he went on to serve as a captain in the King's Own Scottish Borderers, during which time he was injured both at the Somme and at Arras. After the war, he went up to New College, Oxford, and graduated with a first-class degree in history in 1921. Formidable he may have been, but as Master of Balliol he also had a clear sense of the central importance of college life for undergraduates at Oxford. In the college's annual record, he wrote the following in 1960:

> Every true Oxford man would agree that the essence of Oxford is college life. To have one's own rooms, on one's own staircase, making one's friendships with undergraduates and dons, to have meals together, to drop into one's own J.C.R, read in one's own College Library, worship in one's own chapel, to play on one's own field or row from one's own boathouse – all these, taken together, make up the experience men come to Oxford to get and always treasure. It is on this intimacy of daily life that an Oxford education is based. From this it derives its unique value. A college is more than a hostel; it is more than just a private society of teachers and pupils; it is a household, a very large one, of course, but a household all the same. There is nothing quite like it and its Cambridge counterpart in the whole world.[41]

In that household, everybody mattered, even the lowliest of college servants. Although Edward Nelson, as the college's head scout, was a few notches above that rank, the tribute paid to him upon his retirement in 1957, after nearly forty-five years of unbroken service to the college, underlines the point made by Sir David in his description of college life. It was said of Nelson that 'his loyalties were simple, transparent and direct: the College, its good name, its best traditions, its high achievements.' As the rhyme in the Balliol College Record of 1957 had it:

I'm Steward: Nelson is my name
Things have never been the same
Since Nineteen-Twelve, and I aver
That even then things never were...[42]

As will be seen, these were precisely the sentiments and values which Catto would carry with him into his own professional life. As an Oxford don for nearly four decades, he would devote himself to college life in a way that would have commanded the approval of the Master of Balliol.

Not surprisingly, given the future trajectory of his academic career, Catto excelled academically at Balliol. As he approached the end of his time at the college in 1961, a note on his progress recorded that he was 'the most distinguished historian in an exceptionally good year'.[43] Although he undoubtedly had a very significant amount of innate ability and had also been well trained at the RGS, it is equally true to say that he was very fortunate to have been taught by some of the finest historians of that generation. For instance, it was at Balliol that he came under the influence of the great medievalist scholar Maurice Keen, who would also become a firm friend later in life. A modest man who, in truth, had little reason to feel modest about his own achievements, not least since his major book *Chivalry* remains, as his obituary put it, 'one of the great works of history in English of the past 70 years'.[44] Until the Second World War, the topic of cultural history tended to be ignored by most medieval historians, and a clear preference existed for the study of the more traditional subjects of the church, government and the law. That was to change, in part at least, as a result of Keen's approach to writing about the subject, and central to that new approach was that it became impossible subsequently to ignore the culture of those who had ruled Western Europe for half a millennium. In the view of the historian Christopher Tyerman, 'Maurice demonstrated that chivalry existed as a serious feature of medieval politics, religion, nobility and society, not, as previously understood, an exotic distraction.'[45] This approach certainly had an impact on Catto, who would frequently reference Keen's work as part of his own teaching of undergraduates many years later.

Keen had himself been influenced by Richard Southern, another distinguished don at Balliol, who also taught Catto when he was an undergraduate. His book *The Making of the Middle Ages* was a pioneering work, which established Southern's reputation as a leading medievalist. But apart from his scholarship, Keen was also greatly influenced by Southern's teaching style. As Keen himself recalled: 'It was not like being taught in the pedagogic sense, more like being guided on an expedition into unfamiliar, sometimes surprising, but endlessly interesting territory.' According to Keen, Southern also possessed an 'extraordinary knack of knowing what would stimulate and interest a particular pupil at a particular stage'.[46] These were qualities which Catto would display to great effect when he himself became a tutor, and there is no doubt that both Keen and Southern had a considerable influence on him in this respect. In regard to Southern's scholarship, Keen's entry for Southern in the *Oxford Dictionary of National Biography* sums up his influence in the following terms:

> As a tutor and as a supervisor of graduate students Southern trained many future scholars, and influenced many more, but he did not found an interpretive school, and never sought to. To do so would have been incompatible with the importance that he attached to artistry in historical writing, and to understanding the individual in context. 'The first duty of the historian' he wrote 'is to produce works of art ... works that are emotionally and intellectually satisfying ... that portray people whose actions are intelligible within the framework of their circumstances and character'.[47]

As will be seen in a later chapter on Catto's scholarship, this preoccupation with portraying people in a realistic and rooted context also became central to his own scholarship. As such, in regards to their scholarship, a clear line can be traced between Catto, Keen and Southern. Interestingly, an additional link existed, as Southern and Catto had also both attended the RGS in Newcastle, and both had been taught at different stages in their lives by Sidney Middlebrook.

Beyond his academic pursuits, we can also get a sense of Catto's emerging personality at Balliol from his old school's termly magazine,

The Novocastrian (sometimes referred to as 'The Novo'), which, to this day, is still issued to all pupils. In Catto's day, the aforementioned 'Oxford Letters' provided little vignettes into the activities of recent Old Novos, who would be remembered by those still at school. Catto was one of seven Old Novos mentioned in the March 1959 'Oxford Letters', and the overall impression gained by the reader is that although he was certainly diligent regarding his academic work, he was also conscious of his own sense of style and enjoyed an active social life. The first two paragraphs are general, discussing the coming of spring ('...the snowdrops peep through the Balliol lawns...'), and the time of year is humorously contrasted with the 'hibernation' of undergraduates 'facing imminent examinations'. The third paragraph, however, is more specific and begins as follows:

> Mr Rutherford is reported to sleep only during meals – although whether this is a reflection on College food is open to argument. He has however been known to appear at an odd sherry party, as has Mr Catto, whose light also burns well into the night. Mr Catto, it should be explained, spends so much time wondering whether to wear his spats over or under his jeans and rushing with glee from one library to another, signing enrolment forms, that the days are just too, too short...[48]

The days may very well have been short, but Catto nevertheless found the time to establish a series of friendships that not only enlivened his time at Balliol but would also sustain him for the rest of his life. One of the first people he met was a young woman by the name of Katherine Duncan-Jones, who would go on to enjoy an eminent academic career as an English literature and Shakespeare scholar, a fellow of New College, Cambridge, and then of Somerville College, Oxford, before she became a professor of English literature at Oxford from 1998 to 2001. Later in life, she married A.N. Wilson, the writer and author known for his critical biographies, novels and works of popular history. He remembers that his future wife and Catto became lifelong friends during their very first term at Oxford, despite having the occasional disagreement:

> He and Katherine had literally bumped into one another on the corner of Broad Street and Magdalen Street on their first day as undergraduates in 1958. They had immediately gone off to play

Poosticks on the bridge at Magdalen on the edge of Addison's Walk and deep into their seventies, they retained their childishness, their fondness for playing old singles on the record deck: 'American Pie' and Peter Sarstedt's 'Where Do You Go To (My Lovely)?', which was really 'their tune'. There were occasional spats. I never saw him angrier than when she described Colin McMordie as a pouter pigeon. But he was of a forgiving temperament, and if she had been seen round the King's Arms spreading some appallingly inaccurate gossip, he would indulgently describe her as 'Dame Rumour'.[49]

Another friend, James Vallance White, who also met Catto in his first term at the college and would go on to enjoy a distinguished civil service career as a senior clerk at the House of Lords, recalls that Catto had a wide circle of friends and enjoyed a busy social life there. Like most undergraduates, Catto enjoyed socialising, and there was one character during his time at Balliol who threw parties that would become famous among the university's undergraduates at the time. That young man was a fellow called Anthony Bryer, who would go on to become an esteemed Byzantine historian and a professor of Byzantine studies at Birmingham University. When he was a postgraduate at Christ Church, however, Vallance White recalls that 'he had rooms in the Second Quad at which his Saturday lunches were famous'. Robin Milner-Gulland also remembers those parties: 'As an Oxford undergraduate reading history, he already seemed a larger-than-life personality, hosting Saturday parties in his Balliol room to which anyone sufficiently gregarious could come, if bearing food or drink, to relish the gossip and wide-ranging conversation. His wit was sometimes outrageous, sometimes rather boisterous, which disconcerted a few acquaintances but charmed nearly all.'

Catto was undoubtedly charmed and very much enjoyed attending these gatherings, but the friendships he made there and elsewhere across the university during his time as an undergraduate suggest that he was not necessarily a tribal character. Unlike some, he did not just spend his time with friends from school and nor did he restrict himself to frequenting those who shared his political outlook, although this may have been due to the fact that his politics were not always easy to pin down at the time. He always had an interest in politics, but he never campaigned for a particular party whilst he was an undergraduate and, despite his long association with the Oxford Union later in life, he certainly never got involved in student politics. However, there was a period during his time at Balliol when a number of politically active students, especially those on the left, took part in what would become known as the Aldermaston marches. The first of these anti-nuclear weapons demonstrations took place in the spring of 1958, and was organised by the Direct Action Committee Against Nuclear War (DAC) and supported by the recently formed Campaign for Nuclear Disarmament (CND). Support for these campaigns grew rapidly, and by the early 1960s, tens of thousands of people from all over the country marched under the CND's banner. Initially, some of the group's leaders had planned to march in silence to stress the solemn nature of the event, but over time, music was played, and those who attended would have marched along to catchy tunes such as John Brunner's 'The H-bomb's Thunder' – which became something of an unofficial CND anthem – as well as such (perhaps deservedly) lesser-known songs as 'Brother Won't You Join the Line?', 'Doomsday Blues' and 'The Ballad of the Five Fingers'. While Catto could not be described as a politically active student, there is no question that, like many of his generation, he took a keen interest in the world around him. Whether it was as a result of political conviction or simple curiosity is not entirely clear, but Catto had attended Labour party meetings in Newcastle as a pupil at RGS, and he would attend these marches with friends in the late 1950s.

This brief dalliance with the political left did not last for very long, however. As his obituary in the *Daily Telegraph* made clear, his 'early support for CND did not survive one freezing march to Aldermaston'.[50] It seems that he was not impressed with what he witnessed, and it did not take long for him to see through what he would have regarded as hollow ideological posturing. On what was a bitterly cold day and 'with fingers freezing, Catto watched enviously as a bubble-car drew up to distribute warming drinks from a flask to the unilateralist great-and-good (J.B. Priestley, Michael Foot et al) but none to spare for their freezing anonymous fellow-travellers'.[51] He may not have been impressed, but the lack of concern with those at the bottom of the pile would not have surprised him: 'Keenly observant through thick-rimmed spectacles, Jeremy had the historian's recognition that hierarchy existed in all groups, regardless of ideological claims.' His *Times* obituary reached a similar conclusion about the impact which this brief foray into left-wing politics had on him, noting that 'by the time he finished his degree he regarded his fellow Balliolite's utopian dreams with amused scepticism', adding that he 'had come to believe that ideology was a foggy lens through which to see human relations, at best a heuristic and at worst a dangerous delusion'.[52] Perhaps not surprisingly, the only other record of him attending another CND march was a less earnest and more humorous affair. On that occasion, he appeared carrying not a CND banner, but a flag calling for the restoration of the Bourbon monarchy. What his fellow marchers made of that has, sadly, been lost to posterity.

Despite shining on the academic front and forming strong and lasting friendships, Catto's time at Balliol ended with something of a minor scandal. The incident in question was, in many ways, a curious one and saw Catto getting rusticated for stealing books from Blackwell's bookstore. As the drama unfolded and the police were called, news of the incident reached the authorities at Balliol. In a letter from Richard Southern, who was by now a fellow and tutor in modern history at Balliol, a clearly unimpressed Southern wrote to a senior colleague: 'I am very sorry to say that Catto is to be brought up before the Magistrates for the theft of books from Blackwell's. I understand that he has stolen about £30 worth and was actually stupid enough to take them from the shelves in the front of the shop and sell them over the second-hand counter, which seems to me flat insanity.'[53] Although it is not entirely clear what prompted this uncharacteristic bout of criminality, it would appear that Catto was in need of money. The same letter ends with Southern writing: 'The Dean has seen him briefly and the boy really says he stole the books because he wanted money.'[54] After considerable deliberation among the fellows, it was eventually decided that Catto should be rusticated for one term. In a letter to Catto, the college authorities made clear their 'extreme displeasure', but also justified their decision because of a 'natural wish… not to jeopardise your future.'[55] For his part, an ashamed Catto was also clearly relieved. In a letter to the Master, he thanked the college and admitted that 'the decision seems very lenient to me'.[56] The upshot was that Catto was rusticated for Michaelmas term in 1961. He was allowed to return in Hilary term in 1962, and his state studentship was also suspended for that period of time.

Despite being allowed to return, Catto decided on 'strong advice from his tutors'[57] to postpone his studies for an entire academic year. According to Catto's younger sister, who was quite young at the time, the scandal shook their mother, not least as the police were sent to Catto's home. She recalled that her brother briefly worked for the local parks department whilst waiting to go back to Balliol, stumbling across him with her mother at work in the local park one day. Catto then went to

London to stay with an aunt and worked at Reuters for a while, where he had been hired to research and write a history of the company for an important anniversary. Aside from the letters in the college archive, there is no other record of how Catto felt about this incident, but it is reasonable to assume that he would have felt chastened by the experience. Although he displayed a mischievous sense of fun throughout his life, he was clearly not a criminal and nor should he be viewed as a petty thief. The incident could be described as a moment of folly, but in the end, it should not be viewed as anything other than a relatively minor indiscretion. It was certainly a rather sad end to his time at Oxford, but his three years at Balliol were productive and fulfilling, and it should be remembered that he emerged with a top first-class degree as well as high praise from his tutors for his academic achievements. Perhaps more importantly, but unbeknownst to him at the time, a change of fortunes and happier times were just around the corner in his private life.

4

John

'Americans were exotic in those days, particularly in Newcastle.'
– John Wolfe about meeting Catto's family in 1961

'Our father asked me towards the end of his life in 1987 if I thought Jeremy would ever marry and I simply said I thought he was a confirmed bachelor!'
– One of Catto's sisters

'I used to see quite a lot of him when I taught at Oxford...and I find I miss him. Not that I was very close to him. Few people in Oxford were. He was very secretive, as a Catholic homosexual of his generation had reason to be.'
– Professor Blair Worden, a friend and colleague of Catto's

THE SWINGING SIXTIES WERE A TIME OF GREAT CHANGE AND upheaval, and Britain in 1961 must have seemed to many like it was on the cusp of a new and exciting age. In February, The Beatles performed at the Cavern Club for the first time following their return to Liverpool from Hamburg. A month later, the iconic Jaguar E-Type sports car was launched as a two-seater roadster. In the summer of that year, the play *Lady Chatterley*, which was based on D. H. Lawrence's novel, and which had caused such a stir only a few years before, opened at the Arts Theatre in London to positive reviews from critics. But it was also in the sphere of people's private lives that signs began to emerge that the country was moving into a more liberal and less censorious age. At the start of

---

the decade, the Betting and Gaming Act of 1960 paved the way for the operation of commercial bingo halls, followed later in the year by betting shops becoming legal under the terms of the Act. Then, in a move that gave rise to much heated debate, the Suicide Act decriminalised acts (as well as attempted acts) of suicide across the country, and towards the end of the year, the law was changed to allow birth control pills to become available on the National Health Service. As if to underline this more open and less straightjacketed age, the first edition of the satirical magazine *Private Eye* was published in the autumn of that year.

Although Catto would have followed these new developments with great interest, the future seemed uncertain for him after the way in which his time at Oxford had come to an end. However, to use a medieval metaphor which Catto would have understood well, the wheel of fortune was about to turn in his favour, as it was in the summer of 1961 that he would meet John Wolfe, the man with whom he would be close for the remaining fifty-seven years of his life.

Their meeting was the result of an introduction by a mutual friend, Don Levine, a postgraduate at St Catherine's College, Oxford, who had a strong feeling that they would like one another. Their first encounter came outside the American Express offices in London. John, an American who had arrived from the USA a few days before, did not know many places in town, and so it seemed like as good a place as any other to meet. Both were going through something of a transitional period in their lives when they first met. John had digs in Camden Town and was pursuing a master's degree in experimental psychology at University College London, which involved running experiments on rats, chickens and goldfish. (Further experiments on octopuses even took him to Naples for a while.) Catto, meanwhile, having been sent down from Balliol and wondering what his next move might be, was working for Reuters. Through family connections, the possibility had always existed of pursuing a career in the City, but this was never really a serious consideration for Catto, who was determined to return to academic life.

Both men quickly realised they enjoyed each other's company, had many interests in common, and shared a gift for developing long-lasting friendships. One example of this was their friendship with another Oxford man, Richard Booth, whose father, Major Booth, owned many of the shops in Hay-on-Wye, a village on the Welsh and Herefordshire border. Booth, in common with Jeremy and John, shared a passion for books, and Catto was able to help identify books of interesting local history. John, meanwhile, had worked in the New York Public Library as an undergraduate, and his experience with cataloguing proved invaluable in the pair's book quest. To the delight of both Jeremy and John, Booth would later become well known for his creation of Hay-on-Wye as a centre for the Hay Literary Festival.

Having established that they had much in common, their friendship progressed quite quickly, and John met Jeremy's family for the first time at Christmas in 1961. Casting his mind back, he smiles as he recalls that first meeting: 'Americans were exotic in those days, particularly in Newcastle.' But John had no difficulty in being accepted by Catto's family, and one of his sisters remembers that he became a much-loved member of the family from an early stage. However, being a typically English middle-class family of that period, the nature of Jeremy's friendship with John remained, at least initially, something of a mystery. As the same sister recalled many years later:

> It was not discussed really, though I guess as time went on, we all knew. Our father asked me towards the end of his life in 1987 if I thought Jeremy would ever marry and I simply said I thought he was a confirmed bachelor! Our mother died in 1983 and she must have known, but never said. They did not share a bedroom if they both stayed. It was so typically middle class not talking about things, just like with the Catholicism.

After Catto returned to Oxford in 1969 to take up a fellowship at Oriel, John returned to America to take care of some family matters. He returned to England on New Year's Eve in 1973 to live with Jeremy in the Northamptonshire house they would eventually buy together, but he rarely visited Oriel. This was partly because he had his own life to lead. He enjoyed a successful career in IT, having worked as a systems consultant in Boston and then for ICL in the UK, before he retired in 2000. Catto, however, may also have had his own reasons for keeping his different lives separate. Although he was an ever-present fixture in college, which meant there was always the chance of his professional life becoming blurred with his private life, his undergraduates understood that the latter was strictly out of bounds. As such, only a select few friends and colleagues were invited to see his life beyond Oxford. Catto was not necessarily worried that people would disapprove of his inclinations, but he took the old-fashioned view that it was nobody else's business. As a Roman Catholic, it is also reasonable to assume that he must have struggled to come to terms with his own sexuality. In addition, it is also possible that Catto worried that it might damage his future career prospects, although this was probably the least of his concerns.

Whatever the truth of the matter, it has already been noted that one of the key features of Catto's personality was that, even from an early age, he was very adept at sequestering the different parts of his life. Many colleagues, and even some who considered themselves on friendly terms with Catto, have pointed out his tendency to erect barriers: 'I didn't meet or know of the existence of his widower until the funeral. Several people I know, who must be counted as close colleagues, knew nothing of his household arrangements and imagined that he lived alone in Eydon with a housekeeper. It was a very severe compartmentalisation.' This tendency to guard his own private life lent a certain enigmatic air to Catto's persona. Blair Worden, who knew him for many years, wrote the following to a friend following Catto's death in 2018:

> The memorial service for Jeremy himself was excellent, with vivid addresses. He was a remarkable man, and in every way his own man. There were obituaries in the national newspapers which understandably dwelt on his Tory pupils and contacts, but there was so much else to him too, scholarly knowledge and originality of historical perception among them. And he was a famous tutor. I used to see quite a lot of him when I taught at Oxford and later on at the Dacre Trust, and I find I miss him. Not that I was very close to him. Few people in Oxford were. He was very secretive, as a Catholic homosexual of his generation had reason to be.

This last point provides an important explanation for why Catto was so protective of his private life. As Richard Davenport-Hines makes clear in his biography of John Maynard Keynes (who was bisexual), the tendency to compartmentalise was essential to leading a civilised life for men of Keynes' background and generation:

> Most accomplished and effective Englishmen of Keynes's class compartmentalised their lives. It was inherent in their cultural assumptions to categorise and segregate emotions and people according to their worth, to manage their conflicting motives and experiences by keeping them apart....Compartmentalisation was implanted by family circumstances, instilled by boyhood training,

and found in manhood to be indispensable for forming priorities and making choices. If people were to enjoy clear, orderly, civilised, productive lives, without blurs, smudges, mess, waste and overlap, it was essential for them not to mix their friends, aims, urges and trepidation in an undifferentiated hotchpotch. Maynard Keynes exemplified the truth that compartmentalisation is a mark of intelligence as well as requisite to successful intentions.[58]

Catto was not quite of Keynes' generation (and he most certainly did not approve of his economic theories), but in terms of how he segregated his private and public lives, he could almost be described as something of a Keynesian.

Given the age in which they met, it would not have been an easy or straightforward friendship for the two men, and it is worth reflecting for a moment on societal attitudes towards homosexuality in the late 1950s and early 1960s compared with today, as this will provide a clearer context for their friendship. Today, attitudes towards homosexuality are without question significantly different to what they were when Jeremy and John met in 1961. According to a 2019 Pew Research Center poll, 86 per cent of the UK agreed that homosexuality should be accepted by society, and a 2017 poll showed that 77 per cent of British people support same-sex marriage.[59] In 1961, by contrast, although it is true that attitudes towards homosexual friendships were changing, they were doing so at an almost glacial pace. Crucially, homosexuality was still a crime, and there seemed little prospect at the time that this would change in the near future. Some years prior to this, in 1957, the Wolfenden Report published its conclusions, which recommended that homosexual acts between consenting grown-ups should be decriminalised, finding that 'homosexuality cannot legitimately be regarded as a disease, because in many cases it is the only symptom and is compatible with full mental health in other respects'.[60] In the same year, the Church of England passed a resolution which stated that 'this Assembly generally approves the principles on which the criminal law concerned with sexual behaviour should be based as stated by the Wolfenden Committee, and also its recommendations relating to homosexuality'.[61] By the summer of 1961, cinema-goers witnessed the first ever use of the word 'homosexual' in a British film, when the film *Victim*, starring Dirk Bogarde and Sylvia Syms, was released around the country. Despite dealing with the subject of homosexuality in a broadly sympathetic manner, a number of scenes deemed to be inappropriate were cut from the film, and the British Board of Film Censors felt it had no choice but to give the film an 'X' rating, which meant that it was 'recommended for adults only',[62] a classification normally reserved at the time for erotica or horror films.

But despite the Wolfenden Report and the backing it received from the Church, as well as a more liberal attitude being reflected in popular culture, the Sexual Offences Act (which would decriminalise homosexuality) only arrived on the statute books in 1967. In later life, Catto liked to joke with friends that homosexuality had become rather boring over the years and that it had been much more fun during the days before the Wolfenden Report, when it was furtive, but this may not have reflected how he genuinely felt about it at the time. Certainly, the way in which he compartmentalised his life and treated his friendship with John as strictly private would suggest that he was not quite as carefree about the matter as he perhaps liked to pretend later in life.

Nor should this be very surprising. Although Wolfenden brought about a change in the law, it would be a mistake to conclude that this was somehow part of an inevitable march towards a more tolerant and progressive society. Wolfenden and his colleagues themselves felt so awkward about the subject of homosexuality that they could barely bring themselves to use the word. (Indeed, they replaced the Committee's title 'Homosexuality and Prostitution' with the brand name of a famous biscuit, 'Huntley and Palmers'.)[63] One Home Office official even adopted this euphemism and wrote that it might be helpful to 'let the Committee see what a few Huntleys look and behave like'.[64] When the committee interviewed the Lord Chief Justice, his lordship explained that he felt 'physically sick' when trying 'buggers',[65] and made it clear that he felt 'strongly that buggery ought always to be treated as a crime'. For the avoidance of doubt, he added that 'it is such a horrible and revolting thing and a practitioner is such a depraved creature that he ought in my opinion to be put out of circulation'.[66] This was certainly not the voice of a more liberal and tolerant society.

As Wolfenden deliberated, parliamentarians took part in a debate that often seemed divorced from reality. Honourable Members routinely emphasised that they had little or no personal experience of the subject under discussion, which led Lord Snow to comment on 'the curious unworldliness' of the debate. Parliamentarians all sounded like they had 'never met a homosexual, as though these were something strange like the white rhinoceros'.[67] In his excellent book *Sex, Death and Punishment*,

Richard Davenport-Hines summed up this oddly illiberal liberalisation of the law by arguing that the 1967 Act, far from heralding a more liberal age, actually represented little more than a depressing trade-off: 'The liberalization of the law in 1967 marked less a triumph for national toleration than the acme of the Victorian middle-class taste for privacy... There was no attempt to emancipate male homosexuals and little sense of striking a blow against bigotry. Instead the notion of privacy received its ultimate tribute: sexual outlaws were given tolerance within the law conditional on their acceptance of privacy.'[68] Citing people who warned that homosexual acts should be kept private and not 'flaunted in public', he then writes that 'the liberalization of 1967 was not a victory over bigotry, or of the much vaunted "permissive" forces of the 1960s over traditional values...concessions to homosexuals were extended as one side of a bargain, with the acceptance of gay men of notions of privacy, or social invisibility, as the pay-off'.[69]

Viewed in that context, it is perhaps not surprising that Catto chose to compartmentalise his life in such a strict manner. And nor was he alone in that regard. A survey of 127 homosexuals interviewed in the late 1950s revealed that 31% thought their homosexuality was 'very secret', 32% judged it was known only to other homosexuals, and 21% reported that close friends knew but not casual acquaintances.[70] To some extent, these numbers can be explained by the fact that for an earlier generation, the very existence of these kinds of relationships seemed almost incredible. In the interwar years, English jazz musician George Melly's father sat on a jury which acquitted a man accused of sodomy. Asked later if the defendant was guilty, he replied, 'O yes, but half the jury didn't think it was possible and the rest of us didn't think it mattered.'[71]

It was accepted in later years that homosexuality existed, but the language used to describe it remained telling. There was always the suggestion that there was something not just abnormal but also disfiguring about homosexuality. Even Lord Arran, who led the parliamentary campaign to decriminalise homosexuality, described homosexuals in 1965 as 'the odd men out: the ones with the limp',[72] whilst a Roman Catholic priest of the time said: 'You can't be homosexual if you're a civil engineer. Only artists and actors and people like that are homosexual.'[73] At the more extreme end at Westminster, Lord Hailsham, in an essay called *They Stand Apart*, argued that homosexuality was 'a proselytizing religion...contagious, incurable and self-perpetuating', its converts being a 'potentially widely expanding secret society of addicts'. He concluded by warning that homosexuals were on the march, their numbers increasing as a result of 'initiation…by older homosexuals whilst the personality is still pliable'.[74] Others, meanwhile, associated homosexuality with a broader sense of national decline. According to one Tory MP, speaking in the Commons at a similar time, it was clear that 'in the general run, the homosexual is a dirty-minded danger to the virile manhood of this country'.[75] Sir David Maxwell-Fyfe, the Home Secretary at the time, agreed and told the Commons that 'homosexuals in general are exhibitionists and proselytizers and are a danger to others, especially the young'.[76]

Beyond Westminster, public attitudes were not much more welcoming. Surveys held in the mid-1950s indicated that at least half the population saw homosexuality as 'disgusting',[77] with attitudes not changing much by 1963. In April of that year, the *Sunday Pictorial* produced a two-page guide for its readers, presumably designed to be helpful, entitled 'How to Spot a Homo'. The sure, telltale signs, apparently, included 'shifty glances', 'dropped eyes' and, rather oddly, 'a fondness for the theatre'.[78]

Such attitudes, and the language used to express them, would undoubtedly shock many people today, but it is important to remember that although the 1950s and 1960s may not seem that long ago to some, it was nevertheless a different world and, in any case, social attitudes are almost always slow to change. More importantly, all of this should provide a clearer context for Jeremy and John's friendship. Quite apart from his own views, his faith and any concerns he may have had about the impact on his career, it is perhaps not surprising, given the above-mentioned historical context, that Jeremy chose to be so discreet about his friendship with John. Happily, however, their friendship would last for the rest of Catto's life, and by 2017, the law, as well as societal norms, had changed to such an extent that Jeremy and John were able to enter into a civil partnership.[vi] But that was all in the future. Back in 1961, having left Balliol and having met John, Jeremy was now finally beginning to feel more settled. He would eventually return to Oxford, where he made his name as one of the great dons of his generation. In the meantime, his next big move saw him return to his roots in the North East. In 1964, Catto took up a lectureship in modern history at Durham University. It was there that another fortuitous meeting would lead to a lifelong, but in many ways unlikely, friendship.

---

vi Jeremy and John entered into a civil partnership partly as a result of strong financial advice concerning their future financial affairs.

5

Durham Interlude

'He was one of my great mentors. Very intelligent – medieval history, not my field – but great fun.'

– Bryan Ferry on Catto

'...As the brilliant agent of a particular glamour Catto helped make real the finer world of art and culture that had been signified to the young Bryan Ferry by the classicism of the Penshaw Monument, back in Washington...'

– Michael Bracewell on Catto in Roxy Music, 1953–1972: The Band that Invented an Era

'He seemed quite a glamorous figure, blonde, skinny, often in a black polo neck and wearing his heavy-framed glasses.'

– Catto's sister on her brother at Durham in the 1960s

THE UNIVERSITY OF DURHAM WAS OFFICIALLY FOUNDED IN 1832, BUT its origins are considerably more ancient. In the late thirteenth century, a group of Benedictine monks in Durham established a hall at Oxford University, which became known as Durham College. Over subsequent centuries, efforts were made to establish a university within the city itself, but a proposal to enable the college to present degrees was opposed by both Oxford and Cambridge universities, and the plan was consequently abandoned by the time of the restoration of the monarchy in 1660. In the end, an Act of Parliament was required to allow the Dean and Chapter of

Durham Cathedral to appropriate part of the property of their church for the purpose of establishing a university. And with that, the University of Durham was born.

When Catto arrived at Durham in 1964 to take up a lecturing position at the university, there was an unmistakable feeling that Britain was moving into a new era. In July of that year, former Prime Minister Sir Winston Churchill, by now eighty-nine years of age, and having been an MP for sixty-three years, was present in the House of Commons for the last time before his retirement. A few months later, the pipe-smoking Harold Wilson became Prime Minister, when he defeated the patrician Sir Alec Douglas-Home at the general election. The result brought an end to thirteen years of Conservative government, and the new Labour administration wasted little time in ushering in a new age of reform. A mere two months after the election, MPs voted overwhelmingly to abolish the death penalty. Capital punishment had gradually fallen out of use, with the last execution taking place in August of that year. Away from the world of politics, a new age in entertainment was marked, as portable televisions went on sale for the first time and, not long after, football fans were able to enjoy highlights from the weekend's games, as the first *Match of the Day* programme aired on BBC Two. By the end of the year, The Beatles had secured the Christmas number one for the second year in a row with their hit single 'I Feel Fine'. Not everyone was in tune with the sentiment behind that song, however, as violent disturbances erupted throughout the year between Mods and Rockers, whose activities sparked moral outrage across the media and led to hysterical editorials in newspapers such as *The Birmingham Post*, which warned that these two youth groups were 'eternal enemies' in Britain and would bring about the 'disintegration of a nation's character'.[79]

Although Catto, at twenty-five years of age, was still very much part of that youthful generation that had produced the Mods and Rockers, no such concerns troubled him. This period found Catto back in his native North East for the first time since leaving school. Even though he had every intention of returning to Oxford one day, the Durham years gave him the credibility he felt he needed to achieve that goal. His rustication from Balliol had dented his pride, but exile in Durham provided him with the chance to rebuild his reputation. Before ending up there, however, he applied for a position at both Jesus College, Oxford, and Glasgow University. Unfortunately, both applications were unsuccessful, but letters found in the Balliol College archives reveal a series of wonderfully acerbic exchanges between the academics involved in the selection process at Glasgow that could have come straight out of *Lucky Jim*, Kingsley Amis' biting satire on academic life in the 1950s. In a letter to the Master of Balliol, Sir David Lindsay Keir, from L.G. Stones, a history tutor at Glasgow, Stones asked whether he should take Catto or another candidate by the name of Bryer who, unbeknownst to these academics, was the same Bryer famous across Oxford for parties he used to give as an undergraduate at Balliol in the late 1950s. As he weighed up the merits of these two candidates, Stones feared that Catto might not be a right fit for Glasgow: 'I know…that Catto is very good; the problem is only whether he is capable of coming down to the level of John McTavish in the Ordinary class! Would he fit us at all, especially as the most junior man on the staff, with much wood to be hewed and water to be drawn…?' Poor Bryer, meanwhile, found himself subjected to the following withering assessment from Stones: 'With Bryer I have all these questions, plus the problem of whether his second was a mistake or not. All my staff at the moment have firsts, and I do not want a second who deserved no more, and never will.' Sir David's response to his colleague's concerns was equally forthright. Asserting that both candidates were good scholars, he noted that Catto was perhaps the better of the two, 'if only in the sense that he has throughout been a determined, and orderly, well-organised man, with a clear sense of what he wanted to do and how he proposed to do it'. Sir David went on to say that Bryer, by contrast, had 'allowed his Byzantine interests rather to run away with his time and disorganise his work'. In typically caustic fashion, he went on to write that 'his second was therefore not undeserved – in fact I would say it was quite well deserved'. In the end, the Master of Balliol felt that certain nuances of background were all that really mattered: 'He [Catto] comes, as you know, from Newcastle upon Tyne, and he is, by name at least, a Scot – and perhaps a bit by temperament too. Though I myself don't ever feel especially aware of it, and, as you can imagine, I rather like Scottish traits.' Nevertheless, Sir David felt Bryer would probably get on better with the Scots, but it was by no means a certainty: 'Personally I find him a much more attractive type than Catto, and I think he would go down better with McTavish, except of course for the handicap of being very English, whereas I suppose Catto might, in subdued light, pass for a Scot. And undoubtedly his name would be at least an initial help.'[80]

Glasgow's loss would prove to be Durham's gain, as Catto was eventually successful in securing a position at Durham University. A key reason behind his successful application would have been the positive references provided from Balliol. In a letter to Durham's candidate admissions office, it was made clear that Catto 'ought to be one of the strongest in the field'.[81] The letter went on to state that Catto had come up 'to Balliol in 1958 as a Brackenbury scholar and he thoroughly justified his election for he turned out to be one of the most original scholars we have had for some time'.[82] The same letter added that Catto 'is a man of talent who thinks for himself; he investigates difficult and abstruse subjects with penetration, and he got the First Class we all expected of him'.[83] It concluded by stating that Catto's 'performance in the Final Honour School of History in 1961 was of first-class level throughout and he was awarded his First with a formal viva', and that everyone at Balliol 'expected him to go far as an historical scholar'.[84] And with that, Catto was employed as a lecturer in modern history at Durham University on a salary of £1,250 a year.[85]

Catto would stay at Durham until 1969, which was also the year in which he completed his doctorate on William of Woodford, a fourteenth-century Franciscan friar and theologian. The woman who supervised him for his doctorate was Beryl Smalley, a distinguished historian who was best known for her work *The Study of the Bible in the Middle Ages*, which established the foundations of later study of the medieval popular Bible. Smalley was an interesting character in her own right. Like Catto, she was a Catholic, but unlike him she was also a member of the Communist Party. The connection between these two ideas was always hard to discern, and Smalley, who never married, rarely allowed others to gain access to her inner world. In his memoirs, written after Smalley died in 1984, her fellow medievalist Richard Southern, who had taught Catto at Balliol, described Smalley as 'an extremely private person' who was nonetheless 'a fascinating, daunting, and fastidious personality, both visually and mentally' and a 'conspicuous object in the striking elegance and clear-cut severity of her appearance'.[86] Despite being something of a difficult person to handle, Catto appears to have had a good working relationship with her. Towards the end of her life, when she was, according to one account, 'enormously shrivelled and looking like Nefertiti', Catto mischievously, but also affectionately, described her style as 'radical chic'. For her part, Smalley was certainly impressed with the young scholar from Balliol. In her supervisor's progress report, dated 2 March 1968, which was not long before he finished his doctorate, she noted that Catto was working towards his final piece of work with 'unflagging enthusiasm'.[87] It is perhaps easy to overlook the relatively obscure subject of Catto's thesis, but according to Henry James, who read history at Oriel in the years 1979–82, and went on to spend over thirty years as a history teacher at Hereford Cathedral School, that would be a mistake. James has an intriguing theory regarding the subject of his doctorate, and he believes that the choice was a revealing one. He argues that 'to understand Jeremy you need to read his doctorate on William of Woodford', and although he is unclear on whether Catto consciously modelled himself on Woodford, he points out that there were many similarities between the two men: 'Just like Jeremy, Woodford was an influential teacher at Oxford. He was also, like Jeremy, an influential writer. Woodford was a friar and an institutional man, just like Jeremy. Woodford also had no children, like Jeremy. Both thus had great energy for their institutions. Woodford, like Jeremy, used his institutional connections to make links with powerful and influential individuals of his day.'

When he was not busy lecturing or working on his doctorate, Catto found time to lead an active and fulfilling social life, and it was during this time that a chance encounter in a pub in Newcastle would spark a lifelong friendship. At the time, Bryan Ferry was a student at Newcastle University, studying fine art under Mark Lancaster, the renowned artist and set designer. He also shared a flat with Stephen Buckley, who would go on to become a distinguished artist. Many years later, Catto would be interviewed for Michael Bracewell's book *Roxy Music, 1953–1972: The Band that Invented an Era*, and described that first meeting with Ferry and Buckley in the following way:

> In June 1966, I had been to a party in Newcastle with some students from Newcastle University…I didn't meet Stephen Buckley and Bryan at the party, but I was having a drink in a low bar in the Bigg Market, the Royal Court, and they came in. Stephen, who was always the more forward of the two, said to me, 'Weren't we at the same party the previous night?' and I said, 'Yes, we were' – and indeed we had been. So we got drinking, and then we decided we'd go off to a nightclub in South Shields – which, typical of the North East in those days, turned out to be shut. And so we came back.[88]

For his part, Ferry remembers that although he and Catto had seen each other at student events once or twice before, their first proper encounter came at a fairly shabby pub in the city's Bigg Market area, because 'it was the place that had the best music'. At the time, that part of town was somewhat run down, and Ferry recalls that most of the pubs in the area were pretty rough: 'You had to watch yourself and you wouldn't find many students there.'[89]

On the surface, it would have seemed improbable for the Durham history lecturer and future Oxford don and the future lead singer and songwriter of Roxy Music to have much in common, but they formed a connection straight away. They were, of course, both from the North East and bonded over their shared roots. In those days, most major northern cities had a unique sense of their own identity, but Newcastle felt even more different, not least as it was so much further away from everywhere else. However, both men also had a desire to move on to explore new opportunities. Catto was determined to return to Oxford one day, and Ferry hoped that his future would be in London, and perhaps even further afield. Thinking back to when they first became friends, Ferry says that he still has 'such fond memories of him' and that, in particular, he 'loved that Jeremy was always there', adding 'with old friends like him you know how to bounce the ball off the wall, as it always comes back at you with a true bounce'. In addition, he emphasises Catto's sense of humour: 'That was very important. He was clearly very knowledgeable about things, but he was also always very amusing about everything. That provided us with a great link.' That sense of humour, which was such a pronounced part of his personality, also came with a certain 'lightness of touch', which meant that Ferry always felt relaxed in Catto's company. Ferry concludes by saying that Catto 'never went for the obvious answer, and never had an obvious opinion', which meant that he was never anything other than stimulating company. 'He was one of my great mentors. Very intelligent – medieval history, not my field – but great fun.'[90]

Ferry's own words make it clear that a genuine bond existed between the two men, but Bracewell goes further and, in a remarkable passage of his book, insists that Catto had a profound influence on Ferry's 'aesthetic and social education'.[91] According to Bracewell, Catto was 'a connoisseur and scholar, with an interest in aesthetic style that included on the one hand the boutiques of the King's Road (buying clothes from Granny Takes A Trip, as well as from Carnaby Street), and on the other the imagism of Ezra Pound's Cantos', adding that Catto 'represented an elevated, academically assured sophistication and sense of taste – the attributes, in one sense, of an "upper", socially confident class, at ease in both their leisure and their intellectual outlook'.[92] Bracewell concludes that 'as the brilliant agent of a particular glamour, Catto helped make real the finer world of art and culture that had been signified to the young Bryan Ferry by the classicism of the Penshaw Monument, back in Washington'.[93] Catto himself was somewhat more circumspect about his own influence on Ferry specifically, let alone on 1960s popular culture more broadly. In an email to a friend, not long after he had read Bracewell's book, he wrote: 'My career of fraud seems to go on and on. Bryan's historian says I had a deep influence on 60s pop culture…Only you know THE SORDID TRUTH.'[94]

Ultimately, although Bracewell may have exaggerated the influence which Catto had on Ferry and, by extension, on the music and culture of the time, what is certainly true is that what brought these men together was a certain sense of style and a shared preoccupation with aesthetic concerns. Catto described this to Bracewell in the following terms: 'I think that Bryan and I were both in search of style, of various kinds – a desire to be at the edge of things. That was something we wanted to find in those days…The sixties were a period when there was a feeling of hope around; it looked like there were some new ideas emerging, and we looked for them.'[95] But although Catto was undoubtedly interested in those new ideas, he also had a clear preference for 'the Silver Age of Aesthetes' of the 1920s:

> I was extremely keen on that, because I've always been keen on the poetry of Pound. In a way it's beyond understanding I think; it doesn't matter, it's so beautiful…Somewhere in section 'Rock Drill' of the Cantos is the line 'never gin in cut glass had such clarity'. The hard imagist in Pound, struck me as more interesting, in the long run, than my more teenage cult of Decadence.[96]

Ferry agrees that he and Catto, who resembled David Hockney when they met, shared an interest in art, and especially in British art. Moreover, when Ferry was a young art student at Newcastle, Catto helped to arrange Ferry's first ever exhibition of his own work. In later years, Ferry would go on to become a great collector of modern British art and the two men would enjoy visiting art galleries together. Ferry adds that Catto had 'very good and wide-ranging taste', but what cemented that aesthetic bond was that both men 'liked both old and new things…Jeremy was of course a great medievalist, but he was also interested in the modern. He liked the harder edges of Wyndham Lewis more than the softer edges of Bloomsbury.'

The third member of the Durham triumvirate was the aforementioned Stephen Buckley. Originally from Leicester, Buckley, who studied fine art at Durham University under Richard Hamilton, would go on to be described by one critic as 'the Punk Rock of contemporary painting'. He first came to the North East in 1962, during 'the worst winter in living memory'. Despite this, he retains fond memories of the period: 'It was a different world. Trolleybuses were still in existence and the port still had ships. It was quite commercial too, and old submarines and warships were still waiting to be broken up'. Buckley proclaims that the 1960s in the North East were like 'an explosion of excitement' for him and his contemporaries. He remembers Newcastle as a 'vibrant, invigorating and stylish' city, which exuded a 'palpable' sense of history. Alongside his friends, Buckley frequented the city's many clubs, one of which hosted The Animals as their in-house band, and he would visit some clubs up to three times a week. Many of them were not too expensive, but Buckley also adds, with a twinkle in his eye, that they were popular because of 'the bewildering friendship of the town's girls'. His life up to that point had been quite different, with his father encouraging him to read Simone de Beauvoir, which was, he thinks, 'his idea of sex education'.

Buckley recalls meeting Catto for the first time at a Christmas party in Jesmond. He was sharing a flat with Mark Lancaster at the time, before Bryan Ferry took Lancaster's place in the residence. When asked about Catto's sexuality, Buckley explains that Catto never talked about it, but he feels that he was always very 'aware of himself, but uncertain how he could manifest it'. As with Ferry, there was a shared appreciation of style between Catto and Buckley. In his interview with Bracewell, Catto remembers the influence which the young artist had on him: 'Stephen influenced me a great deal – more than I influenced him, in his view of style. I've told you his remark, "The trouble with England, there's too much taste and not enough style." Which is absolutely true....'[97]

Early on in their friendship, Catto, Ferry and Buckley went on occasional trips together, and it was in the summer of 1966 that they embarked on a road trip across Europe and down to Calabria. The trip is described in Bracewell's book, and he writes that photographs of the three men in Italy 'show a supremely cool trio of travellers: Ferry in pink button-down shirt and slick aviator-style glasses; Buckley in pristine white T-shirt and brown fedora; Catto, his hair Hockney blond, wearing jet-black Ray-Ban sunglasses'. To begin the journey, they met at Charing Cross, stuffed their sleeping bags into the back of the car and set off, stopping en route at Canterbury so that Catto could see the cathedral. After that, they crossed to France by boat and stayed the night in Reims, from where they made their way towards Lake Geneva in Switzerland. Buckley recalls that it was unclear where Switzerland started, so they ended up going in and out of the country three times in an hour. Eventually, however, they passed Switzerland and ended up in the Valle d'Aosta before heading to Florence. By now, the car was making some unpromising noises, so they stayed in Florence for three nights in an old and dilapidated palazzo where, as Buckley remembers, 'you could see the leg of a cherub on the ceiling as you sat on the loo'. The next day, they drove to Naples and enjoyed a day trip to Capri, as Catto was very keen to see the graves of the Wittgenstein princes. They eventually reached Calabria, where they spent a number of days, before making their way back to Britain. On the way back, as luck would have it, the car broke down on the outskirts of Monte Carlo. As they were not far from the sea, they took the opportunity to go swimming, and it was there that Catto taught Ferry how to swim. Ferry also recalls that they took turns to drive, and although he himself could not drive, Catto taught him as they went along. Looking back, the trip clearly left a mark on Ferry, who still has very fond memories of their time together. 'We laughed all the way, as we made our way down to the south of Italy.' Speaking to Bracewell about the trip many years later, Catto believed that Italy 'had quite an effect on Bryan':

> I think it was the first time he had been there, and he was affected by both the obvious historic beauties of Florence, where we stayed for a day or two, and by Assisi. And of course Italy in the 1960s was very much a land of style. Italian youth dressed well in those days; now they wear reach-me-down American grunge of the worst kind. In those days, I think both Stephen and Bryan were affected by the people they saw. Crossing into Italy is a different world – it feels like a different world.[98]

On the whole, the Durham years were a happy, exciting and fulfilling time in Catto's life. When he moved there, John Wolfe lived in Oxford, but they would see each other as often as possible, and they also wrote to each other on a regular basis. In 1966, John travelled up to Durham to say farewell to Catto before he moved back to America. He had every intention of returning, which he did in the early 1970s, when he got a job with ICL. In the intervening years, much to his American employer's surprise, he would often take his full two-week holiday allowance in one go to visit Catto in Durham. One of Catto's sisters also visited her brother in Durham and remembers those days with great fondness:

> When I was in my early teens and Jeremy was teaching at Hatfield College in Durham, I went to visit him with our mother in his rooms once or twice, and he was often in Newcastle. He seemed quite a glamorous figure, blonde, skinny, often in a black polo neck and wearing his heavy-framed glasses. He was very kind to me, and on one occasion when I was fourteen and staying with my sister in London, he picked me up in his car (no parking restrictions) and took me to Carnaby Street, out for lunch at Cranks, on to the King's Road and a very cool boutique called Granny Takes a Trip, where he was buying a shirt, I think. It was incredibly exciting. I was later introduced to Bryan Ferry and his friends, helping take some of Bryan's pictures to Durham where he was having an exhibition. Bryan, even before Roxy Music, was ultra glamorous. He came for tea to our house. Jeremy brought various friends home from time to time. And, of course, John Wolfe was on the scene often from 1961, and a much-loved part of our family life. He and Jeremy came in fashionable black PVC coats one year. I was very envious.

6

Prague Spring

'Socialism with a human face'

– Alexander Dubček, First Secretary of the
Communist Party of Czechoslovakia, April 1968

'There's still time for breakfast, I assume.'

– Catto to his host in Prague

1968 WAS A YEAR OF TUMULTUOUS SOCIAL AND POLITICAL CHANGE
across the world, with widespread demonstrations and uprisings taking
place in America and Europe. The Vietnam War sparked a series of angry
and often violent anti-war protests, and the assassination of Martin
Luther King led to race riots in cities all over America. In France, a period
of civil unrest lasting nearly two months was triggered by student protests
and wildcat strikes, which led to President Charles de Gaulle fleeing the
country for the relative safety of West Germany. In Britain, the upheaval
was of a milder nature, but Enoch Powell's infamous 'Rivers of Blood'
speech caused quite a stir, as the incendiary language he used to criticise
Commonwealth immigration threatened to unsettle the country's already
fragile race relations. In Eastern Europe, meanwhile, protests spilled out
on to the streets in Poland and Yugoslavia, culminating with the Prague
Spring in Czechoslovakia, which threatened to weaken the Soviet Union's
totalitarian grip on its satellite states.

It was at this time, and not long before he left Durham for Oxford, that Catto travelled beyond the Iron Curtain to visit Czechoslovakia for only the second time in his life. His first visit to the country had come courtesy of a good friend of his who, in Catto's own words, had 'opened up Czechoslovakia' for him. Christopher Hogwood, an English conductor and harpsichordist, who founded the early music ensemble The Academy of Ancient Music, had invited Catto to join him in Czechoslovakia for a series of concerts in the summer of 1965. The trip included not only concerts, but also a successful attempt to transport a harpsichord from Prague to Marienbad in Catto's car. Beyond this unusual introduction to the country, Catto's interest in Czechoslovakia stemmed from his knowledge of John Wycliffe. This had led him over the years to study the life of the great Czech theologian Jan Hus, who was the inspiration of Hussitism, a key proto-Protestant movement that played an important role in the Bohemian Reformation of the early fifteenth century. In 1968, Catto was in Czechoslovakia to learn more about this important religious movement, but it did not take long to become apparent that his host country was on the brink of a popular uprising of a different kind altogether.

Having been effectively dismantled as a country by the Nazis, Czechoslovakia then, like many other central and Eastern European nations, fell victim to Soviet occupation following the end of the Second World War, and by 1968 it was firmly established as a Communist satellite state. For a few brief months that year, and under the new leadership of the reform-minded Alexander Dubček, who promised his supporters 'Socialism with a human face',[99] Czechoslovakians enjoyed a series of newfound freedoms in a period that became known as the 'Prague Spring'. Those freedoms were quickly crushed, however, when the Soviet leader, Nikita Khrushchev, fearing that other satellite states would be inspired to demand similar freedoms, ordered tanks to enter the country in order to put down the uprising. In the end, there was little in the way of armed resistance to the Soviet invasion. Some protesters flooded the streets, with a few brave souls even confronting the tanks with flowers and taking down street signs to confuse the soldiers. But it was all to no avail, and the experiment in democracy was snuffed out quickly and ruthlessly. The invading army wasted no time in arresting Dubček, and with that the Prague Spring came to an end.

These were certainly heady days in the modern history of Czechoslovakia, and although Catto was not directly involved in the uprising, he did enjoy a quite remarkable walk-on part in the drama that was unfolding around him. As the tanks rolled in, most innocent bystanders quite naturally did what they could to save themselves by escaping the country. Catto, however, managed to not only get himself out of the country, but also found the time to smuggle one of the protestors out in his car, before bringing him back with him to Britain. The man in question was a young Czech student by the name of Hilar Spicka, who was known to friends as Plish. He was the brother of Catto's host in Prague, and thanks to Catto, he was able to settle in Britain and eventually went on to complete a degree course at Newcastle University. Looking back, it is clear that Catto had taken an enormous risk with his own personal safety. Had he been caught by the Communist authorities, he would almost certainly have been arrested, imprisoned, or possibly even shot. Nevertheless, his *Daily Telegraph* obituary does not suggest that Catto was overly concerned about such a prospect. In fact, the impression the reader gets is that he displayed remarkable sang-froid and refused to take the Communist threat as seriously as others did at the time. 'Reporting the Red Army's presence, his alarmed host...was reassured by Catto's response: "There's still time for breakfast, I assume.""[100]

Czechoslovakia was not the only Communist country that Catto visited during this period of his life. In fact, he and his good friend James Vallance White visited a different Communist country every year for several years in a row in the late 1960s and early 1970s. There was no particular reason for these trips, but Vallance White points out that 'there was a feeling at the time, and certainly in the 1960s, that Communism would last forever, and that it would therefore be quite interesting to find out more about such countries'. One year, Vallance White remembers that they decided to visit Romania. Not surprisingly, neither man spoke any Romanian, but Catto liked to joke that it was easy to give a good impression of someone who was capable of speaking Romanian by adding the suffix 'ul' to the end of any English word. So, for example, in Catto's view 'telephone' would become 'telephonul' in Romanian, 'pullover' would turn into 'pulloverul', and so on. Perhaps inevitably, it was another question of language which nearly landed the two men into a spot of trouble during their trip. As Vallance White recalls:

Jeremy and I stayed in Bucharest, in the Athenée Palace Hotel. The hotel was a very poor version of what it was in Olivia Manning's *Great Fortune*. We then drove north to see the wooden churches at Maramures in the northern part of the country. On the way we stopped at Cluj and had dinner near the hotel. There, tables were all decked with a little plastic Romanian flag stuck into a base with the words 'Triasca Partydul', meaning 'Long live the Party'. Jeremy stuck a piece of paper over the word 'partydul' with 'Regul', meaning 'the King'. A party of young people at a nearby table came over to see what we were doing – making me fear a quick transfer to one of Mme Ceaușescu's prisons!

Thankfully however, the party of young people ended up being very friendly, and the evening ended with them joining Catto and Vallance White at an outside table for a drink where they all toasted the King. Thinking back to that evening, Vallance White recalls that 'to them, this was a joke, rather than signs of a monarchist revival movement among the young!' Nevertheless, he also still thinks that 'it did show that the regime wasn't feared as much as, I suspect, the party was feared in the USSR.'

Shortly after his adventures in Czechoslovakia and Romania, Catto would return to Oxford to take up a fellowship at Oriel College. As with the country at large, the late 1960s and early 1970s were undoubtedly a time of change and uncertainty at both the university and at Oriel. But as will be seen, Oxford would also provide Catto with the kind of stability that he had not known for many years. Oriel would go on to become his home for the next four decades, and it was here that he would establish his reputation as not only one of the great teachers of his generation, but also as the quintessential Oxford don.

7

Oriel

'... The Senior Common Room was characterized by a tepid cosiness...'
                                    – Hugh Trevor-Roper, 1969

'...Subversives and troublemakers...'
            – A History of Oriel College, edited by Jeremy Catto

'There was a new seriousness, but also with a convivial side to things.'
                        – John Stevenson on Catto's impact on Oriel

BY 1969, AFTER A PERIOD OF WHIRLWIND REFORM, BRITAIN FELT LIKE a very different country to the one in which Catto had grown up. Only a few years before, then Labour Home Secretary Roy Jenkins had abolished the death penalty, decriminalised homosexuality, permitted abortion, and made it significantly easier for married couples to get divorced. His supporters called it 'the civilized society', but his detractors referred contemptuously to 'the permissive society'.[101] Despite these wide-ranging changes, some things remained reassuringly familiar. In a revival of a ceremony which had first been used in 1911, the investiture of the new Prince of Wales took place at Caernarfon Castle in July, watched by a global audience of over 500 million people.[102] Elsewhere around the country, however, it was a time of fear and uncertainty. In Northern Ireland, the Troubles saw continued violence over the summer months as a march in Derry resulted in a three-day communal riot known as the Battle of the

Bogside. On a happier note, the year also saw the launch of the iconic Ford Capri, the inaugural Booker Prize was won by P.H. Newby's *Something to Answer For*, and *Carry on Camping* became the year's most popular film at the UK box office.

At Oxford, meanwhile, dons and undergraduates experienced change of a different kind. The student revolts that swept across the university during the late 1960s were influenced, in part, by the violent student protests that had disfigured Paris in 1968. The result was that many of its students began to agitate for a broad range of changes to the way the university was governed. The less radically inclined simply called for a relaxation of the dress codes for students, whereas the more hot-headed went so far as to demand that students should have a greater say in how colleges were run. More broadly, frequent student demonstrations were a characteristic feature of university life at this time, with a march against Margaret Thatcher's removal of school milk, as well as a series of anti-apartheid demonstrations being prominent examples. It was also at this time that the protests against the Vietnam War caught the imagination of a generation, even though Britain's involvement in that conflict was confined to the margins. Despite a significant surge in student activism during this period, much of the activity in Britain was relatively subdued compared with what had happened on campuses across Europe. Oriel certainly saw its fair share of student activism at this time, but appeared to be facing other, more pressing concerns. According to one student at the time, 'it felt more like a college that had seen better days and that needed a real injection of focus and vision' to restore it to something approaching its former glory.

One of the fellows already installed at Oriel when Catto arrived was Hugh Trevor-Roper, and there is no question that he would have agreed with the above assessment. The celebrated historian, who was the regius professor of modern history at the university at the time and who would become notorious in academic circles in 1983 when he authenticated the so-called Hitler Diaries shortly before they were established as forgeries, had some forthright views about his adopted college. If Trevor-Roper was to be believed, the late 1960s were not the most auspicious time to be joining Oriel as a fellow. In a scathing account of his first decade at the college, he wrote the following:

> The intellectual level was low, very low; whatever method of
> calculation was used, Oriel always came out at the bottom of the
> list of colleges, measured by results in schools. The teaching was

ineffective; all mental stimulus had long been extinct; the college societies had all died through lack of it; and the Senior Common Room was characterized by a tepid cosiness which was never disturbed by anything so divisive as an idea.[103]

As if that was not enough, in a letter to his friend Bernard Berenson, the American art historian, Trevor-Roper described Oriel as 'the dingiest, dullest college in Oxford'.[104] His withering attacks on the college did not end there. In the same letter, he wrote that the college seemed to him 'like a country club in Carlisle: an old, half-moribund institution where the local squire, the local solicitor, and the local clergyman gathered occasionally for a glass of port, a rubber of auction bridge, and slow conversation about the weather'.[105] Trevor-Roper had previously been a fellow at Christ Church, by any measure a much larger and more glamorous college than Oriel, and therefore much more to his own taste, but when he accepted the role of regius professor, a move to Oriel became unavoidable, as the position was tied to that college. Adam Sisman, Trevor-Roper's biographer, described his relationship with his new college as resembling 'an arranged marriage' and that 'Christ Church had been his first love, and retained his heart'.[106] In other words, Oriel simply could not compete, and Trevor-Roper's relationship with his adopted college would continue to be a strained one for the rest of his time there.

Whatever the merits of Trevor-Roper's assessment of the college, the fellows at Oriel might have been consoled by the fact that he apparently held most dons in fairly low regard, as a letter to a friend made abundantly clear: 'But dons, in general, I fear, are bores. I had thought that this was true only of Cambridge; but alas, it is general. Not only bores but also so silly, and so self-important: they believe that they are an intellectual elite whereas in fact they are, for the most part, an insulated and protected species of lemming.'[107]

Despite Trevor-Roper's excoriating remarks about Oriel, Catto was delighted to have been appointed as a fellow at the college. As a devoted medievalist, Oriel's history brought obvious attractions for him. Founded under the patronage of Edward II in 1326, Oriel can claim to be the oldest royal foundation in Oxford, as well as the university's fifth-oldest college. As a Roman Catholic convert, Catto was also fascinated by the college's central role in the so-called Oxford Movement, a reforming religious movement of high church members of the Church of England, which began in the 1830s and eventually developed into

Anglo-Catholicism. The movement was led by prominent Oriel men, including John Henry Newman, Edward Pusey, and John Keble. Another possible reason for Oriel being an attractive prospect for Catto was that the college seemed to have a tendency to develop a certain type of character. In *Oriel College: A History*, which he himself would edit after his retirement from the college, Catto wrote the following: 'One distinctive feature may, tentatively, be observed. Among the ranks of solid citizens and grave senators of the college, a tendency to resist fashionable ideas is sporadically evident, notably in Reginald Pecock's idiosyncratic theology, Edward Powell's rejection of the Henrician Church, Sir Walter Raleigh's scepticism, William Prynn's defiance of Archbishop Laud, and the Tractarian campaign against progressive Liberalism.'[108] Later in the same passage, he added: 'Subversives and troublemakers, with whom a more recent member of the college, A.J.P. Taylor, gladly identified, were a necessary product of the intellectual independence which every generation of Orielenses nurtured.'[109] A tendency to resist fashionable ideas? Subversives and troublemakers? Was he, by any chance, thinking of himself when he wrote those words? It is certainly possible. Or maybe it is nearer the mark to say that he often approved of those who refused to conform, and secretly admired subversives and troublemakers even if, strictly speaking, he was not quite in the same mould himself.

Oriel would become a natural home for Catto over the next four decades, but as pleased as he was to have arrived at the college, he also knew that he had big shoes to fill, as his appointment had been to replace the great William ('Billy') Pantin, an eminent medievalist, Keeper of the Archives at the university from 1946 to 1969, and a tutor at Oriel from 1933 until his retirement in 1969. Pantin, a small and plump man, who had a habit of wearing a cloak around college, had himself been something of a legendary figure at Oriel, and enjoyed a devoted following among his undergraduates. According to the history of the college, Pantin was an eccentric but much-loved figure, whose rooms were always in a disastrously chaotic state, with 'every available flat surface covered in books and papers, the telephone unanswered because it could not be found under heaps of scholarly debris'.[110] Indeed, his rooms were so messy that undergraduates were often forced 'to read out their essays standing up', as there was nowhere to sit down during tutorials. Like Catto, he was also an idiosyncratic driver and the owner of a large Bristol motorcar, which he enjoyed driving despite it having no reverse gear, the result being that he had to keep driving until he found a roundabout if he wanted to change direction. Unfortunately, towards the end of his time at Oriel, his eccentric behaviour sometimes got the better of him, as he was once found by the college porter sitting stark naked under an umbrella in First Quad. The porter, sensing trouble, rushed up to him and said: 'I'm sorry, sir, but this really won't do.' Seemingly unaware of what was going on, the old don replied: 'Don't worry, it's alright, I'm a mushroom.' This was undoubtedly a sad end for a man who had given so much to his college, but such stories should not detract from the fact that Pantin was a serious and distinguished historian of medieval England, and that Catto had his work cut out as his successor.

Over time, Catto was able to establish his own legend as one of the great dons of his generation. One of Pantin's last undergraduates at Oriel, and one of Catto's first, was a young man from West Sussex by the name of David Manning. Today, Sir David Manning is a retired diplomat, who served in British embassies in Warsaw, New Delhi, Paris, and Moscow, before being appointed as the British ambassador to the United States in 2003. He served in that capacity until 2007 and was involved in the run-up to the second Iraq War. Reflecting on his time at Oriel, he describes the transition from Pantin to Catto as 'bracing'. By this he means that Pantin, who was undoubtedly a charming and intelligent individual, could also be somewhat absent-minded. Towards the end of his time at Oriel, he was perhaps not as demanding in relation to academic standards as he had once been, and there were times when undergraduates had to remind him of the essay they had been asked to write for that week's tutorial. Sir David recalls that his first year at Oriel had been 'pretty slack', but things changed when Catto arrived. 'You had to be ready to produce something serious, and be able to talk intelligently about it.' In addition, Sir David remembers that he and his peers were expected to work a lot harder: 'Getting thirds was no longer acceptable.' Catto was a stickler for getting the basics right, and this meant doing the work, handing it in on time, as well as wearing your gown to tutorials. (Later in the 1970s, however, it appears that Catto became more relaxed about dress codes. As one Oriel undergraduate from that era recalls: 'Jeremy had a mixed attitude to dress protocol for his tutorials. While he insisted on students wearing a gown, and so could perhaps be considered a stickler, he didn't seem to care much what else they wore. I distinctly remember going to tutorials in Trinity term in 1976 and 1977, both of which saw hot summers, in shorts, T-shirt, sandals and my gown.')

Professor John Stevenson, who was a lecturer in history at Oriel from 1971 to 1976, agrees with Sir David's assessment of Catto's emphasis on maintaining high standards, and recalls that the college, having languished somewhere towards the bottom of the academic table of Oxford colleges for a number of years, was now 'trying to pull itself up from its bootstraps'. Catto was very much at the forefront of that process and was, according to Stevenson, part of that 'new thrusting generation of dons', who wanted to revitalise the college: 'There was a new seriousness, but also with a convivial side to things.'

In the end, even if Trevor-Roper was right about Oriel dons in particular, there would be brighter days ahead for the college, and Catto undoubtedly played an important part in that rejuvenation. He achieved this primarily through his teaching, as well as through his singular devotion to his undergraduates and to college life more broadly. In what follows, we will examine these and other aspects of his time at Oriel, starting with his approach to teaching.

8

Teaching

'All Oxford need teach you is to know when someone is talking rot.'
– Harold Macmillan, British Prime Minister (1957–63)
and Chancellor of Oxford University (1960–86)

'Not too many facts, dear boy, not too many facts.'
– Catto to an undergraduate

IN 1909, THE CHANCELLOR OF OXFORD UNIVERSITY, LORD CURZON, declared with the characteristic confidence of a Balliol man: 'If there is any product of which the University of Oxford has special reason to be proud, which has stamped its mark on the lives and characters of generations of men, and has excited the outspoken envy of other nations, it is that wonderful growth of personal tuition which has sprung up in our midst.'[111] Curzon was, of course, referring to the university's tutorial system, which for the past couple of centuries has been the keystone of Oxford's academic excellence, as well as of its international reputation. This method of teaching, which is based on the individual, discussion-based, Socratic method, is said to have attained its unique status in the middle of the nineteenth century. Benjamin Jowett, classicist and Master of Balliol College, is widely credited with having been the guiding influence behind the development of the system. His students said of Jowett that 'his great skill consisted, like Socrates, in helping us to learn and think for ourselves'.[112] After Jowett became Vice-Chancellor of the university in 1882, his teaching method was established as a 'pattern for the whole university'.[113] By the time Catto arrived at Balliol in the late 1950s, he, too, would benefit from this system, under the watchful eyes of Maurice Keen and Richard Southern. What's more, everyone who was subsequently taught by Catto at Oriel over the course of nearly forty years would become familiar with the above description of the tutorial system, and making the most of this system was central to Catto's teaching method, to which he remained devoted long after it ceased to be fashionable.

A good way of describing Catto's teaching method is to begin with what he was *not* trying to achieve. First, although he was committed to the tutorial system, it should not be assumed that he was a dogmatist or that he stuck rigidly to specific theories. According to Lord Sumption, a former Justice of the Supreme Court and historian of the Hundred Years' War, Catto was not a man for systems or theories: 'He certainly thought that the world was a better place for being full of cultivated Oxford arts graduates, regardless of whether they improved the gross domestic product, but he did not believe in overarching theories.'

Secondly, he did not adopt a one-size-fits-all model for his undergraduates, appreciating that his students were all different and that his method of teaching them had to take their individual strengths and weaknesses into account. This is corroborated by Professor Christopher Tyerman, a former professor of the history of the Crusades at Oxford: 'He was very much led by the individual and by their abilities and interests.'

Thirdly, Catto did not view tutorials primarily through the narrow prism of preparing his undergraduates for their exams. According to Professor Simon Skinner, a history don at Balliol, Catto conceived the tutor's role as 'going beyond the subject of the tutorial'. By this, Skinner means that most modern dons see their role today in a narrower, more technical and academic sense. They try at all times to 'teach to the test' and thus 'the preoccupation now is more about churning out post-graduate academic historians'.

Fourthly, and linked to this point, it was not uncommon for Catto's tutorials to veer off-topic and to focus on areas that would not necessarily be covered in the exam. In that regard, Catto's approach was very similar to that of Richard Cobb's. A distinguished historian and essayist, and the author of numerous influential works on the history of France, Cobb, who was a friend of Catto's, was one of the great figures during the latter's time at Oxford and, from the point of view of the modern tutor, certainly had an unusual approach to tutorials. Tim Heald, who edited a book on Cobb's letters and was taught by him at Balliol, recalls in the introduction to his book that at the start of a particular term, he and his tutorial partner were presented with the choice of two alternatives. One was to trawl through all the usual European history questions of the eighteenth and nineteenth centuries, and the other was to root around the less well-known events which were unfamiliar even to Cobb himself. These would include the no doubt fascinating but not entirely useful incident of the so-called 'Umbrella Uprising' in Milan in 1814, when a mob beat to death the finance minister, Giuseppe Prina, with their silk umbrellas on the piazza outside the Duomo.[114] It was clear that Cobb's preference was to opt for the latter alternative, even if that meant studying something that was not going to come up in the exam. Catto approved of this approach and frequently copied it, with the result that his tutorials often ended up as fascinating, illuminating, but also highly entertaining journeys of discovery.

Fifthly, and linked to the point about exams, Catto was not a slave to the demands of the Norrington Table (which ranks Oxford colleges by how many first-class degrees they obtain in final exams). Although he held his students to high academic standards, he also encouraged them to develop a broad range of interests whilst they were at Oriel. He believed that there was more to life than writing history essays, and he wanted his undergraduates to become fully rounded citizens. His view of education and of college life was holistic, and he understood how all the different parts of a university education came together to produce the whole individual. Jeffrey Bonas, who read history at Oriel in the 1960s and came to know Catto in later years, remembers once hearing that one of Catto's undergraduates was unable to accept a place in a university sports team because it would have meant missing an entire term of tuition. Most dons would have agreed with this approach, but Catto told his student to accept his place on the university team because, as he put it, 'it is important in life to do the things we are best at'. As Bonas says, Catto's 'wisdom and his advice were valued by young people just as much as his teaching'. Sir Alan Duncan, the former Foreign Office and International Development Minister, who attended St John's College in the late 1970s and became a long-standing friend of Catto's, believes that this was central to his teaching method and underpinned his overall view of the purpose of education. As he notes in his foreword to this book:

> The insatiable thirst for firsts risks narrowing the purpose and benefits of a university education. Too many professors and tutors

look on extracurricular activity with undisguised scorn. But a university education should be the most potent of all civilizing experiences. Library slaves who know little else of the world will not make their best contribution to its improvement. University life is not just a knowledge machine: it should build characters and confident opinions.[115]

The heirs of Thomas Gradgrind, that brilliant Dickensian creation who was only interested in the pursuit of profitable enterprise, would describe Catto's approach to education as aimless, amateurish and lacking in focus. But that would be to miss the point of what he was trying to achieve. To understand what his ultimate purpose was, we need to return to the point made at the start of this chapter in relation to Benjamin Jowett at Balliol, who encouraged his undergraduates to think for themselves. This imperative was at the very heart of Catto's approach, and central to this idea was the tutorial as it was originally conceived, with its emphasis on the continual testing of ideas through discussion and debate. Today, the tutorial system still has some advocates at Oxford, but the model has changed significantly, and an increasingly small number of dons now teach their undergraduates in this manner. In fact, today's dons are now as likely to simply take in an undergraduate's essay and mark it as they are to engage in a lengthy discussion-based tutorial. The aim now is to 'teach to the test' and to prepare undergraduates for their exams. The relentless acquisition of facts is what matters and writing an essay in the 'correct' manner is what is prized. Discussion and debate are viewed as less important.

By contrast, Catto rarely, if ever, marked his undergraduates' essays in any formal sense, preferring instead to get them to read out their essays before gently probing them on a series of key points in order to elicit a clearer understanding of the topic. For him, it was this exploratory discussion that enabled undergraduates to obtain a clearer insight into the subject being studied. Crucially, it also forced undergraduates to develop their own critical faculties, as they had no choice but to think through the subject for themselves. Of course, facts mattered to Catto, but essays had to be argument-led, with facts playing a strong supportive role. As he told one of his undergraduates who asked him for a last piece of advice ahead of those exams: 'Not too many facts, dear boy, not too many facts.' To some, this piece of advice might have seemed almost perverse, but Catto knew that the real skill in writing an essay rests not on the mechanical accumulation of facts, but on the ability to make a convincing argument. To his mind, the best way to develop those arguments was through the discussion-based tutorial system. He wanted his undergraduate to approach an intellectual problem in an intelligent manner. In essence, therefore, his approach was based on Harold Macmillan's famous dictum that the purpose of an Oxford education was to teach people to think and, as a result, to teach them 'to know if someone else is talking rot'.[116]

But learning how to think was not, in and of itself, enough for Catto. The broader purpose behind his teaching method was to expand the minds of his undergraduates and to create for them a civilising experience that would prepare them for adult life. According to Harry Mount, the journalist, author and Editor of *The Oldie*, who was at Magdalen in the 1990s, Catto's view of education included a significant element of socialisation:

> Jeremy realised that education was much more than tutorials or absorption of facts and theories, crucial as those are. Education at university was also about how to get along with your fellow undergraduates and dons; how to foster amusing conversation, full of anecdotes, jokes and questions and answers. The age of eighteen to twenty-one is halfway between childhood and adulthood. A good education should prepare you to be good company as a grown-up as well as having a full mind.

Daniel Hannan, now Lord Hannan, a former Conservative MEP who was an undergraduate at Oriel around the same time as Mount, agrees with this and argues that the ability to think within a social setting was crucial to Catto's view of education:

> What he was really doing, of course, was teaching you how to think – how to approach an intellectual problem in more than one way, how to develop an argument and, not least, how to do so in a social setting. A great many of his tutorials involved sherry or pink gin, and the most important of his lessons were imparted elsewhere – at the Union, at receptions in his rooms, or at the Canning Club, which brought together dons and bright undergraduates of Tory inclination. He had a strong sense, almost vanished these days, of university life as a symposium – a time when intellectual stimulation ought to be constant and convivial, not confined to tutorials.[117]

Perhaps the best way to get an insight into Catto's teaching method, and to understand the nature of his tutorials, is to hear directly from those who were taught or supervised by him over the course of four decades. What follows, therefore, is a series of accounts, in more or less chronological order, from a broad range of Catto's undergraduate and graduate students, starting with his first students from the late 1960s and ending with some of his last students in the early 2000s.

* * *

Peter de Bruyne *(attended Oriel in 1968 to read law before switching to history. After leaving Oriel, he worked in mining, finance and shipping in Latin America)*
De Bruyne remembers Catto's teaching style as being 'thorough but a pleasure', and that Catto 'combined erudition with being remarkably unpompous', adding that he had 'a sort of controlled impishness' about his personality. De Bruyne was taught the Anglo-Saxon paper by Catto, and he recalls that he 'quite enjoyed' the topic of the later Anglo Saxon manorial charters as his Latin was 'pretty good'. By the end of the course, he told Catto that he felt he had become something of an expert in the field. Catto chuckled at this and said: 'You have a long way to go.'

Sir David Manning *(attended Oriel in the late 1960s. Later, he would become the British ambassador to the United States and is now an honorary fellow of Oriel)*
In Sir David Manning's opinion, Catto 'was a real scholar, who had enormous knowledge of whatever you were discussing, and always had the ability to recommend articles about anything that was being discussed'. In addition, 'his tutorials were demanding – despite the sherries, and gin and tonics – and he did expect you to take the subject seriously and to work hard.'

John Martin Robinson *(attended Oriel as a graduate student in the early 1970s. He is now an eminent architectural historian)*
According to Robinson, 'people can either teach or they can't, and Jeremy had the ability to make his subject interesting', adding that Catto was 'like a fire with warm embers…you wanted to approach him and warm yourself with his learning'.

Andrew Robathan *(now Lord Robathan, attended Oriel between 1970–73. Following this, he was commissioned into the Coldstream Guards, before serving as an MP and minister)*
Robathan 'always looked forward' to tutorials with Catto because 'they were always interesting'. He believed Catto understood the limitations of most eighteen-year-olds and had the ability 'to make history interesting and to bring the subject to life'. Robathan adds that his own 'love of history was largely instilled' in him by Catto, and he remembers that when he eventually emerged from Oxford with a good degree, Catto teased him by sending him a letter, in which he suggested that Robathan's degree had been the result 'more of native good wit than hard work'.

David Mathew *(attended Oriel from 1973–6, and then went on to work in China for Jardine Matheson)*
Mathew feels that Catto made 'a distinction between those undergraduates who interested him and those who did not, and with those who did interest him he sparkled'. According to Mathew, Catto wanted 'to get people to question things', and it was this that really motivated him. In addition, he points out that Catto was always 'very interested in people', and that he had the ability to help you focus on what actually motivated real people to behave in a certain way in the past. With the help of primary sources, Catto would get you to think about, for example, what local gentry families really thought about the Norman Conquest. Referring to the sometimes shadowy nature of medieval history, Mathew argues that Catto 'gave that period of history a personality that was often very difficult to achieve'. Understanding this type of motivation, Mathew believes, was not just a matter of academic interest, but also had a real impact on his own career in China, as it helped him to understand the motivations behind many of the family networks that ran things in China at the time.

John Varley *(attended Oriel from 1974–7. Later, he would become a highly distinguished banker and Group CEO at Barclays Bank from 2004–11)*
Varley had initially wanted to do more modern history when he arrived at Oxford, but he says that 'it then became obvious pretty quickly that I should abandon my ideas about modern history and study whatever Jeremy was teaching', as it was clearly going to be a more interesting experience. He adds that Catto's teaching style was 'a mixture of soft edge and hard edge, even though it was not always easy to detect the hard

edges'. Once he had you reading out your essay, he 'listened a lot and was not especially didactic', in the sense that 'he did not always lead with his own opinions but would nudge you in certain directions'. Varley reflects that Catto's ability in this regard was 'a very considerable skill'. Of course, Catto 'absolutely could have lectured you, even though his tutorials were not lectures, but were instead based on dialogue'. To that end, Catto 'did not do the heavy lifting, but expected you to do most of the heavy lifting yourself'.

James Miller-Stirling *(attended Oriel in 1975, before embarking on a career in shipping, insurance and investment management in the Far East)*
Looking back on his time at the college, Miller-Stirling describes Catto as 'a man of immense excitement and charm, and a man one looked up to'. He recalls how 'the sun used to shine into those rooms he had on King Edward Street…and Jeremy would sit there with his wispy light brown hair, wearing a bow tie, and with those foggy round glasses that made it hard to see his eyes and even harder to know what he was thinking'. But despite this somewhat inscrutable facade, Miller-Stirling always 'thoroughly enjoyed' his tutorials with him and believes that they will 'forever' be in his mind. He recalls that one of Catto's great strengths as a tutor was to make history come alive during tutorials and to 'bring home the realities of living in medieval England'. Although Catto 'never really said a great deal', Miller-Stirling remembers the 'minute and barely readable' comments at the bottom of essays (three of which he still has to this day), which were always 'very succinct' and 'left you feeling both elated and deflated at the sheer brilliance of the man'.

Sir Richard Stagg *(attended Oriel in the mid-1970s. Now a retired diplomat, he enjoyed a distinguished career as British ambassador to Bulgaria, High Commissioner of India and British ambassador to Afghanistan. Since 2019, he has served as the Warden of Winchester College)*
According to Sir Richard, Catto 'was good at putting a different lens on what was going on in medieval Europe', adding that he was 'always keen to talk about what motivated people in medieval times, which made it a real-life subject, rather than just a dry form of narrative', something he found both 'enriching and eye-opening'. When it came to providing his undergraduates with feedback on their work, Sir Richard remembers that Catto 'also had quite a knack for making critical points in a nice way'. He describes 'that smile behind the bow tie' and how Catto would gently ask:

'Do you think that's quite right?' This showed how Catto had 'a knack for getting you to think for yourself', which Sir Richard contrasts with some of his teachers at school, who were very good in their own way, but had 'more of a brutal approach in contrast to Jeremy's more elegant way'. But that gentle art of persuasion should not be confused with weakness: 'He wasn't soft if he thought you had said something daft, but he had a way of telling you that was constructive. The raised eyebrow was very much part of the tutorial experience.'

David Bugge (attended Oriel in the years 1976–9. He went on to pursue a successful career in banking. Today he is a managing director at NatWest Bank in London)
Bugge describes Catto as 'gentle and thoughtful', and adds that he had an 'insightful approach to teaching', which allowed his students to 'develop academic confidence':

> Jeremy would work his way through the topic with questions to us. He would seek to draw out insights that we had not really fully appreciated were there. He opened our minds, and through his questions, he led us to our own more penetrating insights. To form our own views based on evidence rather than just following the line of various academics. We came to trust our own judgements and make our own arguments.

Ken Fincham (attended Oriel from 1976–9. He is now a history professor at the University of Kent)

> I think Jeremy liked the gentle interrogation, to encourage you to discover the shortcomings of your own arguments. A classic technique was to ask one question, then base the next on your response which could be a voyage of mounting trepidation as your position became increasingly precarious or implausible. But in tutorials there was no punchline or denouement, just the silent invocation to think again. Jeremy also enjoyed challenging conventional wisdom, the building blocks of so many essays, and it was stimulating as the ground so often moved beneath our feet.

David Brierley *(arrived at Oriel as an Exhibitioner[vii] in 1979, and then went on to pursue a career as an environmental insurance specialist, leading a team working for Eagle Star Insurance, now known as Zurich)*

In tutorials, Jeremy was very good at asking questions that made you think independently to identify what you were aware of but hadn't thought was important to the question. Jeremy's tutorials made you think hard. He brought interest into the more challenging and difficult aspects of history in such a way that it meant you looked further into a particular topic, more than you would have done otherwise. This was his unique teaching style.

David Freedman *(attended Oriel in the early 1980s, and is now a sales director for Huthwaite International in London)*
In Freedman's opinion, Catto's teaching style was based on 'rigorous examinations of whether undergraduates had a) done the copious prescribed reading; b) understood what we had read; and c) written with clarity and precision'. He adds that 'in the unlikely event that we had also produced anything of style or originality, he would be generous in his acknowledgement' and that 'he could normally spot a bluffer instantly', not least because 'within the realm of the widest medieval English and European span, he simply knew everything worth knowing'.

Simon MacKinnon *(attended Oriel in the years 1980–83, before pursuing postgraduate studies at the University of Pennsylvania. He would go on to enjoy a distinguished business career in Asia, gaining an OBE, becoming an honorary citizen of Shanghai, and receiving the Chinese Friendship Award, which is the highest award given by the Chinese state to foreign nationals)*
MacKinnon recalls Catto's teaching style with great fondness. 'It was the atmosphere with him. You knew there was a tremendous mind, but he never imposed himself as he could have done.' Instead, Catto's approach was based on his ability to 'tease out your logic or lack of logic in your argument'. MacKinnon adds that he remembers one tutorial in particular from which he emerged feeling that he had been 'peppered by a machine gun'. 'I felt completely drained, but the way he did it was very gentle.' He concludes by saying that Catto had 'an extraordinary gift as a teacher' and that his 'overriding memory of him was that he was a very good

vii An award given for excelling academically.

listener, who could pick holes in your argument, but that it was all about improving your analytical skills.'

James Mitchell *(attended Oriel from 1987–90. He would later become an art dealer in London)*
Mitchell remembers arriving at Oxford having mainly studied later history at Harrow School. This had involved looking at lots of documents, which 'made it hard to go back to a world based on very few documents and plenty of conjecture'. Despite this initial challenge, Catto was able to open Mitchell's eyes to the pleasures of medieval history. He recalls that 'Jeremy encouraged you to think and to use the sources that were available'. In the end, thanks to Catto, and much to his own surprise, Mitchell 'really enjoyed' the English History 1 (Anglo Saxon) paper, and it turned out to be the best paper in his exam. Mitchell again credits Catto with that achievement and says that it was 'the mark of the man' that he was the one who helped him to overcome his initial difficulties with medieval history.

Charles Bonas *(attended Oriel in the years 1989–92. He is now a director at Bonas Macfarlane, a leading tuition and consulting firm)*
For Bonas, Catto's teaching method was rooted in his genuine interest in people. 'He valued statistical research, but he was first and foremost interested in people, which came through in his teaching and also made the subject come alive.' Bonas describes Catto as 'a very non-judgmental man, and he never made you feel like you were stupid no matter how appalling your essay was.' The result of this was that Catto was able to instil in his students a profound sense of self-assurance: 'Teaching is about building confidence, and few were better at that than Jeremy.' Finally, Bonas points out that, 'despite all the pink gins, Jeremy was a very serious-minded and disciplined man', who was especially interested in encouraging his students to think about specific areas of history, which would serve to reveal a broader truth about what was being studied:

> Just like he would only reveal fragments of his own life, he liked to study fragments of history and he was ruthless about using facts to make a very specific point. In terms of our essays, he liked things to come out with a punch, and he preferred you to focus on only a couple of sources but have something interesting to say about them. Ultimately, what he liked about medieval history was the chaos and mystery of it.

Dr Kate Selway *(completed her doctorate at New College, Oxford between 1989–93, with supervision from Catto. She is now a King's Counsel at the commercial bar in London)*
Dr Selway recalls that Catto played an instrumental role in helping her to shift her focus from Henry V to Henry VI. 'Jeremy was a very strong guiding force. His vision helped me to make that transition, which helped me to forge a much more interesting path.' As for his style of supervision, Selway remembers that Catto 'did not constantly pester you to come and see him'. The idea was to 'just get on with it', but you were 'always welcome to knock on his door if you needed help'. For Selway, Catto was 'a mine of information', and he would usually spend an hour or so with her, after which she would 'always come away fresh with new ideas and enthusiasm'.

Dr Jonathan Hughes *(supervised by Catto for his doctorate. He is now an honorary research fellow at the University of Exeter)*
When Dr Hughes came over from New Zealand to begin work on his doctorate, a colleague who had put him in touch with Catto said that he would find him a 'very civilised' character, but that he was also 'a young man who was getting fat', the implication being perhaps that he was enjoying college life a little too much. What Hughes found was a man with 'a razor-sharp intellect', whose method of supervision was 'very much based on a light touch approach'. Catto 'made very few demands in regards to written work, which may not have suited everyone', but there is no doubt that it worked for Hughes, who 'experienced a real sense of intellectual bonding' with his supervisor. Hughes often came away from his supervisions 'buzzing with excitement', to the extent that he would 'deliberately not do anything for several hours to allow it all to sink in'.

Nick Lord *(attended Oriel in the years 1992–5. He is now based in Rome as one of the founding partners at Resonate Global Advisors, a specialist global content and events consultancy)*
Nick Lord first encountered Catto after he had failed to get into Balliol. Undeterred, he applied to Oriel instead. When Catto walked into the room, Lord remembers that he smiled at him and said: 'Bloody Balliol!' Thinking back to Catto's style of teaching, he says: 'I don't think he ever taught me as such, but he taught me how to learn and I certainly did learn.' He adds that Catto's 'style of teaching was very subtle, but he knew what he was doing. Just a gentle pull on the tiller and your ship of learning would go in a different direction.'

Simon Kingston *(met Catto at Oxford in the early to mid-1990s, when he was working towards a DPhil. Today, he co-leads the Social Impact and Education Sector at Russell Reynolds Associates)*
According to Kingston, Catto was 'enormously helpful in his intellectual development, helped to gently steer him in new directions, and also helped to find his supervisor'. He believes Catto 'encouraged people to be partisans for their area of interest, but to do so without becoming too specialised'. In addition, Catto was 'a great connector of themes and subjects across time and geography, and his great gift as a teacher was to help you see the endlessly different ways in which human history has evolved, but without falling into the trap of making simplified or glib connections'.

Tom Atkins *(attended Oriel from 1995–8, and now works as an accountant)*
According to Atkins, a phone call from Catto in December 1994 changed his life:

> To say that Jeremy's way of teaching wasn't what I was used to is an understatement. To go from a wood and metal chair in a draughty school Portakabin in Maidstone to an armchair in Jeremy's cosy study should have been a huge shock. But from day one, Jeremy made everyone feel like they belonged. I was a mediocre historian at best, an eighteen-year-old kid being asked to give his thoughts and opinions to a man who had spent his life working on periods of history I had hardly even been aware existed a week previously. Yet Jeremy afforded me, and everyone else he taught, the greatest of respect. It was rare that he would express his own views – in spite of being a world-renowned expert, it was your opinions he was interested in, and it was your views that we would spend the hour and a half exploring, not his own.

Dr Alexander Morrison *(attended Oriel in the late 1990s. He is now a tutorial fellow in history at New College, Oxford)*
Dr Morrison recalls his time at Oriel with great fondness and says that Catto's teaching method was based on a fairly 'laissez-faire approach', in the sense that 'vigorous intervention' was not generally required, as he tended to choose people who could work quite independently. Nevertheless, Catto would 'pick you off if you had done something really stupid', and he would intervene 'if he felt that you might muck up your finals'.

Matthew Bool *(attended Oriel from 1998–2001. He is now a partner at Herbert Smith Freehills in London)*
Bool says that tutorials with Catto were always 'relaxed in style and he always made you feel welcome and at ease'. In terms of his teaching method, Bool recalls that Catto 'loved a good argument and a good discussion', and that he was always 'very good at playing devil's advocate to test you and to make you think'. Catto wanted his students to challenge the premise of the question, to think creatively, and to develop their own opinions. Bool quickly grasped that, having been set an essay, you could of course go to the Radcliffe Camera library, read all the relevant books and then produce an essay based on the overall consensus. But Catto 'really enjoyed it if you were prepared to go against the consensus and he always stressed that your own view was as valid as that of the next historian'.

Marcus Walker *(attended Oriel from 1999–2002 as an undergraduate. He then stayed on for a year to complete a master's in Byzantine studies. He is now the rector at Great St Bartholomew's in London)*
In Marcus Walker's opinion, Catto's teaching style was 'all very didactic', adding that he 'got you to read out your essay and you then had to defend it'. He and his contemporaries used to joke about the fact that Catto would fall asleep during tutorials one moment but would then be fully awake and on the ball not long after. Looking back, Walker believes this may have been a deliberate ploy on Catto's part and was probably his way of keeping his students on their toes.

Erik Hannikainen *(attended Oriel from 1999–2003. He now lives in Venice working on a variety of cultural projects)*
Hannikainen describes Catto as 'always kind, ever generous and constantly amused by whatever was going on in the great world beyond the college gates, and at the same time seemingly indifferent to the passing of time'. As for Catto's teaching style, he remembers that it was 'cosy and relaxed' and felt 'more like a chat after lunch at a country house'. Moreover, tutorials were 'never intimidating, even if the subject was quite new', because Catto 'would very patiently get you to see more points to the argument than you had at first imagined'. When asked what made Catto such an excellent teacher, Hannikainen says the following:

> He made you see the question you were faced with as a great canvas, then made you focus on very small details. Such as the broader

view of society on the brink of the Black Death, then zoom into the minutiae of some chivalric element that was currently obsessing the courts of England and France. Poems such as the 'Vows of the Heron' became microcosms of the great chivalric world of the fourteenth century.

Hannikainen most remembers the paper on chivalry he studied with Catto, recalling that on one memorable occasion, he and another group of undergraduates were taken by Catto to see the Wilton Diptych. 'He then showed us Richard II's cookbook, which was kept in the Bodleian. He wanted us to see the many facets of a period and character, and by giving us these opportunities, he made an already fascinating world truly wondrous.'

Josef Karl Pelikan *(attended Oriel as a postgraduate student in the early 2000s. He now works at the UN as the Chief of Staff and Special Representative for Eastern Europe and Central Asia)*
Pelikan says that Catto was always hugely supportive of his students, and that he encouraged him to stay on at Oriel and even suggested that he should apply for a set of scholarships. 'Without Dr Catto, I would have never had the courage to apply for these, and without his support, I surely would have never been awarded both scholarships.' In addition, Pelikan believes that Catto's tutorials had a significant impact on his future career as a diplomat:

> Dr Catto always provided his supervisees with the impression of being taken seriously as a person and as being appreciated as an interlocutor, although his own in-depth knowledge of affairs was by far larger than that of his supervisees. This approach provided an atmosphere of trust and respect which can be rarely found, and which was very enriching from my point of view. He encouraged students to evolve, develop and to think. Based on my personal experience as a career diplomat, I can only stress the importance of Dr Catto's tutorials, and how they helped me to prepare myself for my professional endeavours.

Clemmie Raynsford *(attended Oriel from 2000–03. She now works for Diageo's corporate relations team in London)*
Raynsford reflects that everything Catto did in terms of his teaching method 'constantly forced you to think for yourself'. As a tutor, Catto

was 'always so measured, refined and minimalist in everything he said and did', but what he said 'always had a great impact'. After her first essay, Catto told Raynsford that he wanted 'an original argument', which gave her a tremendous amount of confidence, as he made her believe that 'despite all the historians and all the books in the Bodleian, there was still room for me to have an original view'. Although he was not fixated on exams, he did provide Raynsford with an invaluable piece of advice:

> After my first poor effort at Trials, when I had most definitely written an A-Level essay – plenty of evidence and very little original thought – he was really kind. He realised I was someone who, when in an exam, started writing almost immediately in an effort to get as much information on the page, as well as to show all the quotes I had memorised. He told me that for the first fifteen minutes of any exam, I was not allowed to write, but only to think, plan and plot what I was going to write. And only after these fifteen minutes was I allowed to write. As he said, 'these fifteen minutes are the 'Alphafactory'. This was his expression for the time when you could move yourself to a First...It has always stayed with me and stays with me in my most impetuous moments now.

Raynsford concludes by arguing that Catto's style of teaching 'transcended normal educational tools and approaches, and his gentle influence and powers of suggestion changed the lives of his students.'

Dr Robert Portass *(taught by Catto at Oriel between 2001–4. He is now a history fellow at Robinson College, Cambridge)*
For Portass, the key to Catto's tutorials was the use of sources. Whereas other historians preferred to focus on the historiography for a particular period, Catto liked to emphasise the importance of using sources properly:

> He was not that interested in historiography. Historians had to do it as a form of due diligence, but the times I really saw him come alive was when he was working with primary sources. He would always return to the manuscripts, return to the chronicles, and he would encourage you to think of them as puzzles. That was an approach that has really stayed with me.

Dr Leif Dixon *(met Catto for the first time in 2004 and was recruited by him to do some teaching at Oriel. Today, he is a lecturer and Director of Studies in History at Regent's Park College, Oxford)*
'Jeremy was very old school on the surface, but there was always an underlying sense of informality about him too. You always felt with him that you were in on a plan, rather than being judged all the time.' All of that, according to Dixon, made him feel 'incredibly valued'. Although he was not taught by Catto, the two men did some teaching together on the Disciplines of History course, and Dixon recalls that Catto's approach to teaching always impressed him. 'For him the key was to respond positively to what the students had, rather than imposing on them or having particular expectations of them.' In addition, Dixon says that he was always struck by 'his very commonsensical approach…he would not use jargon, did not like "isms" or generalisations, but broke down the debates into relatable parts.' Dixon concludes that he learned a huge amount from the way in which Catto 'modelled the clarity of his teaching'.

Alex Young *(attended Oriel from 2002–6, completing both a BA and a master's in modern history. He is now a barrister in London)*
When asked to describe Catto's teaching style, Young emphasises the sense of freedom and autonomy he gave his students: 'He gave you the essay question and provided you with a reading list, but he then just let you get on with it.' When the time came to discuss the finished essay, Young recalls that 'tutorials were very much in the nature of a fireside chat'. Constructive dialogue was always at the heart of Catto's approach, and Young stresses that Catto 'never tried to push an agenda'. Instead, 'it was very much a discussion, rather than about indoctrination'. Nor was there pressure to achieve any particular standard, but Catto's personality inspired loyalty and, in turn, 'a degree of diligence as you didn't want to let him down'. Young also remembers Catto's small acts of kindness, which were nevertheless an important part of his teaching method. After he finished his first year's exams in second place across the university as a whole, Catto sent him a hand-written note, in which he congratulated Young on his results and added the following gentle encouragement: 'Only one person pipped you to the post. You'll have to do something about that next time.'

Josh Pull *(attended Oriel in the years 2003–6. He then became an investment banker before co-founding Keystone Tutors, a leading tutoring company based in London)*

Whilst Jeremy no doubt valued the importance of academic rigour, he also took a pragmatic approach as to what that meant for an undergraduate. His advice before finals was to avoid spending too long in the library reading books cover to cover. Rather he advised short bursts, when one was feeling fresh, and absorbing short articles to find the interesting angle to take away. In essence, he was encouraging us to prioritise original and nimble thinking to make us stand out from (rather than following) the crowd, and emphasised that this was far more effective than working for the sake of it.

William Orr-Ewing *(attended Oriel from 2003–6. He is now co-founder and director of Keystone Tutors in London)*

Oxford was really the beginning of my education rather than anything near its culmination. The idea I most took from Jeremy was that the life of the mind is its own reward: books, ideas, quips, quotes, jokes – and the friendships built up around these – are a feast that we were all invited to enjoy. Enjoyment didn't always mean a lack of earnestness, though. I remember he almost came to tears recollecting a scene in Waugh's *Handful of Dust*.

9

Tutorials

'I was reading out my essay on Anglo-Saxon burials and found that…Jeremy had fallen fast asleep. It was my very first term and I did not know what to do, so I just carried on reading my essay. I went through page three and then page four and, by now, Jeremy was snoring quite loudly…'

– A student recalling one of his first tutorials with Catto

'The puss! Somebody save the puss!'

– Catto during a tutorial

'I will have the Pouilly Fuisse with the fish.'

– Catto to the college butler during a tutorial

THE TESTIMONIES FROM THE PREVIOUS CHAPTER MAKE IT CLEAR that Catto was an exceptionally gifted teacher and that he, in turn, inspired the unwavering loyalty in those he taught over the course of four decades. How did he secure this loyalty?

Firstly, it certainly helped that he enjoyed being in the company of young people. Although Richard Davenport-Hines was not taught by Catto, he could see that he had a uniquely warm relationship with young people, and while 'not a tolerant man…was sympathetic and understanding of the young'. Jonathan Hughes agrees and adds that Catto, like a public-school master, was 'genuinely concerned about the welfare of his students'. This struck Hughes as not only unusual, in that most academics he knew were not that way inclined, but it also meant that Catto had the ability 'to communicate the idea that you were special', with the result that you came away from meeting him 'feeling important'. Hughes also notes that, it was clear that Catto had his favourites, and that 'it was obvious it meant a huge amount to them and had a very significant formative impact on them'.

Secondly, according to Sir Alan Duncan, the answer lay in the nature of his character: 'He was a gentleman and a gentle man…The only word for it is inoffensive. Even when he said outré things, they were somehow both thoughtful and playful, so no one ever took offence.' The historian and author of *The Silk Roads*, Peter Frankopan, agrees and adds: 'He was immensely generous to his students …He could be waspish, but was never unkind or unfair to those with whom he didn't see eye to eye.'

Thirdly, and perhaps most importantly, Catto's students were loyal to him because they could sense that he was a genuinely unique character, which meant that they enjoyed being in his company. He was different to most other dons and he did things in his own inimitable fashion and with his own distinctive style. The result, as the following testimonies from former students will highlight, was that his tutorials provided them with a series of truly unforgettable memories.

* * *

Even though he liked young people and was kind and generous, he could also be tough when he needed to be. It was a part of the tutorial experience which few of his students would ever forget. According to John Varley, Catto had 'high expectations, in particular in regards to your commitment, hard work and punctuality', adding that Catto 'was in an altogether good way very demanding of you, and very trenchant about certain standards'. After a brief pause he concludes by saying that in Catto's tutorials 'you were always on your toes' and that 'there was a tiger behind that velvet'.

David Bugge remembers that Catto could be firm in tutorials when he needed to be: 'He was kind but would ask probing questions. His tone was soft. But he would let the silence linger as you wrestled with his question. He would look at you with those penetrating eyes. He was looking for something from you. He was looking for an intellectual spark on which to engage on a given topic.' One particular moment still sticks in Bugge's mind and had a formative impact on his intellectual development. After reading out a rather lacklustre essay, Bugge recalls that he feared the worst:

He looked at me for quite some time. Disappointment was written all over his face. He asked me a question eventually. I mumbled something. He came back and repeated the question. I waffled again. A third time he repeated the question. I replied: 'I am sorry Dr Catto but I don't know the answer.' He looked at me seriously and after a pause he said: 'David, I don't want you to know; I want you to think.' I never forgot that moment or those words. I was embarrassed. I was humiliated. I was ashamed. Not by Jeremy but by my own failings. I vowed that this would never happen again to me in a tutorial, and from that moment I accepted the challenge. I turned around my sloppy start to life at Oxford and became focused. I worked hard. I decided I would engage fully and develop well-articulated thoughts on any given topic. In short, I turned myself around and then spent a very happy two and a half years at Oriel after this bad start.

But not only did this moment affect Bugge's academic fortunes, it even influenced his approach to his own career. 'Throughout my banking career since leaving Oxford, I kept these same thoughts and attitudes to the fore. Preparing well for meetings and developing my thoughts with rigour allowed me to present complex issues clearly to investors and clients.'

Nick Newman, who was at Oriel in the late 1970s, and is now a cartoonist and writer for the *Sunday Times* and *Private Eye*, as well as an occasional playwright, certainly found that Catto could be 'a very rigorous tutor' and that his expectations sometimes verged on the comical. He recalls that on one occasion, Catto set him an essay on Plutarch. When he gave him the reading list, Newman gave it a quick glance and realised at once that the list was made up entirely of works in Italian. 'But I don't speak a word of Italian', the young man protested. 'Oh, not to worry, I am sure that you will pick it up as you go along', came Catto's nonchalant reply. Given that Newman had a week to produce the essay, it was, to say the least, a tall order.

Tom Atkins, meanwhile, can still remember the 'mauling' he gave one of his essays on fourteenth-century chivalry:

I was being casually dismissive of a particular source that I basically had not read with enough of a critical eye, and I just thought was clichéd and stylised. For some reason, he was reading my essay out rather than the usual practice of me doing it, which made his criticisms all the more embarrassing ('split infinitive – oh dear'). I guess I was trying to be bold and edgy, and instead came across as ignorant and childish. However, rather than tell me this, he would ask me questions about specific points I had made and ask me to think again and to consider aspects of the source and how it was written. To put myself in the mind of the person writing it and look at both the nuances of the writing, as well as the wider context of where the source was coming from. He did not speak harshly or try and belittle me in any way, but he did it in a kind of gentle and patient way that convinces and motivates someone far more than an old-school rollicking does. But it was clear he expected better next time.

At other times, if Catto felt that you had not reached the minimum standard required, he was not averse to using a cutting form of humour to convey his sense of displeasure. Marcus Walker remembers one tutorial for which he had not properly prepared, in which Catto was clearly so cross with him for not having done his work that he refused to speak to him and instead addressed questions to him entirely via his tutorial partner. Walker recalls that this was done to let him know that, at least temporarily, 'diplomatic relations had been severed'.

* * *

Of course, although he could at times be a tough taskmaster, humour was never far from the surface in Catto's tutorials. He understood that, if properly deployed, it could be used to defuse an awkward situation, or simply to make a student feel more at ease. On other occasions, the comedic moments were more inadvertent. For example, Catto had an unfortunate tendency to fall asleep at critical moments during tutorials, which alarmed and amused his students in almost equal measure. Sebastian Grigg, who is now the 4th Baron Altrincham, was at Oriel in the years 1984–7, and then went on to pursue a career in investment banking. Thinking back to his tutorials with Catto, Grigg stresses that 'the frivolous part was only one side of the story', and that 'Jeremy was always extremely interested in the academic side of things'. Nevertheless, he also remembers with great affection Catto's more idiosyncratic habits during tutorials:

It must have been my second or third tutorial with him, and on this occasion, I was on my own with him. I was reading out my essay on Anglo-Saxon burials and found that…Jeremy had fallen fast asleep. It was my very first term and I did not know what to do, so I just carried on reading my essay. I went through page three and then page four and, by now, Jeremy was snoring quite loudly. When I got to page five, he suddenly opened one eye and started making comments about my essay. It was quite extraordinary. Perhaps he had heard my essay like a dog, or maybe he had heard it all before, so knew what to say!

This habit of nodding off was, of course, not restricted to tutorials. Richard Cross remembers that falling asleep was a regular occurrence for Catto, especially in the Senior Common Room after a good lunch:

He could always be found slumped on one of the comfortable armchairs, with his glass of J&B always at an angle, which made it look like it would spill over his trousers at any moment. But what was remarkable was that if you wanted to know the name of, say, some obscure Hungarian duke, you could give Jeremy's foot a kick. He would then wake up, provide the answer and then go straight back to sleep.

When he was not asleep, unexpected but amusing interruptions were a fairly regular feature of Catto's tutorials. Erik Hannikainen remember that his tutorials were 'almost always fun' and 'fascinating', as Catto 'would sit on the sofa and invariably the phone rang, and when it wasn't Debo, Dowager Duchess of Devonshire, it was some incredibly busy MP asking for advice'. Konsta Helle, meanwhile, remembers that one of his early morning tutorials was once interrupted by the Dean, 'who nonchalantly came to collect his sweater which he'd left in Jeremy's rooms at some point'. On another occasion, Helle recalls that he was interrupted in mid-flow as he was reading out his essay by a telephone call from Bucharest. Why anyone should be calling Catto from Bucharest was not immediately obvious, but Catto reached across the sofa to take the call. 'You're where? On the Calea Victoriei…I see…Can you see the Cantacuzino Palace? Right, well, from there you must turn right and then…' After he had finished the call, Catto turned to Helle and, as if to clarify the situation, said simply: 'That was Marc Almond. He's lost.'

At other times, those interruptions came almost straight out of *Porterhouse Blue*. Alex Young remembers one occasion when he and his tutorial partner were plodding their way through a couple of essays on a pretty turgid topic. Catto listened patiently to the essays but with a mounting sense of drowsiness. As ever in tutorials, he had positioned himself in the middle of what could only be described as a very large sofa bed. There were random bits of paper and books to one side, and a telephone within easy reach on the other side. It was not uncommon for Catto to interrupt his tutees if the telephone rang. Very often, it would be important college business, and sometimes the caller might even be a famous and distinguished former student calling for a chat. On this occasion, however, a call came through at just the right moment, as Catto was threatening to doze off during one of the essays. As soon as the phone rang, Catto opened his eyes and answered it without hesitation. 'I'm terribly sorry, but this is a very important call, and I must take it,' he said to his baffled tutees. As they looked on and listened to the unfolding conversation, they could not make much sense of it. 'Aha, yes, I see... Right...Hmmm...How very interesting...' In the end, and just before he put the phone down, Catto eventually told his interlocutor: 'Yes, fine, John, very well. I will have the Pouilly Fuisse with the fish.' John was the college butler, and his call provided just the shot in the arm which Catto needed to get him through that particular tutorial.

Apart from these distractions, tutorials were sometimes interrupted by other even more absurd and improbable external factors. Although Catto merely tolerated dogs, he was very fond of cats and enjoyed calling them 'purries'. Marcus Walker recalls an episode when Polly, the famous Oriel cat, who belonged to the Provost, was attacked by two hooligan ducks in Second Quad. Catto always liked to imply that the Provost was guilty of not feeding his cat properly and that it preferred him over the Provost as he used to give it cream as a treat. In any case, Walker remembers that during one of his tutorials, as his tutorial partner was reading out her essay, the sound of miaows of distress began to echo around the quad. Catto, ever alert to the plight of his beloved purries, 'leapt from his normal recumbent position on the sofa, and with a speed nobody thought possible, jumped on to the table in front of the window, leaned out of the window, and started shouting, "The puss! The puss! Somebody save the puss!"' Thankfully, and to everyone's relief, Polly was saved by the college porter, who rushed on to the scene to shoo away the ducks. The following Sunday, duck was served at high table, prompting Catto to quip that the duck 'may not have been the duck in question, but perhaps one of its family members'.

* * *

The lubricating effects of alcohol were an important part of Catto's tutorials. When asked by a colleague to sum up his thoughts on his own teaching style, Catto said that 'it works if you give them gin', while Nick Lord recalls being told that 'you will learn as much in the bar as you will in tutorials'. But the offer of drinks could also be viewed as a reward for hard work. David Brierley remembers that 'at the end of the tutorial, we were always rewarded with an offering of a bran or whisk'. Alexander Morrison believes that Catto 'looked on tutorials as a social occasion', with drinks served appropriate to the time of day, so undergraduates might be offered 'some prosecco in the morning, and some port or sherry later in the day'. Gin was another favourite tipple, according to one of Catto's former undergraduates:

> Our tutorials seemed always to take place in the period before lunch and Jeremy would invariably offer drinks (usually sherry) towards the end of the tutorial. One day he began the tutorial with an apology as he confessed to having run out of sherry. He then fidgeted his way through the next hour or so, visibly distracted, before leaping to his feet with a great cry of 'gin, we can have gin'. There was no sherry but, in an emergency, gin would have to do. 'All's well that ends well!'

Whatever the drink of choice, Catto's habit of serving alcohol during tutorials surprised many undergraduates when they first arrived at Oriel. David Freedman remembers 'being taken aback by the leap he encouraged from sixth form deference to adult undergraduate ease'. After his first tutorial in Catto's flat in King Edward Street, Freedman remembers that his new tutor 'thrust very large pre-lunch gin and tonics' into his hand, and that 'the last part of the morning quickly moved from the strictly academic to the predominantly social'. It was, Freedman suspects, 'an aspect of educational conviviality that is no longer countenanced or even comprehensible today'.

Clemmie Raynsford had a similar experience and recalls that 'arriving in Catto's tutorials from an all-girls Catholic school on the coast was a truly unique experience'. Her memories of those tutorials are particularly vivid, with the fire 'always burning, no matter what time of year it was'. She found the setting 'quite informal', as if you were simply 'going to see him for a chat', and then 'the pink gin would eventually appear'. But although this approach may have been unusual, Raynsford also points out that by serving drinks, Catto was 'treating you like an adult and preparing you for a much more adult conversation'.

Ralph Perry-Robinson, who was at Oriel in the mid-1980s and is now a sustainable planning consultant, remembers that Catto did not necessarily object to undergraduates enjoying a few drinks, even if this distracted them from their work. He once apologised in advance about the probability of being a little hungover for a tutorial, to which Catto's response was: 'Not to worry, dear boy, I always like my fruit with a little wax on it.'

Even when it came to preparing for exams, the promise of an alcoholic refreshment was not necessarily off the menu. Josh Pull remembers that Catto had a very clear line on how best to prepare for exams:

> During my finals, I had finished my penultimate exam and had a three-day gap before the last one. Bumping into Jeremy that evening he suggested a 'whisk or bran'. Overriding my half-hearted protests that I still had one exam to go, we proceeded to have a fairly late night of convivial drinking and discussion. At a time when it was becoming increasingly popular amongst undergraduates (no doubt fully endorsed by many tutors) to avoid drinking at all for the entire summer term until finals were complete, Jeremy would endorse the opposite approach, encouraging us to remain relaxed and above all to keep enjoying life.

Finally, although Catto believed that gin should be consumed, there were times when it had to be used for a different purpose. Nick Newman recalls that he had spent all night ahead of one of his tutorials putting together an essay for Catto, with the result that he felt somewhat bleary on the day of his tutorial. As he rushed along to Catto's rooms in Second Quad, Newman managed to hit his head on a fire extinguisher. Undeterred by this unfortunate incident, he arrived on time and sat down to read out his essay for Catto. But the meeting with the fire extinguisher had left its mark, and as 'large blobs of blood' dropped from Newman's head on to the floor, Catto promptly got up and disappeared into the nearby kitchen, only to emerge, to Newman's astonishment, with a large bottle of gin, which he then used to tend to the wound. Looking back, Newman agrees that as Catto was not the kind of man to waste even a drop of gin if he could help it, this must have been a very serious situation indeed.

In summing up his unique approach to tutorials, Dr Leslie Mitchell, an historian and emeritus fellow of University College, Oxford, who knew Catto over many years, points out that 'as a tutor, he did things which would not be allowed these days'. Mitchell recalls one incident in particular when he enlisted Catto to teach a group of summer school students from Tennessee. Catto enjoyed the experience of teaching these young Americans so much that he invited them back to Oriel one evening for a drinks party. Mitchell remembers that the party involved 'a knockout punch' being served by Catto which, given how old the American students were, would have been illegal in their own country. Catto then took things further by asking the boys to perform a 'rebel yell'. To those not familiar with this particular ritual, the 'rebel yell' was a terrifying battle cry used by Confederate soldiers during the American Civil War. Soldiers would yell when charging so as to intimidate the enemy and boost their own morale. Catto was very amused by all of this, and no doubt his young American friends will have enjoyed the experience too, but in our own more earnest and puritanical times, Mitchell believes that 'this kind of tutoring is now totally impossible'. He adds that in terms of his sense of humour and the sheer enjoyment he derived from such unusual teaching methods, Catto was 'part of a golden age of tutors, who did not exist before the war and do not exist anymore today'.

10

Scholarship

WHEN CATTO DIED IN 2018, THE OBITUARIES QUITE understandably focused on certain aspects of his life. His witticisms and idiosyncratic use of language loomed large throughout, and a series of anecdotes were produced in an attempt to shed some light on his uniquely engaging personality. In addition, his wide-ranging network of contacts beyond the world of academia featured heavily. However, references to his scholarship were often rather cursory and, in some cases, appeared to dismiss his credentials as a scholar. For example, some of the obituaries seized on the fact that Catto never wrote a book, and the conclusion readers were encouraged to draw was that his scholarship was the least significant part of his legacy. There are some who would undoubtedly agree with the view that places great emphasis on the publishing of books by academics to burnish their reputations as serious scholars. Writing about Hugh Trevor-Roper, who, like Catto, also never published a book, his biographer Adam Sisman once said that 'the mark of a great historian is that he writes great books on the subject which he has made his own. By this exacting standard Hugh failed'.[118] Others would argue that the quality of an academic's scholarship can often take many different forms and that it is too reductive to focus simply on the publishing of books.

Whichever view one supports, and before returning to this point, it is important to begin by tackling the question of why Catto never wrote a book. As the following accounts from friends and colleagues will show, there are many theories as to why he never published and a straightforward answer to the question does not necessarily exist. According to Professor John Watts, fellow of Corpus Christi, Oxford, and a noted specialist in the political history of late-medieval England, the reason is that Catto viewed the writing of books as somehow beneath him. There was, according to Watts, 'something about the solemnity of the book he found slightly repulsive'. Professor Kantik Ghosh, a fellow and tutor at Trinity College, Oxford, who specialises in medieval English literature, holds a similar view: 'He was of course immensely learned but had a wonderfully patrician disdain for publication. He was very fond of academia but was at an angle from it. He was amused by it and perhaps thought that writing books was a touch vulgar.' That certainly rings true, in the sense that Catto undoubtedly disliked solemnity and pomposity, but it may not provide a full explanation for why he never published.

On a more practical level, the writer, journalist and historian Giles MacDonogh believes that Catto was not a natural writer, and therefore shied away from publishing a book: 'It was always said about Jeremy that he found writing hard, and that he is best remembered as an inspiring teacher and that is no mean feat either'.[119] Others have commented on this too. Professor Blair Worden, an eminent historian and a leading authority on the English Civil War, agrees to the extent that the experience of writing was 'agony' for Catto. It is certainly possible that he found writing to be a challenge. James Clark, who was supervised by Catto for his DPhil in the 1990s and is now a professor of history at Exeter University, adds that 'Jeremy was something of a stylist and was always searching for bon mots or well-turned phrases, which is hardly helpful when writing to deadlines.' But if that was the main reason, then it would not explain why he was so comfortable with producing a steady stream of insightful and well-written articles over many years. Indeed, according to Dr Jonathan Hughes, Catto was actually 'remarkably prolific, especially towards the end of his life', having produced a very significant number of learned articles over the course of his time at Oxford.

According to some, Catto made it harder for himself to publish a book when he chose to not publish his doctoral thesis on William of Woodford. This is important because publishing the thesis might have made the next step to publishing a book much more straightforward. Kantik Ghosh partially agrees with this and has often wondered why Catto never published his thesis. The work in question was produced by him at Balliol in the 1960s, and is, according to Ghosh, 'absolutely brilliant, still worth reading, and full of valuable insights'. It is typed on very thin paper which, owing to the passing of time, makes it quite tough to read these days, and making a digital copy of it would help to keep it preserved. In any case, it seems that this may have been a missed opportunity for Catto.

For others, the key to understanding why Catto never published a book was his clear preference for writing articles. According to John Whitehead, 'Catto was more of a miniaturist, as opposed to a painter of great canvasses', which means that he was simply better suited to the essay format. Dr Robert Portass agrees with this argument and points out that Catto was 'a supremely gifted essayist, and that that was the format with which he was most comfortable'. A similar view is expressed by Jonathan Hughes, who prefaces his remarks by saying that 'it does not matter' that Catto never published a book. 'It would be a bit like asking why Chopin never wrote a symphony,' he adds. More importantly, Catto was simply 'not that interested' in publishing a book, and that 'everything he wanted to say and express could be distilled into an essay'. In other words, Hughes believes that Catto would have agreed with James Campbell, the great historian of the Anglo-Saxon period, who once said that 'most books should have been articles, and most articles should never have been written'.

Some have argued that Catto's preference for the essay format was the result of his research interests. James Clark believes that this was perhaps the key reason behind Catto's decision: 'The nature of the work he did for his DPhil thesis was not easily translated into a monograph. His work on manuscripts made for fascinating reading, but it did not make for a broad overview of a period like the work produced by Richard Southern or Maurice Keen. His core area of knowledge was hard to translate into narrative form.' Clark adds, however, that although Catto may not have produced a monograph, what he did provide, often in the form of an essay, 'carried with it a huge amount of carefully weighted judgement'.

In Jonathan Sumption's view, Catto's attitude towards writing books was similar to that of Kenneth Bruce McFarlane, the historian who dominated the medieval history school at Oxford when Catto first became an academic historian. In the *Oxford Dictionary of National Biography*, McFarlane's biographer wrote the following about his attitude towards writing books: 'McFarlane preferred to write lectures and papers rather than books. Some were of seminal importance and all touched major problems and raised new lines of enquiry. Everything he wrote had the stamp of authority, based as it was on first-hand investigation and an instinctive distrust of received opinion.'[120] Sumption adds to this by pointing out that McFarlane was 'a perfectionist who never signed off on a book while he thought that further research might improve it (it always could).' Catto took the same view, which is why Sumption believes he never wrote a book, something which John Stevenson agrees upon: 'Jeremy's problem was that he was too clever and he suffered from being a perfectionist. He could always see what was wrong with what he had written. He certainly worried about his own productivity, but he was almost too fastidious in his own work to write as easily as he might have wished.'

Sumption and Stevenson would appear to have a strong case, as it is certainly true that Catto was an admirer of McFarlane's approach to publishing. In a December 1972 review of a collection of posthumous lectures by McFarlane called 'Lancastrian Kings and Lollards Knights', Catto concludes with the following tribute: 'But it is a major contribution to the religious and to the social history of the fourteenth century, and the modesty of the volume's size should not deflect anyone from the importance of its contents.'[121] There are some who dispute this view, however. Christopher Tyerman for one sees it as 'a bit too neat' as an explanation, and points out that Catto was happy to publish works that provoked discussion and debate, even if the research could still be improved upon. He adds that although Catto may have 'admired McFarlane, he was not a McFarlanite', suggesting that perhaps a bigger influence on Catto was Hugh Trevor-Roper. A more persuasive explanation according to Tyerman is that Catto had a heavy teaching job as a young man and put a lot of time and effort into that, which ate into any kind of large-scale research project. This dedication meant that publishing a book was always going to be harder for him than for those who were not as devoted to their teaching commitments. Robert Portass agrees and adds that Catto 'was also too busy, in terms of his life, but also in regards to how his mind worked, in the sense that, although he wore his learning very lightly, he was interested in all sorts of history'. As such, it was difficult for Catto to have the kind of single-minded dedication that is often required to produce a monograph.

Leif Dixon adds an interesting follow-up thought by pointing out that Catto 'did not have a long production line of graduates', largely as a result of devoting so much of his time to his undergraduates: 'Jeremy preferred undergraduates to graduates. He admitted to me that he found graduates a bit dull at times and felt that they could be excessively serious and narrow.' James Clark picks up on this point: 'It was the seriousness Jeremy didn't like and he affected that he didn't understand the graduate student's anxiety that their doctoral research was a make-or-break step towards a career.' According to Clark, Catto found 'such practical, material concerns rather vulgar'. In terms of cultivating a production line of graduates, Clark share's Dixon view, and says that in Catto's time, Oxford supervisors were beginning to act like their US counterparts, and vigorously promoted their graduate students, individually and collectively, as the leading edge of the next generation of scholars. 'This only provoked Jeremy to do the opposite, to affect a kind of bafflement if questions of funding or postdoctoral opportunities were raised. Topics of this kind he would classify as "serious", meaning he would side-step a discussion of them if he could!' Of course, none of this meant that Catto was somehow anti-specialist, but he certainly preferred teaching undergraduates as their minds were more malleable, which meant that he could have more of an influence on their development. According to Dixon, Catto had 'something of a saviour complex, which meant that he wanted to have an impact and he felt he could have more of an impact on undergraduates than on graduates'. The result was not just that he never published a book, but also that 'there was no "Catto school", which may have hurt his reputation as much – if not more – than not producing a book'.

But apart from his commitment to his undergraduates, Tyerman also adds that perhaps an even more important explanation for Catto never publishing a book can be found in the fact that he was part of the generation that did not equate the quality of an academic's scholarship with the publication of books: 'The younger generation rather sneers at not publishing, but many of Catto's generation, men such as Prestwych or

Armstrong, did not publish either.' To really understand what this means, it is worth reflecting on how academic expectations have changed at Oxford over time, and what impact this may have had on Catto.

When Catto was an undergraduate at Balliol in the late 1950s, dons would have been under very little pressure to publish their research, and there was no expectation that a book had to be published at some stage. Some dons, like Maurice Keen, did publish, notably his great work on chivalry. But others never produced a book. By the time Catto himself was a don in the early 1970s, expectations had not changed very much and, as Tyerman points out, 'the idea that a fellow was primarily a teacher still held'. This changed, however, in the late 1970s and early 1980s, largely as a result of the squeeze put on university funding by the Thatcher governments. The question became about how academic output should be measured and, over time, this meant that the faculty's research needs became more important than the college's teaching needs. In truth, there had always been some creative tension between these two areas, but following the reforms under Thatcher, the balance shifted in favour of the former. Today, dons are governed by the Research Excellence Framework (REF), which is a system that grades universities for the quality of its research output. The stated aims of this system are to inform the allocation of block-grant research funding to Higher Education Institutions (HEIs) based on research quality; provide accountability for public investment in research and produce evidence of the benefits of this investment; and provide insights into the health of research in HEIs in the UK. Critics argue that there is too much focus on the impact of research outside of the university system, and that that impact, however it is measured, has no real relevance to the quality of research. Some argue that the REF actually encourages an element of quantity at the expense of quality in published research, and discourages research which might have value in the long term. Others have even gone so far as to suggest that the system has encouraged the 'commodification' or 'proletarianisation' of academia,[122] in the sense that output is now measured in a similar fashion to the work of, say, a factory worker in Stalin's Russia. On the other hand, supporters of the REF system believe that it has helped to standardise the quality of research and that it performs a vital task in terms of holding academics to account. Some feel that, if anything, the pressure has somewhat lessened over the past decade, and that critics have tended to exaggerate the pressures put on academics to publish.

Regardless of the relative merits and demerits of this system, the idea that Catto was essentially a product of his generation in regards to publishing books is perhaps the most convincing explanation for why he never published. Of all the reasons proffered by friends and colleagues, this is the one to which nearly everybody returns in some form or another. Kantik Ghosh certainly thinks that it was 'partly a generational thing'. Oxford during the early stages of Catto's time had people, in his view, who were very learned, 'but who did not see the point of publishing unless they had something new to say'. Stevenson shares this view, and believes that it was partly due to Catto being from a certain generation that 'would have looked down on the publish or perish idea'. The world of the REF, Stevenson adds, 'was not the world he grew up in'. Alexander Morrison, who describes Catto as 'a very significant intellectual figure', agrees with this interpretation and explains that Catto, in part at least, never published a book because 'the idea that tutorial fellows should also be researchers is a relatively modern idea, and was not around' when Jeremy was at Oxford. He adds that Catto was part of the generation that believed that 'you published something if you had something worthwhile to say'. Dr Leif Dixon describes Catto as an 'old-fashioned polymath' and agrees that he 'belonged to the school of thought that believed that you should not publish unless you had something new or interesting to say, and only if you could say it well'.

Whatever the truth of the matter, it would be a mistake to assume that Catto was not a serious scholar, or that he failed to contribute anything of lasting value to the world of scholarship, solely because he never published a book of his own. Professor Ian Forrest, who succeeded Catto at Oriel, and is now head of humanities at the University of Glasgow, believes that the idea that Catto was not a proper scholar was 'garbage of his own myth-making'. By this he means that Catto did not 'blow his own trumpet, did not promote himself and did not like people who did'. But despite this reticence about his own work, there is no doubt in Forrest's mind that to this day 'specialists in the field rely on his work', adding with firm conviction that 'it is absolutely foundational'. Specifically, five points stand out in regards to Catto's scholarship: (1) his ability to illuminate the overlapping and interconnecting worlds of the medieval period; (2) his work with literary historians; (3) his facility with medieval language and texts combined with a pan-European understanding of the medieval period; (4) his supreme skill as an essayist; and (5) the international dimension to his scholarship.

John Watts argues that Catto 'was one of the most important and fertile historians of the Late Middle Ages, and particularly of the worlds of learning, religion and government, worlds whose numerous interconnections he delighted in demonstrating'.[123] His single most important contribution, according to Watts, was the way in which he thought about matters and how this influenced other historians. Catto resisted the temptation to think in categories. Instead, he showed how the worlds of churchmen and statesmen overlapped in medieval times, which was critical to gaining a clearer understanding of the practical realities of the medieval world.

According to James Clark, Catto's work with literary historians was a crucial aspect of his scholarship:

> Jeremy continued to develop and extend our understanding of religious and intellectual culture in later medieval England at a moment when the weight of numbers and publications in medieval research lay elsewhere. From the 1970s to the 1990s, more and more conspicuous contributions were seen in the early medieval (e.g. McKitterick, Nelson) and central medieval (e.g. Bartlett) periods, and the focus of research on the post-Black Death period had shifted decisively from the cultural scene to kingship and political culture (e.g. Ross, Hicks, Carpenter). Jeremy had been supervised by the intellectual historian Beryl Smalley, but it was another mid-century Oxford late medievalist, K.B. McFarlane, whose influence seemed ascendant at this time. It was no surprise that in the absence of other historians alongside him, Jeremy gravitated to those working in literary studies where later medieval texts and themes still held attention. His essays engaged with the research of Anne Hudson and other literary specialists, adding to their insights with his acute understanding of the Latin learning of the Wyclifite era and after. This is surely where his lasting contribution lies. Research on the 'vernacular theology' of the half century after the first condemnation of Wyclif is burgeoning still, and it owes much to Jeremy's reading of the academic, fraternal and monastic learning that surrounded and stimulated it. For those working in this field, I would add that Jeremy's deft but determined challenges to received interpretations have and will continue to inspire fresh research and further debate. For those of us who knew him well, these clever revisionist forays show his instinct for mischief, tempered just a little by the thoroughness of his treatment of the sources.

Elizabeth Solopova, a fellow and lecturer in medieval English literature at Oxford, who collaborated extensively with Catto on a series of projects, argues that Catto was 'absolutely a first-rate scholar' and that 'his contribution to scholarship was very significant'. Specifically, she cites Catto's facility with medieval language, and his ability to provide readable and literary translations of medieval texts. He was able to do this not only thanks to his superb technical comprehension, but also because his wide-ranging understanding of the medieval world enabled him to elucidate the actual meaning behind these texts. That broad understanding was based on his ability to look at things from a pan-European perspective. Kantik Ghosh, meanwhile, argues that Catto 'looked at the broader picture and had a very good understanding of how the history of ideas related to other European societies'. Ghosh remains a huge admirer of Catto's scholarship and describes his passing as 'the demise of an archive', adding that Catto's 'loss is still keenly felt by those in his field'.

Despite never having written a book, the enduring quality of his essays and articles remains second to none. Solopova argues that 'his published output was both very extensive and very significant'. Ian Forrest agrees entirely and is quite bullish on Catto's record: 'He was not a non-publisher. He had a big publication record.' Moreover, as Forrest points out, 'they did not have to squeeze those articles out of him…there was a steady stream of constant work'. Another who agrees with this point is Julian Munby, who is an archaeologist and fellow of the Society of Antiquaries of London, as well as Head of Buildings Archaeology at Oxford Archaeology. He collaborated with Catto on the history of the university and points out that Catto's area of expertise meant that he 'started off in an area that is pretty difficult. You have to be able to read Latin, know about theology, and when you pick up an ancient manuscript you have got to know if they are saying something new and interesting'. He dismisses the modern fixation with publishing books and argues that 'if you make a contribution to a topic, it will last for a hundred years'. He concludes by saying that Catto was 'a brilliant essayist', who made precisely such a contribution through his many essays over the years. In that regard, it could be argued that Catto and Trevor-Roper shared much in common. Writing about the latter, John Kenyon has pointed out that 'some of Trevor-Roper's short essays have affected the way we think about the past more than other men's books'.[124] This point is further supported by both Richard Davenport-Hines and Adam Sisman in the introduction to *One Hundred Letters from Hugh Trevor-Roper*, where they write the following: 'The bulk of his publications is formidable…Some of his essays are of Victorian length. All of them reduce large subjects to their essence. Many of them…have lastingly transformed their fields.'[125] When asked about Catto's scholarship, Davenport-Hines goes further, making the comparison between the two men more explicit. Within the essay format, Catto's great ability was that he was 'never prolix, always wonderfully focused on target, and never diffuse…he was an essential historian'. He concludes that Catto was 'a master of the short and perfect essay, and in that he followed Trevor-Roper'.

Beyond the study of medieval history at Oxford, Catto's contribution to the world of scholarship also had an important international dimension. Professor Sir Niall Ferguson, the eminent historian and senior fellow at the Hoover Institution and Harvard, who writes and lectures on international history, economic history, and the history of the British Empire, agrees entirely that Catto's reputation as a scholar should not be underestimated. Citing Catto's work on the history of Oxford University, Sir Niall says that 'the history of the university is just an exceptional achievement, and nothing like it has ever been done for any American university, not even close'. Picking up on this American theme, James Clark believes that Catto's written work 'will stand for a generation', and he points out that Catto's name 'will resonate more in American and Canadian scholarship circles than in British ones today…and would be much more well known and indeed revered over in the US'. The reason for this, Clark suggests, is that 'medieval Latin texts are studied more in the US now, whereas the numbers in Britain have dropped'.

The final word on Catto's scholarship must go to John Watts who, following Catto's death in 2018, and in an effort to correct the often misleading impression given by some of the obituaries, penned a longer piece for Oxford University's history faculty, in which he paid tribute to Catto's scholarship. To expand on some of the above-mentioned points and to put everything that has been said in this chapter into a broader and fuller context, it is worth producing that tribute here in full:

While he produced a number of edited texts and several multi-authored volumes – most famously two volumes of the history of the University – Jeremy's preferred format was surely the essay: short, pointed, and readable. He produced well over forty such pieces, covering a wide range of topics. They are remarkably learned, but they are never learned for the sake of it. Many of them range broadly and touch lightly on the details, but these succeed so well because the scholarship behind them was so extensive and reliable. As for the more heavyweight pieces, they invariably pack an interpretative punch. Describing the contents of Peterhouse MS 223, what he called a radical preacher's handbook from 1383, Jeremy surveyed more than two dozen texts, ranging in time from Augustine to John Wyclif and covering more than 280 folios of crabbed Latin. His deep knowledge of the reading habits of later medieval scholars allowed him to say what was conventional in this collection and what was not, and to discern the purposes for which it was created. The important pay-off for the reader – delivered in a tightly-managed 11 pages – is that, even in the later 1380s, after the condemnation of Wyclif's teachings, an influential prelate could continue to esteem the great heretic's views on the truth of holy scripture and to join him in promoting the preaching of parish priests over the fakeries of the friars; so it was that the radicals of the Wyclif generation lay the foundations for the re-spiritualised church of the Lancastrian period. Or, to choose another example, Jeremy's 2004 essay on the 'triumph of the hall in fifteenth-century Oxford' uses a painstaking account of institutional change – complete with maps and ground-plans – to launch a novel and provocative argument that the so-called 'rise of the undergraduate colleges' was really the apotheosis of the educational model of the ancient halls.

This draws attention to another marked feature of Jeremy's essays: they are often sparked by a sense of fun – a mischievous desire to deflate pompous claims and subvert widespread assumptions; to introduce what he gleefully called 'a stiffening wind' to areas of cosy consensus. Jeremy's sketch of 'Renaissance Oxford' is one memorable example – here in the home of Duns Scotus, the Renaissance is well underway by the 1420s and 30s (and maybe rather past its best by the time of John Colet's lectures on St Paul, which Jeremy found wholly conventional); it is peopled by spiky old scholastics whose Latin would have horrified Erasmus, even though they were just as philologically alert and as bent on returning ad fontes as any Italian; its Ciceronians were the progeny of the fourteenth-century foundations of William of Wykeham, but they cultivated eloquence for essentially the same political and social purposes as Thomas More. 'It may be an overstatement,' Jeremy wrote, surely a twinkle in his eye, 'to see Netter, Pecock or Gascoigne as humanist theologians...' but that is precisely what he was suggesting, and – after reading him – the starchy, muddy fifteenth century never looks quite the same again.

And if the Renaissance was well underway before 1450, so was the Reformation. Its architects were not Henry VIII and Thomas Cranmer, but Henry V and Thomas Arundel. Jeremy's invocation of 'Thomas Arundel's reformation' was a good-humoured but calculated riposte to the assaults of certain literary scholars against the man they accused of closing down the golden age of Middle English literature. But it was also a deeply serious, and very persuasive reinterpretation of the spiritual world of the early fifteenth century: not as an era of repression, but as a time in which the institutional church, supported and led by a sober and imaginative king and a cluster of well-educated civil servants, found a way to finesse the need for conformity with the provision of spiritually and socially-rewarding forms of worship.

In this amalgam – of church and state, of policy and principle – two of the central axes of Jeremy's work, and perhaps his life, are exposed. When he wrote about intellectuals and divines, as he did often, he was at pains to emphasize their connection with the real world. Thomas Aquinas may be most famous to us as a systematic thinker in the schools of Paris, but, in an early article, Jeremy linked his treatise De Regno ad Regem Cypri to the predicaments faced by Thomas's relatives and other Italians in the wake of the final collapse of the Hohenstaufen rulers of Sicily. Explaining Wyclif's ideas on the Eucharist in a famous essay, Jeremy challenged what he called the 'intellectualist' approach to understanding them: for one thing, it inappropriately stabilized what was actually a developing and passionate line of thought; for another, it overlooked the ritual centrality of the eucharistic miracle in the lives of contemporary Christians – Wyclif may not have meant to undermine this most holy thing, but his attack on transubstantiation could not be understood in any other way by people at the time.

And if intellectuals were worldly, so by the same token were statesmen, warriors and bureaucrats capable of sensibility and spiritual reflection. Jeremy wrote again and again, and very affectingly, about the ideal of the Mixed Life, a form of monastic contemplation suitable for, and sought by, the kings, lords and 'graduate careerists', as he called them, of the fourteenth and fifteenth centuries. As much as Archbishops Chichele and Arundel, it was these men that built the renewed church of Lancastrian England. Bearing what he neatly called 'the burden and conscience of government', they pursued new and more enlightened forms of statecraft – councils, memoranda – and joined monastic and episcopal colleagues in the making of ecclesiastical polity. This was surely the underlying purpose behind Jeremy's cultivation of generations of Oxford men and women: that, in some way, they should echo their Lancastrian forebears in harnessing learning and spirituality to their careers in the world. In his well-known essay on the religion of the fourteenth-century nobility, Jeremy quoted a devotional tract called the Cloud of Unknowing. It urged its readers that those who 'stand in activity by outward form of living, nevertheless yet by inward steering after the privy spirit of God ... [could be] partners in the highest point of this contemplative act'. It seems a fitting text for his life and work.[126]

11

College Man

'Oriel was hugely lucky to find someone willing to devote his energies to the college.'

– Sir David Manning on Catto

'A very committed servant of the college.'

– John Varley on Catto

THE COLLEGE SYSTEM, WHICH REMAINS IN PLACE AT OXFORD TO THIS day, came into being about 800 years ago. At the outset, this nascent system lacked organisation or facilities. The result was that students and their teachers established themselves in small groups based in local inns and lodging houses, and it was from these ad hoc groups that today's university, consisting of a series of constituent but autonomous colleges, gradually evolved. As the university took shape, friction between the hundreds of students living how and where they pleased led to the decision that all undergraduates would have to reside in approved halls. The first 'colleges', therefore, were not actually colleges at all, but monastic halls. Over time, these medieval bodies were replaced by colleges. What differentiated them from the earlier halls was that colleges were often generously endowed and had permanent teaching staff, which helped to create more of a sense of continuity. The remnants and basic architecture of these colleges, which can still be seen in today's colleges, also added a community atmosphere. They were designed with a dining hall, a chapel, a library, a series of common rooms, as well as accommodation for both students and dons. In other words, colleges, as conceived historically, were living communities that created interconnected spaces for learning, socialising and cohabitation. Today, there are forty-three different colleges, each with their own history, customs and traditions, and it is this which gives the university much of its unique and distinctive sense of identity.

When Catto became a fellow at Oriel in 1969, he involved himself in all aspects of college life right from the start. Unlike many dons today, he did not merely view his college as a place of work. Nor did he limit his activities to his teaching responsibilities or leave for home once his official teaching hours had been completed. Oriel was his home, and over the course of four decades, he always saw his residence in Oriel as an essential part of his role within the college community. As generations of his students would confirm, he was a constant and very visible presence throughout their time in college. It undoubtedly helped that he was one of the few remaining unmarried dons who was able to make the college their home. Nevertheless, what made his dedication to college life especially remarkable was that his desire and willingness to be ever present in college was already becoming unusual even during his time at Oxford. Indeed, even as early as 1964, only one in five Oxford dons was resident in college.[127] By 2006, Catto did not stand entirely alone in his devotion to college life, but he was certainly part of a dying breed of men devoted to serving their colleges.

For the first few years at Oriel, he lived in a set of rooms on King Edward Street, just around the corner from the college. But even though he did not live in college, his rooms quickly became a focal point of college life. Tutorials would be held there during the day, and a steady stream of colleagues and undergraduates would be invited to drinks parties in the evenings. All those who knew Catto would confirm that he was always a very generous host. Alan Hollinghurst, the novelist and Booker Prize-winning author, remembers 'happy memories of evenings forty-five years ago, when I and one or two other friends called in pretty regularly at his rooms in King Edward Street to partake of the "river gin"'. Hollinghurst adds that Catto 'was always very hospitable, and funny, and dealt with our strong divergences of political opinion with his usual enchanting fantasy and camp'. Later generations of undergraduates would become familiar with the suite of rooms overlooking Oriel's Second Quad, and those who either had their tutorials in those rooms or attended drinks parties there will have a vivid visual memory of the setting, which resembled Uncle Monty's sitting room in the film *Withnail and I*, complete with groaning bookshelves, well-worn sofas, old rugs, paintings (in particular the painting of Thomas Catto), dimmed lights and, of course, the year-round fire. For many years, the rumour among undergraduates was that Catto had these rooms enlarged at a time when the incoming Provost had not yet taken up his own residence in college by instructing the builders to annex two adjacent rooms from the Provost's apartments. When the new Provost arrived, the building works were complete and could not be reversed. Whether the story is true or not has never been fully established, but it only added to the Catto mystique over the years.

Beyond conducting tutorials and hosting drinks parties, Catto was always at the heart of college social life. Whether it was inviting guests to dinner at high table on a regular basis, attending evensong on Sundays, or even turning up to the college bar for an impromptu drink, Catto was always very much part of the fabric of college life. Even those who were not taught by him knew who he was and would sometimes be invited to his rooms for drinks. Indeed, from the moment undergraduates arrived at Oriel, they would realise that they were part of a community, and much of this was down to Catto. At the annual Freshers' Dinner, Catto would break the ice, and help shy and nervous undergraduates feel instantly more relaxed by encouraging them to place bets on how long the Provost's speech would last. The winner would often be generously rewarded with a case of wine. At other times, he would lighten the mood at college dinners by running a betting syndicate about how many people round the table would take snuff. Catto would point at someone down the end of the table and whisper into his neighbour's ear: 'Do you think she has the nose for snuff?'

Guest nights, which gave members of the college the opportunity to invite guests to college dinners, were another important feature of college life, and Catto always enjoyed being involved with these occasions. Richard Cross, who was a professor of medieval theology at Oxford and a tutor in theology at Oriel for over a decade, and is now the John A. O'Brien Professor of Philosophy and former chair of the philosophy department at the University of Notre Dame, met Catto for the first time in 1993 when they became colleagues. Cross recalls that they got on very well straight away, stressing the attractions of Catto's convivial nature, which made him such a central part of college life for so many years. But not everyone, he adds, appreciated that side of Catto's character.

After college guest nights, Catto would always have people back to his rooms until well into the early hours, and it was usually around 1 a.m., when things were getting a bit out of hand, that those present would hear a loud banging on the ceiling from the don who lived above Catto demanding that the noise be kept down. Cross also remembers that Catto was very fond of his guests smoking at these gatherings. 'Of course, you always had to smoke at his parties, and this was especially true after the smoking ban came in, which made smoking indoors illegal. And yet his rooms never smelt of smoke, as he always had a fire burning all year round, which acted as a natural ventilation system.'

Another colleague who would come to value Catto's commitment to college life was Nigel Biggar, a theologian and ethicist, who was the regius professor of moral and pastoral theology at Oxford from 2007 to 2022. Biggar came to know Catto when he was chaplain and a fellow of Oriel from 1990–99, and he recalls that his first impression was that he found talking to him at high table quite difficult because he was 'constantly ironic' in his conversation. 'As a Scot', Biggar explains, 'I play a straight bat and find English indirection difficult.' As an example, he remembers asking Catto one evening at dinner what he specialised in. The question was met with Catto's characteristically mischievous smile and the simple reply: '1468'. This 'carapace of irony', as Biggar describes it, was possibly a form of 'self-protection' for Catto. But, as time went on, Biggar found him to be 'very astute and often astute about people', adding that 'there was wisdom behind the carapace'. Reflecting further, Biggar says that he 'never found him to be unkind', and although 'he could be waspish, he was never bitter'. Perhaps most importantly, Biggar describes Catto as 'one of a dying breed of college men who had the time and inclination to devote themselves to college life'. As Oriel's chaplain for much of the 1990s, Biggar says that he was 'constantly aware' of Catto's support of the chapel (even though he was a Catholic), and he stresses that Catto 'was there on Sunday evenings every time', which was just 'one instance of how he kept college conviviality alive'. Biggar, clearly impressed with Catto's dedication to college life in all its forms, concludes by noting that 'you have to have a core of people who keep that going, as it is very time-consuming'.

Finally, as the following tributes from his students make clear, generations of Orielenses were grateful for Catto's devotion to college life and saw it as one of the defining features of his legacy. According to Sir David Manning, one of Catto's first undergraduates, 'Oriel was hugely lucky to find someone willing to devote his energies to the college.' For Sir Richard Stagg, Catto 'was very much someone who was in college all the time, and available and welcoming all the time'. He was 'a wonderful force' and his approach to college life, according to Sir Richard, is 'a model that has long since gone'.

Ewen Cameron Watt believes that 'Oriel was not just a home' for Catto, adding that 'he loved the college deeply and had its best interests at heart'. Alexander Rufus-Isaacs, meanwhile, reflecting on Catto's commitment to college life, suggests that 'stalwart would be too weak a word to use…he was really more of an institution within the college and, indeed, the broader university'. John Varley describes Catto as a 'very committed servant of the college', who was 'always very visible and had a very strong sense of the college's standing, status and reputation'. Although Catto was perhaps not that interested in, for example, the fortunes of the first XI cricket team, he always understood that these things still 'reflected on the glory of the college'. Konsta Helle, one of Catto's last undergraduates, remembers that Catto was a college man first and foremost: 'In and around college, Jeremy was nothing if not a fixture; he was in formal hall (often beaming and waving coyly to us when coming to high table); he was in chapel (ever disliking Howells' canticles); and he faithfully came to Saturday of Eights Week[viii] (Torpids was by then probably too wet and cold for him).' Helle recalls that such was his impact on college life that when he retired at the end of Trinity term in 2006, 'it felt like the light had gone out of Oriel and the esprit de corps was beginning to wane'.

viii Eights Week, also known as Summer Eights, is a four-day regatta of races which constitutes the University of Oxford's main intercollegiate rowing event of the year. The regatta takes place in May of each year, from the Wednesday to the Saturday of the fifth week of Trinity Term.

A portrait of the quintessential Oxford don. © *Diccon Swan*

Jeremy wearing his RGS Newcastle blazer, aged 17. © Annabel Flowers and John Wolfe

'Americans were exotic in those days…' Jeremy and John looking dashing during a trip to London, c. 1962. © John Wolfe

Jeremy and a friend larking about in London, c. 1962. © John Wolfe

Was the owner of the Rolls-Royce brave enough to allow Jeremy to drive it…?
c. 1963/64. © John Wolfe

Jeremy (lying down) with friends alongside the Cherwell in
Oxford after a day of punting up the river, c. 1964. © John Wolfe

Jeremy and John enjoying themselves in the sun, c. 1964/65. © John Wolfe

Jeremy in relaxed mood during his trip to Italy with
Bryan Ferry and Stephen Buckley, Summer 1966. © John Wolfe

'A supremely cool trio…' Jeremy (left) with Bryan Ferry (right) and Stephen Buckley (centre) in Newcastle, Autumn 1966. © John Wolfe

Jeremy's political opinions may not always have been fashionable, but those quite outrageous flares were certainly tailor-made for the 1970s. © *John Wolfe*

Jeremy with William Hague in his rooms at Oriel, c. 1982.
(Note the framed photo of Margaret Thatcher on the mantelpiece). © John Wolfe

Jeremy in North London at the time of the 1987 general election (and possibly gloating about
a third consecutive win for Margaret Thatcher's Conservative Party). © John Wolfe

Jeremy enjoying a moment of peace and quiet in Venice, 1987.
© *James Vallance White*

Jeremy brandishing a bottle of Tabasco (presumably intended for the preparation of a Bloody Mary), c. 1987. © *John Wolfe*

'Whisk or Bran…?' Jeremy with two of his students, Simon Kingston (left) and Patrick Nold (right) in his rooms at Oriel, c. 1995. © John Wolfe

'The heart of darkness, or the English Congo, where indigenous people do abominable things under shady trees…' Jeremy looking relaxed in the garden at Eydon in Northamptonshire, c. 2010. © John Wolfe

Jeremy on the steps of the Garrick Club in London with his sisters, Annabel (left) and Jane (right), August 2015. © Annabel Flowers and John Wolfe

Jeremy staying afloat in Singapore, 1985. © Sir Alan Duncan

Jeremy's rooms in Second Quad, Oriel College (Did he really annex a part of the Provost's apartments to enlarge his own rooms…?). © Oriel College

Floreat Oriel: Jeremy visibly moved at the wedding of one of his last students, Summer 2012 (Note the groom wearing an Oriel tie). © Josh Pull

12

Pastoral Matters

'Always make sure to have a dinner jacket ready…'
 – Catto, as Senior Dean, to Simon King, prospective Junior Dean

'I am sure that if you put a condom over the fire alarm, it won't go off.'
 – Catto to a student during a party

'One last point…Change your rooms…I've seen many a man ruined through having ground-floor rooms in the front quad', said my cousin with deep gravity. 'People start dropping in. They leave their gowns here and come and collect them before hall; you start giving them a sherry. Before you know where you are, you've opened a free bar for all the undesirables of the college…'

As anyone who has ever read Evelyn Waugh's *Brideshead Revisited* will know, that exchange precedes Sebastian Flyte being sick through the window of Charles Ryder's rooms, and ends with Flyte's embarrassed Old Etonian friend explaining away his friend's excesses by saying that 'the wines were too various', and that 'it was neither the quality nor the quantity that was at fault', but 'the mixture'. As the narrator then explains in a quasi-philosophical manner: 'Grasp that and you have the root of the matter. To understand all is to forgive all.'[128]

Much like Sebastian Flyte's friend, Catto knew all too well that it was often the mixture, rather than the quality or the quantity of the wine, which led the young into trouble, and his natural generosity of spirit meant that he was always inclined to understand and to forgive. This was important because, aside from his teaching responsibilities, one of Catto's most significant roles was that of Senior Dean at Oriel. In essence, this position meant that he was charged with keeping undergraduates in line and disciplining them when – as inevitably happens with young people – they crossed the line of what was deemed to be acceptable standards of behaviour. The other side of the role involved providing students with a sympathetic ear if they were going through a difficult time. It is a role that requires tact and sensitivity, as well as an understanding of what motivates young people to behave in certain ways. During at least some of Catto's time at Oriel it would be no exaggeration to say that the college was known for its rowdies and rowing hearties, and that the young men who were regularly getting themselves into various scrapes certainly kept Catto busy as Senior Dean. To many who knew him well, including John Varley, Catto's appointment to the role seemed at first 'quite improbable', but it was clear nevertheless that he 'took it very seriously', because he always had the college's best interests at heart. In dealing with disciplinary matters, his instinct was usually to give his students the benefit of the doubt. His accommodating attitudes were shaped by his thoroughly realistic view of undergraduate life. As he once told a colleague: 'In the first year, they are finding their way, and in the second year, they have a bit of fun. It's only in the third year that they actually do some work.' Catto felt, therefore, that it would be neither sensible nor fair to punish them too harshly for their misdeeds. In that sense, his methods resembled those employed by the best kind of boarding school housemasters. Reflecting on his current role as Warden of Winchester College, Sir Richard Stagg points out that 'some housemasters have a great knack of giving the boys a sense of freedom within certain constraints, as well as the illusion that things are more free than they actually are'. Catto, he believes, also had that ability. He 'did not tolerate revolutionary activity, but he was much more tolerant of other activities and forms of behaviour, and he created a framework in which people could feel comfortable'.

In helping him to discharge his pastoral responsibilities as Senior Dean, Catto was always expected to work closely with both the college's Dean and the Junior Dean. As he reached the end of his tenure during the late 1990s, Catto enlisted the services of Simon King, and offered him the position of Junior Dean. King, who was doing a DPhil in Oriel at the time and now runs GMTL, a corporate intelligence company, was unsure of what his responsibilities would include, so he asked Catto what he would need to do to perform his role to the requisite standard. Without hesitation, Catto replied that King 'should always make sure to have a dinner jacket ready'. The younger man was understandably perplexed at this reply and asked why on earth that would make a difference, but Catto just smiled knowingly and said: 'Because that way you will make the undergraduates feel guilty, as they will think they've dragged you out of a dinner to discipline them.' Aside from that amusing vignette, King argues that Catto's modus operandi was to tread softly and to carry only a moderately large stick. His instinct was always to be lenient, if at all possible, so long as the behaviour in question was not too egregious. Looking back, King recalls one incident involving a group of Oriel boaties who had broken into a student's rooms at neighbouring Christ Church one evening before throwing all of the poor fellow's possessions out of the window. As the Senior Dean at Oriel, Catto was brought in by the authorities at Christ Church to answer for the behaviour of the young hooligans from his college. In the end, although Catto was not necessarily speechless with admiration at the behaviour of his students, he made the point to his opposite number at Christ Church that the students in question were essentially 'good chaps' and that they would 'go on to finish their degrees and then work in the City', so it would be unfair to ruin their careers because of this one lapse of judgement.

Ralph Perry-Robinson recalls a similar incident when his rooms in Oriel Street were destroyed by a certain dining society to which he belonged. Catto did not fine him, and the perpetrators were not punished either. When asked about the incident, Catto smiled and waved away the incident by saying that it had been 'a better class of trashing'. This was typical of Catto's sense of generosity, as well as his sense of humour, of which several generations of undergraduates were the grateful beneficiaries.

Giles MacDonogh was an undergraduate at Balliol in the mid-1970s and knew Catto through the Union. He recalls that, as Senior Dean, Catto 'had to sort out a large number of vexatious issues, including a man called Rosser who had been falsely accused of mistaking the bath for the lavatory, and another called Booth, who eventually owned up to being the culprit'.[129] In addition, 'there was a creepy ex-hairdresser turned mature student called Raymond, and a boy called Mellon, who became the object of Raymond's passion'.[130] But the best story involved a friend of MacDonogh's who was at Oriel at the time.

In my first year my best friend was at Oriel and, for a brief moment, he became infatuated with a girl who was one of the small female contingent at Hertford College. The girl – who is now a very senior columnist on the Guardian or the Observer – was decidedly cool towards him, but one evening, fortified by Dutch courage, he took action and climbed into Hertford after dark to confront her. He chose as his entry point an open window over the main gate. He landed softly, too softly as it turned out, on a double bed; and the occupants strongly objected to the threesome. They turned out to be the philosophers Geoffrey and Mary Warnock. Geoffrey Warnock was also the college principal. 'Who are you?' said the Warnocks, switching on the lights. My friend responded that he was 'Tom Smith from Iffley'. The philosophers were not going to be fobbed off so easily and Geoffrey Warnock might have detected something of the accent of a fellow Wykehamist: 'You don't look like Tom Smith from Iffley: you're wearing a bow tie!' Even worse, he had tied the tie himself, something exceedingly unlikely in a proper Tom Smith of Iffley. The friend was soon forced to reveal his identity. The next morning he was up before Jeremy. Jeremy lightened the friend of a £10 fine to pay for the Founders' Port and it was agreed that a bunch of flowers should be sent to Mary Warnock to soothe her ruffled feathers. 'I suppose, in a few days time,' said the friend, looking at his feet, 'I shall find this pretty funny.' He cast a glance across the desk at the Senior Dean whom he discovered to be quietly sobbing with laughter. Jeremy finally blurted out 'I find it bloody funny now!'[131]

Thinking back to his time at Oriel in the 1970s and Catto's appointment as Senior Dean, David Mathew reflects that Catto was in many ways 'a strange choice' for the role, not least because he was 'the most un-authoritarian figure you could imagine'. Mathew recalls a story which saw him getting into trouble with the college authorities over the misuse of 'some very powerful fireworks'. Essentially, Mathew, in a bout of high spirits, had inserted these fireworks into some champagne bottles, before setting them off from a pair of flower boxes in Oriel Square. Unfortunately, when the rockets crashed back down to earth, they landed at the feet of Provost Turpin. The Provost had many virtues, but he was not a man who was primarily known for his sense of humour. Having been caught red-handed as the culprit, Mathew recalls that he was 'inevitably called in to see Jeremy' about the incident, before being fined £20 as a punishment. In the end, however, the cheque handed over by Mathew was never actually cashed. Many years later, he asked Catto about this. 'Oh, I couldn't do that to you', Catto smiled. 'I only wanted to make a point.' But Catto was not the only one to find the incident amusing. When Hugh Trevor-Roper heard from his friend that the Provost had escaped unscathed, he joked that Mathew's 'aim was not very good: it should have hit him'.

It was at a similar time during the late 1970s that Oxford had an unusually large number of homeless people wandering the streets. They were such a prominent feature of the landscape at the time that the undergraduates even gave them nicknames. There were figures like 'Snowy' and 'Karl Marx', who inhabited a bench at the back of the old Radcliffe Infirmary. And then there was 'Pete the Poet', who was seemingly just a mass of hair and lice, and could often be found not far from Oriel College. To help this particular man, two undergraduates at Oriel took it upon themselves to give him a bath. One of them, Alexander Rufus-Isaacs, who was at Oriel between 1976 and 1979, explained that he and his friend brought 'Pete' back to Oriel and proceeded to give him a bath in the baths below the Rhodes Building in the college's Third Quad, which were usually reserved for the college's rugby players after a match. Alerted by the commotion, and just as 'Pete' had taken off all his clothes before lowering himself into the bath, Catto and another fellow came down to the baths and ordered him to be taken out again. No punishment was handed out, and Catto quite clearly was amused by the incident, even though he had to pretend to take the matter seriously. As Rufus-Isaacs says, 'Trampgate' showed that Catto was really quite the 'benevolent disciplinarian'.

In another incident, Laura Brady, who read PPE at Oriel in the mid-1980s, went on to pursue a career in the Foreign Office, and worked in Moscow during a pretty turbulent time in Russia's history in the early to mid-1990s, remembers witnessing at first hand Catto's indulgent attitude towards discipline. She recalls celebrating her birthday with some friends one year when a fellow undergraduate at Oriel decided to take a potshot at her through her window with an air rifle. As luck would have it, the pellet missed her, but went clean through one of the birthday cards and became wedged in the birthday cake. As the Senior Dean at the time, it fell to Catto to deal with the matter. Today, it is hard to imagine that such an incident would be tolerated, but Catto was able to see the funny side, not least as nobody had actually got hurt. Sebastian Grigg remembers that Catto was always 'profoundly familiar with undergraduate madness and managed to smooth the whole thing over'. For her part, Brady brought up the event many years later during a speech at a college gaudy, and had the good grace to joke that although Moscow in the 1990s was undoubtedly a dangerous place, her time at Oriel in the 1980s prepared her for this like no other experience.

James Mitchell was another individual who benefitted from Catto's generosity, after getting himself into trouble with the police for a 'silly prank' that ended with him spending a night in the cells at Her Majesty's pleasure. Mitchell remembers that, after a big win at rugby over a rival college in the late 1980s, he and his friends celebrated their victory at a James Bond-themed party, to which Mitchell brought a fake gun as part of his outfit. At the end of the night, and after perhaps a few too many drinks, Mitchell made the mistake of waving his gun at a passerby on the High Street on his way back home. What began as a bit of tomfoolery escalated quickly. The police were called, Mitchell was arrested, and was subsequently released on bail after spending a night in Oxford's prison. When he got out, he made his way back to Oriel and decided to report the incident to Catto. As he stood at the entrance to Catto's rooms, he feared the worst. Upon entering, however, he found his tutor propped up on the sofa and with a big grin on his face. 'So, tell me all about what you got up to last night, you wicked old thing…' According to Mitchell, Catto seemed 'really quite excited by it all and found it very amusing'. Mitchell was still unable to see the funny side of the incident and protested that the matter might be viewed as serious by some, but Catto waved away his protestations: 'It's good to see there are still some young people with a bit of spirit.' In the end, Catto was right and nothing else came of the incident. Looking back, Mitchell feels that 'the story sums him up really'. Catto had 'seen it all before' and even had the generosity of spirit to overlook the fact that one of his students had spent a night in the cells.

Marcus Walker also experienced Catto's lenient attitude towards matters of discipline in his first year at Oriel in 1999. For the occasion of the bicentenary of the birth of Cardinal Newman, one of the college's most illustrious alumni, Walker and a friend decided that the college authorities might appreciate a re-enactment of Martin Luther's famous protest against papal indulgences in 1517, so they went ahead and nailed a copy of Luther's *Ninety-five Theses* against the college chapel door. Perhaps not surprisingly, the college chaplain, a man not best known for his sense of humour, was appalled and fought hard to get Walker expelled from the college. In the end, and to Walker's great relief, he got off without even having to pay a fine. To this day, he is convinced that the Provost at the time, who was a Protestant Ulsterman, came to his rescue as he secretly found the incident to be not entirely unamusing. But perhaps even more importantly, Catto as Senior Dean also saw the humorous side of the story. He later admitted to Walker that he had found the incident to be 'amusing in the old-fashioned way' and that, if anything, such behaviour 'should be actively encouraged' rather than punished.

By the late 1990s, Catto had been at Oriel for nearly thirty years, and it is safe to assume that he had seen most variations of student hijinks during his time. On this occasion, however, it was not a student, but Catto himself, who almost got himself into trouble when he turned up at a party to join the students already assembled for a few drinks. Having been a fairly regular smoker in his earlier days, he found himself in the mood and asked one of the students whether he might be allowed to smoke a cigarette. The student replied that nothing would give him greater pleasure than to offer Catto a cigarette, but that if he did so the very sensitive fire alarms in that part of the college would be triggered instantly. Catto was naturally disappointed by this reply, but it was only a temporary setback, for which he had a solution. 'I am sure that if you put a condom over the fire alarm, it won't go off,' he suggested to the student, whose eyes bulged out of their sockets in true H. M. Bateman style after what he had just heard from the Senior Dean. Undeterred, Catto looked around and, with a mischievous look in his eye, said: 'I am sure that one of you strapping young men must have one on your person.' It did not take long for a condom to be produced, whereupon Catto instructed one of the students to place it over the fire alarm. Unfortunately for those assembled, the condom failed to quell the alarm when the first cigarette was lit, and as soon as news of the incident reached the Dean, he was ready to punish the perpetrators. Until, that is, Catto gallantly stepped in and admitted that he had been the one to suggest the use of a prophylactic to muffle the fire alarm. With that, and to everyone's relief, the matter was dropped. It is not known what the Dean made of it all, but it is reasonable to assume that no action was taken, in part at least, because he probably did not wish to see the words 'Oriel Senior Dean triggers fire alarm with a condom' splashed across the newspapers.

Unlike all of the above-mentioned Oriel undergraduates, Harry Mount was never taught by Catto, but knew him socially, and saw Catto's liberal and generous attitude towards discipline as one of his defining characteristics. Although Catto could be prudish about certain matters, his liberal attitude sometimes even extended to acts of physical nudity:

> I was once staying at a house in Northamptonshire with several undergraduate friends when one of them, a good-looking young man from a different university, proceeded to get extremely drunk and whip off all his clothes at the table. Jeremy took it all in his stride – neither censorious, awkward or perturbed. He let it all go on without attempting to rebuke or punish anyone who was there. He never told off anyone in my experience, knowing that it wasn't his job to rein in youthful exuberance – and that severe punishment, i.e. rustication or being sent down, could destroy someone's life.

Without perhaps realising it, Mount touches upon an important point with this last remark. Although the biographer should normally hesitate before playing amateur psychologist, it does not seem unduly venturesome to argue that Catto's indulgent approach to disciplining his students may have stemmed from his own experience in his final year as an undergraduate at Balliol, when he was sent down for stealing books from Blackwell's. His letter to the Master of Balliol showed that he appreciated the relative leniency shown in dealing with the case, and it is certainly possible that the experience may have influenced Catto's own views on how to handle disciplinary matters.

Whatever the truth of the matter, Catto's responsibilities as Senior Dean did not just revolve around disciplinary concerns, but also extended to softer pastoral considerations. If he sensed that his undergraduates were going through a difficult time: he could be surprisingly gentle with them, which meant that they always felt like they could approach him if they needed his help or guidance. According to Peter de Bruyne, Catto was 'a man to whom you could take your problems. Sometimes his advice was very conventional, but sometimes he could be deeply unconventional, which would make you laugh.' De Bruyne, who is Chilean, remembers arriving at Oxford in 1968 via Millfield School and a crammer[ix]. As a result of his foreign background, he felt like a bit of an outsider at times. Moreover, he felt that certain sections were trying to 'run down the place as a centre of privilege', and he found this to be surprising as well as

---

ix A specialised school that trains students to pass entrance exams to universities.

depressing. Sensing that Catto might be able to help him with this, he spoke to him about the matter. 'Jeremy sighed and said that things had always been like that and then proceeded to give a series of historical parallels.' De Bruyne felt instantly better and believed Catto handled the situation in his typically astute way by putting things in their proper context. Even if his students thought a situation was very serious, Catto, who always had an eye for the bigger picture, had a way of making them see that things would turn out for the best.

David Bugge endured a torrid start to life at Oriel and remembers that Catto had a remarkable instinct for understanding when his undergraduates were going through a difficult time:

> I am not sure why but I really lost my way. I was rather alone in life and had a very dysfunctional family. It was an unhappy time at home. I failed my Latin twice and was facing execution. I took a telephone call from Jeremy at home in the holiday. I sensed very clearly from his tone and words that I was as close as it was possible to be. But he had stood up for me. He believed in me and saw that I had lost my way. He knew I was a good young man. But he let me know in no uncertain terms that I had better change as I had one last shot.

For Bugge, being given a second chance by Catto was a real turning point in his life. He met Catto again some thirty-five years later and was able to thank him: 'I was able to look him in the eye and thank him with all my heart. It was a moment of huge good fortune in my life and I am eternally grateful to him. It gave me a platform for the rest of my life.' Looking back, he describes Catto as 'rather an enigma', and adds that 'one-to-one conversation could be quite difficult, as he probably only shared his private life and private thoughts with a few people'. Nevertheless, Bugge is also clear about the very significant impact which Catto had on his life: 'In life, we all meet a handful of people who have a big impact on us. Jeremy was such a man for many at Oriel. He was certainly a hero of mine.'

Nick Lord remembers sensing that Catto was always on the side of his students. He recalls standing outside the Porter's Lodge one day chatting to a friend, when there was a loud crashing noise and the Provost came rushing out, shouting 'STOP, THIEF!' Lord and his friend spotted the thief and ran after him down Oriel Lane. They managed to catch up with him, pinned him down, and waited there with him until the police arrived. The Provost thanked the two undergraduates and sent them back to college. About three hours later, the porter knocked on his door and hand-delivered a bottle of champagne to him. It had been sent by Catto and contained a card with the simple inscription, 'You're a hero.' Lord recalls this story because he feels that when things did go wrong for you, the good things you had done counted in your favour. He points out that Catto 'was always an ally behind the scenes' and he 'always had a sense that [he] had my back'.

However, it was often tricky to be sure whether you were in his good books or not. Catto had a series of gestures that he would deploy if he saw you in the street or across one of the quads. If he was happy with you, out would come 'the bow and arrow' and he would pretend to fire an arrow at you. But if you had done something to displease him, he would slowly 'pull out the gun' and pretend to shoot you. Although looking back, Lord concedes that he may have got the two gestures the wrong way round, and admits that he and his friends would spend hours trying to decipher these Catto gestures of approval or disapproval.

Catto's generosity of spirit meant that he was always willing to help his undergraduates if they needed him, and he understood that a friendly chat and a drink could often put things right. Mark Newman, who was at Oriel in the early 1990s, and is now an Assistant Director for Economic Affairs at the Qatar Foundation, remembers Catto fondly:

> Jeremy was my moral advisor during my three years at Oriel as a postgraduate. Jeremy's interpretation of that responsibility largely entailed invitations to drinks. The drink offered was always a pink gin. I do not recall the taste; I do recall the potency. During my first year, I encountered a setback in my studies. I was in crisis mode. I went to speak with Jeremy. He dropped what he was doing, counselled me to exchange the sixteenth century for the seventeenth century, made a brief phone call to make the necessary arrangements, and poured us some pink gins. Jeremy's nonchalance, mirthful manner, and kind support were inspirational and made a world of difference.

On the rare occasions when his undergraduates failed their exams, Catto's instinct was to see things in perspective. Tom Atkins found out about this side of Catto's pastoral care following his death in 2018:

On his death, my friend shared the story of when, after a disappointing set of mods, Jeremy took the time to write to him at home and tell him to enjoy the summer, play plenty of cricket, and come back to college in the autumn refreshed and ready to go again. In what was always a pretty intense environment, I think he appreciated that most people were putting enough pressure on themselves without the threat of censure for not working hard enough.

Although Catto always saw things in perspective, David Brierley remembers that he also had the ability to rise to the occasion when bad news had to be imparted:

I was asked about prospective Oriel candidates from my school, Hulme Grammar, in Oldham, and my opinions were taken on board. This contributed to a young man, Richard Hilton, eventually becoming my brother-in-law. Richard arrived in October 1980. In January 1981, his father died suddenly, and Jeremy had the role of breaking this tragic news. This was done with enormous empathy, kindness and care. This demonstrated his gentle side.

Even when it was time to leave Oriel, Catto's pastoral care did not end there, and his undergraduates knew that they could always rely on him for advice and guidance. He was utterly loyal to his undergraduates and wanted to see them flourish. If this meant using his extensive contacts to help them along the way, then he was more than happy to oblige. Dr Christian Glossner, who did his DPhil at Oxford from 2004–7, and is now a managing partner at Congentis in Zurich, remembers that on one occasion one of his friends, who was in his last year at Oriel, was having a drink with Catto in his rooms when the conversation turned towards the young man's plans for the future. 'What are you planning to do after you leave?' Catto asked. 'I hope to become a banker,' replied the young man. 'Wait one moment,' said Catto, before picking up the phone to call one of the high-profile banks in the City. The young man looked on with growing disbelief as Catto asked to be put through to the CEO. 'Just say that it's Jeremy,' Catto told the receptionist on the other end of the line, who then promptly put him through. 'I have a young man with me who would like to become a banker.' When the CEO asked what the young man was reading, Catto explained that he was a classicist. 'Classics?'

came the reply. 'That's exactly what we're looking for!' For Glossner, this story confirmed what another friend had told him when he had arrived at Oriel, namely that the old boys' network still existed, 'so long as Catto was still alive and well.'

This unconditional loyalty to the college's men and women meant that he even liked to praise and promote Oriel's black sheep. Sometimes this was taken to rather alarming lengths. Henry James remembers a 'brilliant address' that Catto gave in St Mary's Church to mark Founders Remembrance Day, in which he pointed out that an old Orielensis had sat in all of Hitler's cabinets between 1933 and 1945. After a theatrical pause, Catto looked up and explained to his audience that 'Oriel had a duty to remember both its good men and its bad men'. No doubt, his tongue was firmly in his cheek when he made the remark, but the underlying sentiment was genuine and heartfelt: 'Floreat Oriel.'

13

Admissions

THE UNIVERSITIES OF OXFORD AND CAMBRIDGE ARE UNUSUAL BY comparison to most other universities across the country, as they conduct face-to-face interviews with prospective undergraduate candidates for places on every degree course. As a result, the 'Oxbridge interview' has become famous, and even people who have never even thought of applying to either Oxford or Cambridge will believe that they are familiar with how the dreaded interview process works. Over the years, thanks to embellished media stories, countless myths have been turned into a form of received wisdom. In the popular imagination, candidates are quizzed, probed and expected to answer fiendishly difficult questions by eccentric dons who are determined to catch them out at every given opportunity. Either that, or they are made to perform absurd tasks, such as being able to catch a rugby ball as soon as they enter the interview room. The truth, as so often with such matters, is rather less exciting. Dons at Oxford and Cambridge interview candidates for the simple reason that a significant part of the teaching that takes place at both universities happens in small classes, which are more commonly called tutorials (or 'supervisions' at Cambridge). As such, interviews are, in essence, a small version of tutorials, and dons are trying, often in little more than an hour, to assess a candidate's ability to study, think and learn in this type of pressured environment.

Even before attending interviews, it could improve a candidate's chances if they met Catto at an open day, as a young Finn by the name of Konsta Helle discovered in the early noughties. 'It was sunny and almost oppressively hot, but Jeremy had his gas fire going in his rooms. When I told him I was Finnish he immediately asked me to come to his bedroom and showed me a biography of Mannerheim. He then bluntly told me "I'm losing my Finnish boy, Erik [Leif-Erik Hannikainen]. I could do with another one. Would you like to apply?"' Helle did so and spent the next five years at Oriel.

Given his own almost total lack of any kind of sporting prowess, it is highly unlikely that any of the candidates interviewed by Catto would have encountered a flying rugby ball, but he did have his own idiosyncratic methods. David Mathew recalls arriving at his interview with Catto feeling nervous and anxious: 'When I knocked on his door, I was astonished to find Jeremy welcoming me and looking like David Hockney, which he did in those days.' But any nerves he may have had were quickly settled when Catto smiled at him and said: 'I think I know what you would like. Gin.' As Mathew recalls, 'he then sat there and plied me with gin and tonics before the questions came'. Encouraging interviewees to drink alcohol would, of course, be unthinkable today, but Mathew remembers how adept Catto was at making him feel at ease in what he knew to be a very pressured situation.

Tom Atkins, who came up to Oxford from a state school in the mid-1990s, was also surprised by the relatively relaxed atmosphere he found at his interview:

> My school had not, as far as I was aware, sent anyone to Oxford, certainly not within the memory of any of the teachers there, and going into the interview I had no idea what to expect. I guess I was expecting a grilling across a table about my academic prowess, rather than a fire, a comfy sofa and some genial men gently probing me about an exam paper I had done a couple of months before and whose contents I had largely forgotten about the moment I put the pen down.

But once the interviewee had been put at ease, there is no doubt that Catto could also be a tough interviewer. When asked about his interview with Catto, Ken Fincham, who had come up from Tonbridge School, replies without hesitation that he still has 'a very vivid recollection of his interview with Catto'. He recalls that at one point the line of questioning moved on to the topic of the French Revolution. To his growing dismay, he quickly found that every opinion he expressed was questioned and probed by Catto, before being repackaged in the form of another question. Fincham admits that he had never before felt under that kind of academic pressure. 'I could really feel the walls closing in on me,' he recalls, but then Catto's tone suddenly changed and, much to Fincham's relief, he said simply 'you're probably right', before moving on to a different line of inquiry. Catto was not trying to be deliberately difficult but was rather doing his best to keep Fincham on his toes.

Marcus Walker remembers how rigorous and well-prepared Catto was for the interview. Walker, who was born in Jerusalem and spent his childhood in the Holy Land, Moscow and Cairo, produced a dissertation on the question of why Britain had withdrawn from Palestine in 1948. Looking back, Walker recalls with a smile that he 'successfully blagged' that he had 'not quite read all of Paul Kennedy's *Rise and Fall of the Great Powers*', as he had suggested in his personal statement. Thankfully, this did not actually come up in the interview, but Walker remembers the degree to which Catto was in command of his brief regarding Britain's withdrawal from Palestine, even though it was a subject that was far removed from his own area of expertise. Walker is still clearly impressed when he thinks back to how Catto cross-examined him on all manner of different sources relating to the period. 'He had mugged up on Palestine to such an extent that he was really able to engage properly. It was very impressive.'

Alexander Morrison arrived at Oriel via Sevenoaks School. After an unsuccessful interview at University College, Oxford, he took a year out, but Catto saw potential in the young man and gave him a place at Oriel. Morrison would go on to win the Gibbs Prize before becoming a Prize Fellow at All Souls College, the university's leading graduate research institution. Uniquely among Oxford colleges, it has no undergraduates and its members automatically become fellows. Graduate and postgraduate students at Oxford are eligible to apply, and admission is secured through an examination that was once described as 'the hardest exam in the world'. When Morrison got in, Catto, who enjoyed cultivating friendly feuds with his fellow academics, could not resist the temptation to send a simple three-word telegram to the University College don who had turned Morrison down: 'Ha. Ha. Ha.' And in characteristically mischievous fashion, to celebrate Morrison's successful election, he then invited his colleague from University College to a high table dinner at Oriel, but without telling him that Morrison would also be present at the dinner.

When he was not interviewing official candidates for a place at Oriel, Catto was always generous enough to provide the children of friends with help and advice regarding interviews. Wilf Stephenson remembers that when his son was applying to Cambridge, he was undecided about which subject he wanted to study at university. When Stephenson mentioned this to Catto, he suggested that he should send his son to him and that he would be happy to advise him. Not surprisingly, given that the choice was between history, maths and Japanese, Catto advised the son to apply for history. But he also offered to give the son a mock interview, an offer which Stephenson's son was only too happy to accept. Catto told the father that he would only need about forty-five minutes with his son, and Stephenson recalls that 'on the stroke of forty-five minutes, the phone rang and it was Jeremy'. Catto told him down the phone that they had nearly finished, before adding: 'Do you think you could find us another bottle of tonic?' Clearly, the mock interview had gone very well indeed.

There were, however, persistent accusations of bias levelled against Catto throughout his time dealing with the admissions process at Oriel. Specifically, the suggestion was that candidates had a better chance of being admitted to read history at Oriel during Catto's tenure if they were male and had been privately educated. An example of this alleged bias can be found within the college's archives in the shape of a formal complaint that was made against the college in the late 1990s. In a letter from the parent of an unsuccessful female candidate to Tony Benn MP, the parent asked Benn to take his daughter's case up directly with the Provost, Ernest Nicholson. In this letter, the disgruntled parent begins by declaring the following: 'As a socialist, I have always felt it incumbent on me to challenge prejudice and privilege. Having persuaded my daughter of this, she applied for a place at Oriel College, Oxford to read Modern History.'[132] After she failed to secure a place, her father's letter went on to say that 'there are some issues arising from the selection process' which he believed 'should be pointed out to give future applicants a fair chance of

the best opportunities provided by public money'.[133] Having noted that
the college was, according to the university prospectus, 'committed to the
principle of equal opportunity', and that it welcomed 'men and women
applicants from every kind of background and school', the parent pointed
out that at his daughter's interview 'there were 26 candidates for 8 places
for Modern History and only 3 candidates were female'.[134] In addition,
his daughter apparently 'met none who were from state schools', and she
had told him that 'undergraduates at Oriel reported that it is very rare
for females and people from state schools to win a Modern History place
there'.[135] He concluded his case with the following:

> Overall across Oxford University, some 47% of places go to state
> school pupils, so I believe that the evidence is sufficient to question
> the accuracy of the prospectus, at least in the department concerned.
> Moreover, it does seem that effectively a policy of gender and class
> discrimination is being tacitly operated. That the college receives
> public funding despite its own considerable wealth, makes it a
> matter of public concern.[136]

In his reply to the parent, the Provost began by reaffirming that he
and his colleagues were 'indeed committed to the principle of equal
opportunity', adding that they were 'anxious to increase the number of
applicants from the state schools and from women'.[137] The Provost then
continued in a more personal vein, by explaining that he had himself
come from 'a poor home, was state-school educated', and was 'not
"Oxbridge" by origin'.[138] Reading the letter, the parent could have been
left in no doubt that the Provost took this matter seriously and that
his own 'passionate commitment to equal opportunity'[139] was genuine
and heartfelt. As a result of the complaint, the Provost had taken steps
to speak to his colleagues in the history faculty and, having done so,
he assured the parent that he was 'satisfied' by his colleagues that 'their
choice of students for next year was made on a careful assessment of
academic achievement and promise amongst the twenty-six candidates
whom they interviewed, and was fair', adding that it was 'not an
outcome' he 'would welcome too often'.[140] By way of providing the
parent with further contextual information, the Provost then compared
the admissions for that faculty with other departments: 'May I add,
incidentally, that on the other hand all of the candidates admitted to
read English were women and almost all the candidates admitted to read

Law were women and from state schools. That is the way things have happened in these subjects this year, whilst in other subjects there was a more of a usual mixture.'[141] Sensing perhaps that this did not necessarily constitute a solid defence of the history department's record, he then went on to explain that he had spoken at length to 'the woman who was closely involved in the history selection process', adding that she had been 'involved in the process of selection from beginning to end, that is, in reading the written work submitted by the candidates, in conducting the interviews, and in the meeting afterwards when admissions were finally decided'.[142] Having done so, the Provost felt able to assure the parent that he had 'complete confidence in the integrity of this young woman and in her commitment to equal opportunity'.[143] The result of this, according to the Provost, was that although his colleague found the parent's daughter to be 'academically impressive', there was also in her view 'no doubt that the candidates finally selected were rightly placed ahead of her when the final decisions on selection were made'.[144] The Provost ended his letter with the following: 'The truth is that competition for places is fierce', adding that the parent's daughter not gaining a place 'was not a reflection on her intellectual ability, which is considerable, but only on the competition here'.[145]

Quoting these exchanges in full does not, of course, prove anything either way. Even so, it is important to note that the care and attention to detail devoted to this case does indicate that the college was in no way cavalier or complacent about the question of admissions. It also suggests that admitting the right people was taken very seriously by the college. But beyond this specific example, if one examines the statistics over a longer period of time, it is difficult to avoid the conclusion that Oriel historians in this period tended to be a certain type of person. It is also true that the numbers of public-school boys admitted to read history at Oriel were always higher than in other subjects across the college, and that even after the admission of women to the college in 1985, there were always fewer women reading history than in other subjects. Nevertheless, it is not clear what conclusions can be drawn from all of this. Unfortunately, there is no record of how many state-school-educated pupils or how many women applied to Oriel to read history during Catto's time at the college. This matters because it is possible that Catto was forced to pick from a narrow pool that contained very few from those categories, which meant that he would often have had no choice but to choose a large number of public-school candidates. On the other hand, it is also possible that fewer women and candidates from state schools applied to Oriel precisely because the college had developed a reputation for not admitting many candidates who fitted those profiles. Alternatively, it cannot be entirely ruled out that Catto was instinctively biased in favour of a particular type of candidate. As a man from a certain background and generation, who had himself attended an all-boys school, it would not be hugely surprising to learn that he preferred to surround himself with young men from a similar background. Equally, it has also been argued that the man who had been to a relatively minor private school and hailed from the North East enjoyed being in the company of people from grander social backgrounds.

One person who is qualified to shed some light on Catto's approach to admissions is Dr Leif Dixon. He spent two years working alongside Catto on Oriel's admissions process in the early 2000s and was, therefore, able to observe him at close quarters. On the one hand, what he took from Catto was that admitting students to Oxford 'was a very important and interesting thing to do'. He also admired Catto for his dedication to the cause. 'Jeremy poured a lot of time and energy into admissions, and I could not have been better served as a professional model.' In addition, Dixon recalls that Catto 'had a quite democratic tendency with admissions in the sense that all four colleagues who helped with the admissions process had their votes measured in an equal manner'. At no time, in other words, did Catto pull rank, which 'astonished' Dixon and made him feel 'very empowered'. On the other hand, Dixon also maintains that 'although Jeremy did not do it deliberately, he tended to favour the type of person who could respond fluently to his kind of interview'. What Dixon means by this is that Catto's interviewing style was 'quite traditional' in that it involved questions about essays and the analysis of gobbets of text, which were skills that 'could be coached' and which would, therefore, give candidates with a private education a distinct advantage. And although Dixon insists that Catto 'did not carry any prejudice as such', he also thinks that 'among the marginal candidates, he picked the ones with whom he was most comfortable'. This meant not only public-school boys, but also those who had family connections to the college. Similarly, Dixon adds that 'Jeremy was not against admitting women, but thought that men were more interesting'. Unlike Dixon himself, Catto was 'not that concerned with the proportion of students who would go on to get firsts'. As a way of further clarification, Dixon notes that he and Catto would sometimes discuss these matters, and that Catto did not believe in social class or that, at any rate, it was all much more complicated than the simplistic private-versus-state-school divide implied. As usual, he would joke that the real access cases were those boys from boarding schools, given the horrors that they had been forced to endure. Although this was said with a wry smile, it was Catto's way of suggesting that issues of class were rather complicated and nuanced, and that it was wrong to make general assumptions about candidates. More seriously, however, Dixon says that Catto 'did not accept that some people were from systemically disadvantaged homes', and that this may very well have coloured his view of the admissions process.

The nature of this process means that it is difficult to be certain about what motivated Catto, but given the accusations of bias, it is important to tackle this directly. Even if it is true that Catto favoured certain candidates over others, it is worth remembering the broader context. Specifically, it is essential to see the admissions process through the prism of the overall purpose of the university and how, over time, interpretations of that purpose have changed. To some dons, the driving force behind admissions has always been a purely academic one, with the aim being to pick the brightest and most academically able. The university exists to train future scholars or, at the very least, to pick those who will go on to take their rightful place in the world of work and contribute meaningfully to the country's economic well-being. Aside from academic considerations, many of today's dons also see the admissions process as a vehicle for social mobility. The idea is that Oxford's principal function should be to provide bright and able young people from disadvantaged backgrounds with the opportunity to receive a transformative education that will shake up the country's class system and propel those young people into a higher social class.

Maurice Bowra, who was Warden of Wadham College from 1938 to 1970 and also served as the university's Vice-Chancellor from 1951 to 1954, held a rather different view. He believed that 'commoners should not be cut all to the same pattern or taken solely on the chance that they will do well in Final Schools'. It was important to accept some candidates who might be academically undistinguished but who would 'plainly benefit by extra-curricular activities and add to the variety of college life'.[146] Russell Meiggs of Balliol agreed, and argued that 'if the only function of the University is academic, the college system is an extravagant medium', adding that 'a considerable part of the defence for the college system lies in its contribution to total development'.[147] At

Christ Church, Steven Watson suggested that the criteria used at college entrance should recognise 'the need to civilize those who are born to great responsibilities' and 'the desire to be tender to claims of loyal old members'.[148] Hugh Stratton brilliantly captured the nature of these different views in the following terms:

> The Left suspected that the Right's idea of a decent commoner was an amiable, well-connected public-school dunce, keen on rugger and beagling but usually too drunk for either, likely to pass without effort (or qualifications) into the upper-middle ranks of government or business, to the ultimate detriment of British power, prosperity, and social justice, but sure to turn up to Gaudies and quite likely to donate silver or endow a trophy or two. The Right suspected that the Left's idea of a decent commoner was a bespectacled black beetle from a nameless secondary school who would speak to nobody, swot his solitary, constipated way to an indifferent degree, then forget the College the day he left it for a job in local government, where his chief effect on the national life would be as a chronic claimant on, and voter for, the National Health Service.[149]

Catto had a romantic view of Oxford's ultimate purpose, and it is fair to say that he was firmly in the camp of Bowra, Meiggs and Watson. The idea that the university should exist simply to train the next generation of scholars would have seemed to him unacceptably narrow. Picking people on the sole basis that they might be more likely than other candidates to emerge with a first-class degree was never at the forefront of his mind. He certainly wanted his undergraduates to be clever, but he also saw the value of assembling a diverse cohort of undergraduates who would contribute to college and university life in different ways. Nor, as Dr Dixon has pointed out, was he persuaded by the arguments put forward by the class warriors, who aimed at using the university as a way of creating a more level playing field across society. Instead, the medievalist in him knew that Oxford had originally been founded to educate the men who would go on to serve the church and the state; they were not only men of learning, but also of character and ambition. A similar idea pertained later in the nineteenth century, and the young men who were admitted were chosen for their ability to serve the British Empire and to run the great offices of state. In Catto's own time as an undergraduate in the late 1950s, a similar idea still held sway, even though the university was by then beginning to take on more candidates from state grammar schools. In any case, Catto was undoubtedly influenced by his own background and upbringing, and he would have been conscious of picking candidates who had the potential to go on to lead interesting and worthwhile lives in politics, the City, academia and the Church. None of the above is designed to provide an apologia for Catto's approach (assuming that one believes that such a defence is required in the first place), but it should hopefully help to place the question of admissions, and Catto's attitude towards the process, within a broader context.

14

Women

'Very sorry, Miss Minerva, but perhaps you are not aware that this is a monastic establishment.'

— An 'Oxford don' in Punch magazine, 1896

'He was far too polite to ever say so, but it was always fairly obvious that he did not want me there.'

— Oriel's first female historian about Catto

FOR MOST OF ITS LONG AND ANCIENT HISTORY, STUDYING AT OXFORD University was the sole preserve of young men. The oldest constituent colleges began life as male-only institutions, and it was not until 1879 that the first women's colleges – Somerville and Lady Margaret Hall – came into existence. But although these pioneering women attended lectures at the university and sat for regular exams, they were not officially full members and, critically, their qualifications were not formally recognised until as late as 1920. Vera Brittain, who matriculated in that year, described the atmosphere in the Sheldonian, when women were first admitted to degrees, as 'tense with the consciousness of a dream fulfilled'.[150] It had certainly been a long time coming.

Things were not much better at the other place and, if anything, they were even worse. Although Oxford took far longer to grant women degrees than almost any other university in the country, Cambridge University was even slower to get off the mark. Girton College, for example, which had been founded in 1869, only awarded full degree status to women in 1948. The rivalry between these two ancient universities is of such intensity that neither institution enjoys finishing as runner-up behind the other. In 1920, Jane Harrison, the eminent Cambridge classicist, was clearly piqued by Oxford nudging ahead of Cambridge, as she said that it was 'so like Oxford & so low to start after us and get in first!'[151]

It is important to understand why it took the universities so long to confer degree status on women. For some, there appears to have been a genuine fear of allowing women access to a previously all-male environment. In 1896, during a debate in Congregation on degrees for women, the satirical magazine *Punch* poked fun at the problem in a mischievous cartoon, which showed the Greek goddess of wisdom trying to enter Oxford, only to find her way blocked by a college don. 'Very sorry, Miss Minerva,' he explains, 'but perhaps you are not aware that this is a monastic establishment.'[152] For others, the worry was that the arrival of women would distract the men from getting on with the serious business of academic work. This concern was also acknowledged, albeit with a note of some resignation, by certain women at Oxford. In 1914, the head of one women's college was so outraged by this matter that she felt she had no choice but to write to her students to warn them of 'a very tiresome complaint that the men examinees are disturbed by the way our students sit in their tight skirts and show their legs'.[153]

But once this initial hurdle of allowing women to gain access had been cleared, and as attitudes gradually softened over time, colleges one by one became co-educational institutions. To those in favour of admitting women, it was not merely a matter of equality or fairness. More pragmatically, colleges that failed to admit women would continue to lag behind other more progressive colleges, in particular in regards to academic performance in exams. Oriel, however, remained stubbornly opposed to the idea and would not admit women until 1985, which meant that it became the last Oxford college to do so. But despite this opposition, there had in fact been calls to admit women long before 1985. In December 1968, the governing body 'noted' (but did not accept) a motion passed by the Junior Common Room in favour of the admission of women.[154] This was during the 'year of revolutions' across Europe, when students' demands at Oxford were at their most radical. At Oriel, this manifested itself in calls to remove traditional features of college life, including high table, the separation of common rooms, as well as challenges to the college authorities' right to act independently of undergraduate opinion. Nevertheless, the authorities at Oriel remained firm and unbending on the question of admitting women to the college. By the early 1970s, a move in favour of admitting women was once again gaining some momentum, but motions such as these were repeatedly struck down, as the fellows were never quite able to secure the two-thirds majority required to pass them. The question continued to be debated for the rest of the decade, but without any change in the outcome.

All of this was to change, however, in the period following Michael Swann's brief tenure as Provost, which came to an end in the early 1980s after no more than nine months. The college had to move quickly to find a suitable replacement. Hugh Trevor-Roper, who had been raised to the peerage in 1979 and had left Oxford to become Master of Peterhouse College, Cambridge in 1980, still took a keen interest in the internal politics of Oriel, and he was convinced that only one man was qualified to take on the role. In a letter written from the House of Lords to Eric Vallis (appointed Treasurer at Oriel in 1974), Lord Dacre expressed the following view:

> What is needed, in my opinion, is someone who will not be put off by the Swann episode (i.e. someone who already feels committed to the college), who is willing to live in that unprivate, unprotected house, who is committed to academic revival and knows how to achieve it, and who is both tough and flexible: for he will have to outmanoeuvre, rather than frontally challenge, the existing oligarchy. Also, someone who is a scholar, capable of communicating his interest to undergraduates, politically sophisticated, and socially agreeable: for the whole philistine ethos of the place needs to be changed. If such a person can be found, we should not object to another (but very different) long reign. Is there anyone who combines these qualities…? …I can think of only one person so qualified, viz: Jeremy Catto. He has the right views and the right standards. He knows what he wants and how to achieve it, but is at the same time very tactful and contrives to make no enemies. He is hospitable, convivial, sophisticated, and undergraduates like him. He would be a much-needed unifying force in the college, and yet would quietly but firmly change its course. He is no younger than Turpin when he was elected, and he is older than Maurice Bowra when he was made Warden of Wadham. Would he be willing to

stand? I don't know, but perhaps he could be persuaded. Would you persuade him? Would the Fellows vote for him? I doubt it. But if his name were inserted only towards the end of the 90 days which are allowed for election, when their little minds are wonderfully concentrated by the prospect of being hanged (on a silken cord, by the Lord Chancellor), perhaps then, after careful and dire threats of a dark future, who knows...?[155]

The very next day, Dacre wrote a letter to Catto from Chiefswood, his home in Scotland, in which he almost pleaded with Catto to put himself forward for the role, even though he instinctively understood that Catto had certain misgivings about the job:

You may protest, 'give not this rotten orange to thy friend'; and indeed, in its present state, it looks pretty rotten. But perhaps it is only verging into putrescence – a mere spot of mould on the outer rind and if correctly treated could be converted into delicious marmalade or exciting curacao. Is it not your duty? Would you not enjoy it? I hear you protest, it is a bed of nails, a crown of thorns. Well, at your instance, I was willing, however reluctant, to lie in that bed, to wear that crown; so why may I not return the compliment? You will say, the Fellows would not vote for you; why then for me, who would reign longer? I answer, both persons and circumstances are now different. Your sweet temper will conciliate those whom my asperity has repelled; and the Fellows, by now, are living in an atmosphere of crisis; so will not the imminent threat of being hanged, with a silken cord pulled – not without some relish – by the Lord Chancellor, wonderfully concentrate their minds? Let your friends perform their part: will you be willing to stand? I hope you will.[156]

In the end, Catto did not throw his hat into the ring. The likeliest reason for this is that, despite his friend Lord Dacre's endorsement, it is unlikely that he would have been able to secure enough support from the college's fellows to emerge triumphant from the chasing pack. That was certainly the view of Eric Vallis, who replied to Lord Dacre in a letter dated 8 September 1981, in which he wrote the following:

Nothing would give me greater pleasure than to be able to support – and do something about – your suggestion regarding Jeremy: I have known him longer than I have any other Fellow and would endorse unreservedly all that you say. But sadly, I am bound to say that he could not command anything like enough support to make it possible for his friends to get him to the starting gate; and many would say it would not be a kindness to Jeremy even to mention his name…[157]

With Catto out of the running, the college wasted little time in finding a successor to Swann. Sir Zelman Cowen, who took up the role of Provost in 1982, was welcomed by Catto in typical fashion. When he arrived, Catto's first words to him over high table were: 'Oh Provost, I do hope you're not going to swan off.' That he did not do. Instead, he decided, albeit with considerable initial caution, to involve himself in the debate on the admission of women to the college. As he wrote later:

> Oriel had been deadlocked over the issue for years. Some wished to preserve the traditional college. Others felt that society had changed and that our anomalous situation discouraged applications from good students. When I was quizzed by the delegation of Oriel fellows who came to see me in Canberra, I was asked my view of the desirability of opening the last male preserve to women. I replied that the question should wait until I got to Oxford, rather than divide the college further by making a statement before hearing the views of its members.[158]

But when a motion to admit women was brought before the college shortly after his arrival, that initial caution disappeared, and the new Provost recorded:

> I strongly believed the college should admit women, and I decided it was time to act. I consulted among fellows, among the students and among our alumni…There was searching debate and calm discussion. Whatever had divided the college in earlier times, the decision to admit women was taken quickly, decisively and with no lasting division; as one fellow later wrote, within a year we had forgotten what all the fuss was about.[159]

Nell Butler was one of the first female undergraduates to arrive at Oriel in 1985, and went on to pursue a successful career in television, creating among other programmes the hit series *Come Dine with Me*.

She provides an interesting glimpse into the atmosphere surrounding the college at the time and recalls that there were 'only about twenty-five women in the first year', which meant that female undergraduates were still 'very much a minority'. It was an exciting time for those young pioneering women, with Butler recalling that there was a feeling among the new arrivals that they had come 'to raise the academic standards' at the college and had 'as much right as anyone else to be there'. Once they had arrived, however, it became clear that there were some male undergraduates who, along with some of the dons, had not wanted women to be admitted. Butler remembers the chant of 'no women' going round the dining table from time to time, and says that some of the women found this oppressive and intimidating. For her own part, though, she points out that 'slightly posturing men held no fear' for her and that she always suspected that the men 'secretly quite liked having us around'.

Catto's position on the admission of women remained consistent over the years, as he was part of a small group of fellows who persistently voted against their admission. Given his views, it is interesting to speculate how this issue might have been resolved if Lord Dacre's campaign to install Catto as Provost had succeeded. Sadly, we will never know for certain. But what we do know is that, eventually, when the vote was put to the fellows in 1984, Catto bowed to the inevitable pressure and agreed to vote in favour of the admission of women. For many years he had refused to be moved on the matter, and his stance on this important question was not always easy to understand. In later years, whenever the question of admitting women came up, Catto was, as ever, adept at diffusing the situation with humour. He would point out that Oriel had, in fact, been the first college to appoint a female fellow and that this had happened back in the early fifteenth century. After pausing for effect, he would go on to explain that, at the time of her appointment, she had been dead for fifteen years, but that that was not viewed as a defining characteristic at the time and was therefore not held against her. To some, all of this will have been seen as evidence for Catto's apparent misogyny. His dogged refusal to admit women to the college and his tendency to make light of the situation will have provided irrefutable evidence for the fact that he simply did not wish to share the college with female colleagues or undergraduates. The relatively low numbers of women admitted to read history even after women were granted access to the college will, according to some, offer up further proof of his entrenched bias in favour of male undergraduates.

Jane Potter, now Hannah, was the very first female undergraduate historian to arrive at Oriel after the college admitted women. After her time at Oxford, she had a long career in banking in London followed by a stint in Geneva. Thinking back to her time at Oriel, she says that she 'thoroughly enjoyed tutorials with Catto' and adds that he was always 'perfectly polite and helpful'. However, as a shy girl from a northern comprehensive, she also says that she felt somewhat anonymous at times. 'I did not know him very well, because by and large he did not take much notice of me. Others were taken out to lunch at the Grid or invited to his rooms for sherry, but I was just ignored.' By the others, Hannah means the Old Etonians and Old Amplefordians who seemed to make up a large proportion of the intake for history at Oriel. 'He was far too polite to ever say so, but it was always fairly obvious that he did not want me there.' Reflecting on what might have motivated Catto to object to the admission of women, Hannah does not think that he was a straightforward misogynist, but rather that he was a classic product of his generation and that women were 'a bit of a mystery to him'. She remembers that he once said to her at a college dinner, 'I was wondering what you would wear.' This was said in such a way to suggest that he had never considered what women might wear to a formal college occasion. In the end, Hannah met her future husband at Oriel and is grateful for her time there, but she maintains that she got in partly because she was Catholic, and that she would probably not have been awarded a place if Catto had not been put under pressure from the college authorities to admit more women.

However, on the other side of the argument, there are women who were taught by Catto over the years who remember things differently. On the vexed question of sexuality and gender, Clemmie Raynsford 'always had a sense that he was a homosexual man and that, perhaps, he laughed more loudly at the jokes from male undergraduates and maybe smiled at them more sweetly', but she also felt that 'he liked having women in tutorials as an effective foil for some of the more negative or arrogant tendencies of the male undergraduates'. She adds that Catto never gave the impression that he was 'angry that the college had admitted women'. In fact, in tutorials, Catto would 'often speak with reverence about the female historians he admired'. In the end, Raynsford is convinced that 'everyone was a human being' to Catto.

Kate Selway, having been supervised by Catto for her doctorate for four years, says that she 'never encountered any kind of misogyny'. In her experience, Catto 'was always witty, amusing and charming' with her. Was he ever reserved with her at the start? 'Yes, but I was quite reserved too and I was also quite in awe of him. But I never had any sort of feeling that he was remotely misogynistic.'

Nell Butler was not taught by Catto but remembers him as a 'very memorable person around college', who was 'quite flamboyant in a donnish sort of way'. She adds that she and the other female undergraduates were 'all aware in a light sort of way that he was not pro women arriving'. Nevertheless, it was also clear that he was 'not ashamed of the views he held'. Catto, according to Butler, could be 'quite waspish', but was also evidently 'a very cheery presence', who 'did not look sourly across the quad' at the women who had arrived at Oriel. In addition, she was 'never personally offended by him, because he was always open to debate and discussion'. Looking back, Butler says that this was typical of the period, in the sense that the 1980s were 'much more accepting times, and it was just accepted that people had different views' about all manner of questions. This greater sense of tolerance may also have meant that although the debates leading up to the decision to admit women were often quite tense, the sting was taken out of the issue pretty quickly once women had been admitted. Butler agrees and confirms that 'within a year or two' very few people felt the need to revisit the issue.

On balance, even if the charge of outright misogyny cannot be levelled at Catto, his refusal to admit women to the college must have some other explanation. First, as something of a traditionalist, he believed that the college had operated successfully in the past and that there was no compelling reason to change. According to a former colleague who worked alongside him for many years, Catto felt that admitting women would be 'a step into the unknown, and a risk not worth taking'. Secondly, the same colleague has argued that Catto was also keen on admitting a certain type of person, or, as he put it, Catto's 'History Boys', as he felt that he 'was good at teaching them and they responded well to him'. In other words, it was not a question of disliking the thought of teaching women, but more a case of understanding his own strengths and weaknesses. Thirdly, friends who knew him well have pointed out that Catto's position on the question of admitting women was, in the end, simple and straightforward, and that it boiled down to questions of choice and plurality. That is to say, he did not object to the admission of women to the university per se, but as so often throughout his time at Oxford, he remained wedded to the idea of defending the rights, privileges and freedoms of individual colleges. This meant that, as independent and autonomous institutions, colleges should have the right to offer a different choice to prospective students. He did not object to all women's colleges, such as St Hilda's or Somerville and he, therefore, felt that it was important, for the sake of balance, to have at least one male-only college at Oxford.

In the end, after the decision to admit women was taken in May 1984, it was implemented gradually, and the first cohort of twenty-one female undergraduates arrived in October 1985. In hindsight, it could be argued that the only drawback of admitting women came as a result of an unfortunate accident which led to the ending of a longstanding and much-cherished college boat club tradition. After being admitted to the college, women took to college sport with great enthusiasm. Rowing, in particular, became a favourite sport among the new female undergraduates, and they also enjoyed the boat burning ritual associated with success on the river. On one occasion, however, one of the new cohort jumped over the burning boat after a bump supper, which led the governing body, ever mindful of the dangers of burning undergraduates to a crisp, to ban the practice of boat burning altogether. Reggie Burton, an old classics fellow, who had been appointed to the college as far back as 1932, and who still remembered the days before First Quad was paved and grassed, looked back nostalgically to a time when the 'pyre rising nearly thirty feet'[160] had been lit by the Provost, who was then carried shoulder-high out of the hall to mark the college being head of the river for the first time in ninety years. Apart from that, the vast majority who gave the matter any thought at all would go on to agree with the aforementioned fellow who said that within a year or so of admitting women to the college most people had forgotten what all the fuss had been about. That almost certainly – at least eventually – included Catto himself.

15

College Finances

'The performance of real estate property as an asset class has been atypical over the past 500 years.'
　　　　　　　　　　　　　　– Catto during a finance committee meeting

'In this home of lost causes, no architect has been employed.'
　　　　　　　　　　– Review of Oriel College's Island Site, Daily Telegraph, 1986

CATTO WAS OFTEN HEARD TO SAY THAT HE LIKED THE IDEA OF HIS students becoming either bankers or diplomats. It was not entirely clear whether he was being serious or not (and with Catto one could never be fully certain), but his impeccable reasoning was that if they became diplomats then he could go and stay with them at different embassies around the world, whereas if they became bankers, they would be able to donate large sums of money to their beloved alma mater.

For Catto, this last point was especially important because he cared deeply about his college's longer-term future and played an unusually active role in its financial administration. The commitment to such an endeavour inevitably involves endless rounds of committee work, which can often be a draining and rather thankless task, but is absolutely essential to the smooth running of a college. The nature of what is discussed at such meetings can often be rather dry, but Catto was adept at injecting an element of levity into proceedings. A former Provost recalls how on one occasion Catto said little for most of the meeting, before delivering the following verdict on a proposal for the college to invest in real estate: 'The performance of real estate property as an asset class has been atypical over the past 500 years.' The line was uttered in a deadpan manner, but with his customary impish smile evident for all to see.

Despite the humour, Catto took his responsibilities very seriously, and securing endowments for the college was especially important for him. Jeffrey Bonas, who is a founder member of the Oriel College Development Trust and worked alongside Catto for many years in that capacity, is full of admiration for Catto's work in this area of college life. 'Jeremy was for many years a trustee of the Oriel Development Trust, which raised millions for the College. He came to events, gave us ideas, and introduced us to donors, many of whom he had taught and, as a result, were inclined to be generous.' In addition, Bonas adds that so committed was Catto to raising endowments for Oriel that he may even have dipped into his own resources over the years to help the college. 'I think he did gift the college but I do not remember any details. I certainly knew him to be personally very generous.'

One of his old students, Henry James, has an intriguing theory about his interest in endowments. According to James, Catto's doctorate on William of Woodford, who was a leading fourteenth-century friar, is arguably a revealing choice of subject. James feels that there are several parallels between the two men, but he adds that there is a particular similarity in regards to endowments:

> Woodford was essentially a conservative man and he was opposed to change. He opposed the new and threatening ideas of Wyclif and his followers. For example, Wyclif et al wanted to dis-endow the Church of its lands, whereas Woodford wanted the Church to keep hold of its endowments. Jeremy was a great believer in endowments and spent a lot of his time and energies in increasing the endowments of Oriel.

Whatever the truth behind his motivation to involve himself so closely with college endowments, the administration and finances of the college genuinely mattered to him, and there can be no question of his dedication to the cause. Wilf Stephenson, who was treasurer at Oriel from 2005 to 2021, remembers that he first met Catto not long after he arrived at Oriel in the summer of 2005. Looking back, he chuckles and reveals that, characteristically enough, his first introduction to

Catto came not during a meeting of the finance committee, but over dinner, at the end of which Catto made him try some snuff, which was something he had never tried before. Another early encounter with Catto came during a meeting in college to discuss that year's relatively poor performance in exams, which had resulted in a slide down the Norrington Table. The various dons lined up to defend their departments, and when one don protested perhaps a bit too vociferously, Catto leaned across to Stephenson and in a stage whisper said to him: 'He's only having a go because PPE has done so badly.'

Over the years, the two men would sit together on countless committees, and Stephenson recalls that there were times when he had some tough decisions to make. This included cutting back on certain activities that were considered as non-essential. One of those, to Catto's great dismay, was the daily Senior Common Room breakfast. According to Stephenson, this had quite simply become an 'unaffordable luxury' for the college to sustain. Indeed, so lavish was the affair, Stephenson adds, that 'it felt like something from a country house weekend party', and he believes that Catto was so upset by the decision that he 'never quite forgave' Stephenson for culling it. On a more serious note, however, Stephenson believes that Catto was 'completely dedicated to the college, to undergraduate life and to the running of the college'. He adds that Catto was unusual in that regard, as many dons did not involve themselves in college life quite to the same extent, and he concludes that Catto was an 'old-fashioned bachelor don who lived in college for a very long time and was very much part of the fabric of college life'.

In addition to the college's endowments and finances, the upkeep of its buildings was also of great importance to Catto. Over the years, he was intimately involved in a series of important building works at the college. Sandy Hardie, who served as Oriel's bursar from 2001 to 2005, remembers meeting Catto for the first time as part of the selection committee that eventually chose him as bursar. Not every don took as close an interest in the running of the college as Catto who, according to Hardie, was 'very interested in the fabric of the college'. Reflecting on Catto's involvement in these administrative matters, Hardie believes that Catto had a series of qualities that made him a very effective operator behind the scenes. At governing body meetings, he was 'an unobtrusive presence' and usually sat 'at the far end of the table', from where his 'occasional and brief interventions' were always 'courteous and un-polemical'. Yet this understated approach should not be confused with ineffectiveness. Hardie points out that Catto 'preferred to exercise influence informally'. He was good at handling colleagues, especially the Provost, and he was 'a natural conciliator whose instinct was to take the personal heat out of any difference of opinion or policy'. All of which meant that Hardie could often rely on Catto to get involved in all manner of projects to improve the buildings of the college:

> I was determined to do something about the Lodge, which was among the scruffiest in Oxford. The money became available, and I put together the ad-hoc committee to steer the thing from design to completion. Jeremy was an essential presence, because he cared about the fabric, and his support was invaluable, not least because we went outside Oxford for our architect and chose what at the time was an unorthodox approach to the project.

More significantly, the college history credits both Hughe Browne and Catto with the idea of building a tunnel to connect the Island Site with the main part of the college. 'If a tunnel could be made between the main college site and the alleyways behind Oriel Street, this new quadrangle could be fully integrated into the existing college and treated as a contiguous extension.'[161] This was quite difficult to accomplish, 'because of the services running below Oriel Street', but the plan was 'successfully brought to completion in 1985-86'.[162] When combined with a series of other improvements to the college's buildings, the completed work led to a complimentary editorial in the *Daily Telegraph*, which would have pleased Catto:

> In Oriel, the latest development is bucking the modernist trend. A small, bourgeois courtyard is being slowly and carefully restored so that every room is a different shape and character. An old street lamp lights the scene, and a tunnel bored through ancient foundations connects this almost Italian side-street with the rest of the college…The secret? In this home of lost causes, no architect has been employed.[163]

16

History Faculty

'Catto did not want to be disliked, but did not mind being misunderstood.'
— Leif Dixon

'If the history syllabus is still a mangrove swamp, with crocodiles, through which every individual must cut a personal channel, it is a swamp full of unexpected forms of life.'
— Catto's assessment of the Oxford history syllabus, 2006

THE NINETEENTH-CENTURY VOLUME OF THE *HISTORY OF THE University of Oxford* describes the development of the university's history faculty in the following terms:

> Modern History was introduced to Oxford in the 1850s and established on its own as an honours degree course by 1872. Beginning (at the latter date) with the fall of Rome and concluding for England at 1847, elsewhere at 1815, history was a subject that was hardly 'modern', nor was it an innovative or experimental study of recent, let alone contemporary, issues and events. Instead, the study of history began and continued as an epic illustration of the qualities required of England's governing élite.[164]

As the above extract makes clear, part of the rationale behind the formation of the history syllabus was to produce a group of people who would go on to play leading roles in British public life. And as the *History* shows, the architects of the syllabus largely succeeded in achieving their original aim. Examining data from Balliol graduates, it points out that between 1873 and 1914 'there were more students reading history at Balliol than at any other college', and that 'these young men led the country and empire in almost every field'. It goes on to say that 'the greatest number chose multiple careers devoted largely to public service and education, which enabled them, if they wished, to exercise decisive authority', and that 'it was characteristic of the standing of Balliol men in public service that ten of the college's history graduates were among the delegates at the Peace Conference in Paris in 1919'.[165]

The syllabus evolved over time, and under the stewardship of William Stubbs, the control over its content became more centralised. Stubbs was regius professor of modern history from 1866 to 1884, and the changes he introduced 'shaped the History school for at least three generations', with Stubbs giving 'the school an ordering, unifying principle of study in the systematic and organic narrative of constitutional history', which he described as the 'unravelling' of the 'string which forms the clue to the history of human progress'.[166] Nonetheless, some college tutors, who were zealous guardians of their own freedoms, objected to these centralising tendencies. To provide this opposition with a certain structure, a few set up dining clubs, which met regularly to discuss the development of the syllabus. The most prominent example of these were the so-called Modern History Association dinners. According to Simon Skinner, these dinners (which are still in existence to this day in some form or another),

> ...owe their origin to opposition among college tutors to reforms which they attributed to outsider professors who, in their view, fetishised research training at the expense of tutorial pedagogy – the old tension between Mr Chips tutors who regarded themselves as preparing men in the widest sense, i.e. intellectually and culturally, for life, public office, the professions, and research-orientated professors preoccupied with the production of scholars.

Skinner adds that 'while quietly researching and writing very important medieval history, Jeremy undoubtedly identified with the former ethos'.

Although Catto frequently attended these dinners, it would be a mistake to assume that he was some kind of blinkered opponent of the faculty's reforms. In fact, he was, in many ways, always keen to work with his colleagues, rather than against them. Dr Catherine Holmes, a tutorial fellow in medieval history at University College, Oxford, who worked alongside Catto for a number of years, points out that his approach to faculty business was strictly collegiate: 'He was a genuine faculty person in that once a decision had been taken, he accepted it, even if he didn't like it, and did his best to put it into action.' Although he sometimes enjoyed playing up to a certain reactionary stereotype, the truth is that he was a much more subtle operator than many people appreciated. According to Leif Dixon, Catto 'did not want to be disliked, but did not mind being misunderstood'. Indeed, he even at times rather 'enjoyed being underestimated' by his colleagues. Christopher Tyerman agrees and recalls that in a speech at his retirement dinner, Catto 'only partly in the desire to be perverse, shocked and angered fellow retirees by praising the then new reforms to the history syllabus'. Tyerman adds that Catto had 'a natural interest in international and comparative history and was keen on measures that would engage the young'. He concludes that Catto was 'a right-wing radical not a conservative'. Put differently, if Catto had been a character in Tom Sharpe's novel *Porterhouse Blue*, it is unlikely that he would have warmed to Sir Godber Evans, the proto-Blairite and insufferably self-righteous Master of the eponymous college. And whilst he might have had a soft spot for Skullion, the pugnacious and reactionary college porter, he probably would not have placed himself fully in his camp either. Instead, Richard Davenport-Hines believes that 'Jeremy was a Whig really, in that he believed in managed progress'. He adds that Catto was 'out of step with the "move fast and break things" attitude of the modern world', and that 'never hurry, never pause was more his style'.

Both Martin Conway and Simon Skinner, who worked alongside Catto for many years and attended countless faculty meetings with him, agree and believe that Catto was in fact a much more nuanced, thoughtful and moderate presence at meetings than some might have imagined. According to Conway, Catto 'was always far too astute to let himself be labelled as reactionary, and actually played a big role in reforms of syllabus and ethos. He cared about important things, but was not some Bill Cash backbencher in the faculty'. Skinner adds that Catto was always open to sensible changes: 'I don't think of Jeremy as in some simple sense anti-reform. I think he was very ready to reform when that changed things towards an ideal which was no doubt traditional.' In terms of specific changes to the faculty for which Catto campaigned,

Conway emphasises the role he played, when he was director of graduate studies, in ensuring that funding was available for graduate students to learn foreign languages. 'This had been removed as some form of budget economy, and Jeremy was keen to restore it as a means of boosting the study of European history. He therefore approached the Dacre Trust and got them to agree to make a donation to the faculty, which gave us an ample fund, which I believe still exists.' Skinner, meanwhile, points to Catto's reforms in that role when he shifted postgraduate admissions to prospective supervisors and away from a central admissions board. This meant encouraging applicants to make direct contact with possible Oxford supervisors before they applied, which greatly expedited the entire process of graduate applications. Skinner describes this as 'in practical terms one of the biggest and most important changes' of his professional life.

John Stevenson, another long-standing colleague of Catto's, agrees with all of the above:

> I don't think he could be described as a reactionary and he was certainly alive to the need to inject historiographical thinking into the syllabus – in that sense he was alive to new approaches to history and certainly not hidebound. I would describe him as a cautious reformer, and this was confirmed by the way we in the early 1970s at Oriel had evening sessions in Jeremy's rooms with the history undergraduates discussing a key book in historiography, like Braudel or Collingwood, over and above the normal tutorial round. One of the thrusts in the 70s and 80s was to inject new approaches into a still pretty standard syllabus (three papers in 'English' history, essay/dissertation, no explicitly historiographical paper...).

In addition, Stevenson recalls that Catto also backed him in a campaign in the 1990s to make the Bodleian more efficient in dealing with the new computer age, as it was proving very difficult to search the catalogue in a way which now is taken for granted. In that regard, Stevenson thinks that 'Jeremy was certainly a progressive voice'.

Blair Worden first met Catto in 1974 when he returned to Oxford after a stint at Cambridge. He and Catto became colleagues at the faculty, and Worden recalls that Catto played a vital role when a decision had to be made regarding the appointment of a successor to Hugh Trevor-Roper as regius professor in 1980:

The overwhelming opinion of the faculty was in favour of Keith Thomas. Hugh and Jeremy were keenly opposed to the idea. Hugh had had a feud with Keith which did not bring out the best in either of them, and was alert to Keith's intellectual weaknesses but not his strengths. I think Jeremy regarded him as a deadening force, and feared having Keith, who was already very influential in the faculty and university (Jeremy used to call him the Duke of Newcastle), in Oriel. There was a faculty committee, to which Jeremy belonged as the Oriel representative, which met the Patronage Secretary. The members expressed their opinions in turn. Everyone was for Thomas until the last two. The Crown (that is, Mrs Thatcher) could ignore the faculty's opinion if it wanted to, but would have hesitated to overrule a unanimous or almost unanimous view. Then, to everyone's surprise, Margaret Gowing, the professor of the history of science, said she thought Keith would be a terrible appointment, and spoke of his crushing effect on his pupils (Jeremy used to call him Doubting Thomas). She suggested Michael Howard (Professor of War Studies at King's College, London) instead. I'd talked to Hugh and Jeremy about alternatives to Keith, but Howard's name hadn't occurred to any of us, even though he was a friend and pupil of Hugh. Jeremy, the last to speak, had to think very quickly, and said he thought Howard would be the better appointment. In fact, he was a very worthy appointment, and hadn't been thought of because military history was then so outside the swim. Had it not been for Jeremy's intervention, I think Thomas would almost certainly have been appointed.

Later in the mid-1980s, Worden points to another decisive intervention when Catto had an influence on the revision of the syllabus.

As usually happens with new syllabuses, the committee's proposals to the faculty meeting tried to get too much in. No one knew how to cut the proposed syllabus down, until Jeremy said, 'Why don't we make the [compulsory] History of Political Thought paper an optional one?' This hadn't occurred to anyone and was instantly accepted. The Political Thought paper derived from the desire of the founders to prepare undergraduates for public life, which was Jeremy's view too. But he evidently regarded the abstractions of political thought as dispensable.

Aside from the views offered by his former colleagues, perhaps the clearest insight into Catto's own attitudes towards faculty reforms can be obtained from a piece he wrote for Oriel College shortly after his retirement in 2006. Contemplating the end of his academic life would have given him the opportunity to reflect on the broad range of changes during his time at the university. What emerges very clearly from this piece, which he called 'Last Impressions', is Catto's fundamentally optimistic view about the overall direction of the faculty's reforms during his time at Oxford. Given that it provides the reader with a clear explanation of his own thinking on this matter, it is worth quoting it here in full:

> Historians looking back over their own times are apt to suffer from a species of deformation professionelle: taking the context too seriously, as if what they have done and failed to do exemplifies some larger social or intellectual change. Perhaps the only real change experienced by Oxford historians is the rhythm of their own ageing: certainly, no degree either avant-garde opinions, or of recidivist prejudices for that matter, can delay the process, as the National Gallery has recently indicated by exhibiting a painting of some of our best, dearest and still active colleagues under the withering caption British Intellectual Life, 1960-1990. College tutors at the end of their run would be lucky to be displayed over even that conditional label. But that is no cause for regret. From my perspective, Oxford history in the last forty years seems to have been, in general, at least as successful as its record in the previous forty years. I have to qualify that at once. Success, for historians, is not only or even primarily the contribution of the development of professional historical study, essential as that is, but the practical achievements and contribution of former Oxford undergraduate historians – about 12,000 of them in forty years – to the material and intellectual wealth of the nation and the world. The great historians of the past, Macaulay, Clarendon, Machiavelli, were active in affairs and regarded their historical work as pointers to better action in the future. Certain and systematic information on the achievement of Oxford historians in the last three decades of the twentieth century has not been, perhaps cannot be collected, but when I remind myself of the Oriel historians' achievements in business, the City, politics, diplomacy and endless other fields – and there is no reason why they should be notably different from other

colleges' historians – it is not possible to see them as anything but an immense force for good. As Faculty Board officers know, they have been outstandingly well-disposed and supportive for future historical study in Oxford.

On the surface, an Oxford historical education in 2006 is quite different from what was on offer in 1969. The syllabus has been transformed. No continuous English history, no constitutional history, no compulsory political thought, no compulsory languages; instead, papers devoted to historiography and historical philosophy, taken twice, a vastly more variegated diet of further and special subjects and an obligatory dissertation. The current syllabus is no doubt only a stage in a development which began long before 1969. This was the progressive loss of confidence in the programme of undergraduate study set in place a century before. It had been obvious since at least the war that the Oxford history syllabus, if taken seriously as a coherent intellectual exercise, was too positivist and too legalistic to offer an adequate general education in the subject, and even less could it be a basis for professional historical work. Not that its original core, set in place by Stubbs in the 1870s, was deficient in intellectual fibre: he had made constitutional history – the development of law and liberty – its organizing theme, giving significant form to the conflicts of the past and offering some structured interpretation of events from King Ethelbert of Kent to Mr Gladstone. It was a noble theme, but it had systemic defects even to start with, disadvantages which grew more serious as time passed. For one thing, it was insurmountably Anglocentric. Constitutional development could be stretched to include America and the Empire, but it was incongruous even for the European liberal democracies and quite irrelevant to Empires of central and Eastern Europe and to the ancient civilizations of the Orient. For another, the history of the twentieth century stubbornly refused to develop in any constitutional way. The syllabus must have looked rather forlorn in 1918; by 1945 it was entirely discredited. Of course, there was a riposte: the Oxford history school had nurtured in just these years both alumni distinguished in public life and excellent professional historians. But that was because they did not treat the syllabus as a coherent whole. In practice, as older historians will remember, it was just a husk, an archipelago of topics of interest to tutors or undergraduates, or rather a mangrove swamp through which the enterprising student could carve an individual channel. The papers in constitutional history, which should have formed the organizing principle and were compulsory until the late 1960s, were merely a bore or a destructive exercise.

The vast majority of the college tutors – who in the end reformed it, not the professors – sought a new syllabus: in my experience, there were no true believers at all in the existing system. The question was where to find a new intellectual core. On that there was no agreement. At my first faculty meeting, six schemes, including the current syllabus, were struck down by large majorities. This was very worrying for my more serious-minded colleagues, who fretted that the Oxford School was falling behind Cambridge, Harvard and – worst of all – the sixieme section at the Ecole Normale Polytechnique, the home of the Annales. It did not seem to bother undergraduates, nor did it dry up the stream of graduate students seeking Oxford higher degrees. In fact the energy and enthusiasm of historians in their third year, Special Subject phase or early graduate years seemed to me notably more intense than in 1958, when I came up to Balliol. It focussed round a number of charismatic figures, and bore out the observation of Richard Southern in 1961: 'the greatest developments in historical thought have been on the periphery of the old syllabus'. There, the influence of adjoining disciplines was more keenly felt: social anthropology, art history, environmental studies, the history of science and philosophy, Oriental and African history. They appeared on the historical horizon in Special and Further Subjects or in the new joint schools, and soon conquered the living heart of undergraduates and graduate history.

The charismatic historians of 1970, whose students still dominate the Oxford History Faculty, provided the reason why the Faculty could be calmly confident in the ruins of its syllabus. Jack Gallagher, one of the earliest and the avatar of a new African history, had left before I came back. But most powerful of all, Hugh Trevor-Roper, the Regius Professor, was at the heart of the Faculty establishment, his appointment in 1957 (which may not have been possible without Prime Ministerial intervention), as a polymath interested above all in the history of ideas, a challenge to its Anglocentric and institutional rump. Formidable on the surface, but friendly and enjoyably mischievous with those who broke through his reserve, his graduate students were as variable as his interests, a leaven in the historical profession rather than a school on the model of Geoffrey Elton's or Jack Plumb's disciplined ranks. Peter Brown was another rising star, whose genius had just been recognized with the publication of his Augustine of Hippo in 1967: he breathed life into the late antique period and the 'Dark Ages'. Every term the fame of his lectures attracted new recruits with each passing week, recruits whom he would lead on imaginative journeys into the Persian hills or the North African bled, far away from Magna Carta and the Bill of Rights. Many of the enthusiasts who sat at his feet (literally, in his packed lectures) are now mature scholars who have transformed our understanding of that era. Then there was Richard Cobb, an unclassifiable historian: with as much lateral imagination as any annaliste, and a dedication to solid work in the archives which few of them could match, he was a formidable but elusive intellectual force focussed on the marginal and the unpolitical individual. Only he could have written about people who had gone through the French Revolution without realizing it had happened. They, and several others similar, in terms of the formal bias of the syllabus, were at the periphery – but their magnetic force rearranged and reinvigorated its worn and tired parts.

In time, as we have seen, the college tutors managed to effect several reforms of the syllabus, which removed any trace of its constitutional origin. They have hardly succeeded in giving it any alternative organizing principle; but this has proved not to matter. The immensely enriched experience of history available to undergraduates, which originated in the 1960s, has had its enlivening effect on the historical profession. But much more important, it has imparted to Oxford historians now active in all kinds of business and affairs an imaginative stretch and insight into human life which was not so easily available in the narrower institutional and political study of an earlier generation. If the history syllabus is still a mangrove swamp, with crocodiles, through which every individual must cut a personal channel, it is a swamp full of unexpected forms of life.[167]

17

Clubs and Networks

'He treated us like grownups, which was hugely valuable to our development.'
    – Professor Sir Niall Ferguson on Catto's influence at the Canning

'It was a relationship which I suspect slightly echoed that of Disraeli with Queen Victoria.'
    – A.N. Wilson on Catto's relationship with Princess Margaret

'He was one of the people who turned me into an Anglophile.'
    – Radek Sikorski, Polish Minister of Foreign Affairs

WHEN CATTO DIED IN THE SUMMER OF 2018, MANY OF THE OBITUARIES commented on his clubbable nature, and it is certainly true that for much of his life he was an inveterate and enthusiastic joiner of clubs. Groucho Marx's dictum of refusing to join any club that would have him as a member was not one to which Catto subscribed. Instead, he always enjoyed being in the company of like-minded souls, initially as a member of the Travellers Club, then as a longstanding member of the Garrick Club and, finally, the Beefsteak Club, and he relished convivial conversation with friends across the club table. At Oxford, too, he played an active role in several clubs and societies, notably the Oxford Union, the Canning, and the Grid.

It is through these clubs and societies that the full extent of Catto's extraordinary network can be appreciated. Moreover, this inclination to join clubs and to establish networks were two of the most important ways in which he distinguished himself from the majority of other Oxford dons. Unlike many of them, he had no intention of confining himself exclusively to the academic world. The idea of locking himself away in some dimly lit corner of a library, only to emerge for the occasional lecture or tutorial, did not appeal to him. He had a strong sense of the bright world beyond Oxford, and even though he preferred to operate from the shadows, he was always instinctively drawn towards the traditional centres of power and influence. He also liked to impress upon his students the importance of cultivating their own networks, because he understood that, beyond the tutorial and the lecture hall, what really mattered was to play an active role within society, and making good contacts along the way was essential to that endeavour. As he once told a student, who asked him for some advice just before he was about to leave Oxford: 'Never refuse an invitation to a cocktail party.' Although this may have sounded like a slightly whimsical piece of advice, it was a rule from which he himself very rarely deviated throughout his life, as he knew only too well that chance encounters at parties could change a person's life.

As a result, Catto's network, according to Peter Frankopan, was 'as big and varied a web of contacts as anyone in the country'.[168] Over time, it would contain such a bewildering array of characters that it often seemed like he knew everyone. Although he was cautious of name-dropping, it is true that he enjoyed the company of a young Benazir Bhutto at the Union in the late 1970s, was a regular drinking companion of Harold Macmillan throughout the 1980s, and also interviewed Chelsea Clinton for a place at Oxford in the late 1990s. He spent time with Princess Margaret on a number of occasions, and his unmatched network included prominent politicians, diplomats, lawyers, artists and even the odd rock star. It was the type of network that would be unthinkable for a modern-day Oxford don to cultivate. Such is the degree of specialisation, not to mention the constant pressure to publish research, that today's dons, even if they had the inclination, would struggle to find the time to acquire the kind of network that Catto enjoyed.

Oxford Union
Although his network was impressively broad, there is no question that the world of politics loomed especially large in his imagination. He relished the proximity to power, spent a considerable amount of time on his political networks, and came alive in those moments when he found himself in the company of politicians. Many of those political contacts

were acquired through the Oxford Union, a student society that dates back to the nineteenth century. In the early part of that century, student members of the university were restricted in the matters they could discuss and the opinions they could air in public. Tired of the curtailment of their freedom of speech, twenty-five young men met near the end of 1822 and established a set of rules that would govern a new society, with the result that in March 1823 the United Debating Society was born. Many of its former presidents have gone on to hold high office in the UK and across the Commonwealth, including William Gladstone, Ted Heath, Boris Johnson, and the aforementioned Benazir Bhutto.

One of Catto's early Union protégés, who would go on to enjoy a highly distinguished political career, was Alan Duncan, an undergraduate at St John's College, who became Union President in 1978. Sir Alan (as he is now) remembers that his first encounter with Catto came at the Union. He recalls that they hit it off straight away, as they shared the same sense of humour, but also because the older man was impressed with the younger man's appetite, uncommon among many Union hacks then and now, for wanting to help run the Union from a financial and staffing perspective. In addition, it was clear that the two men were on the same page ideologically. When they met, Britain was on the verge of electing Margaret Thatcher as the country's next prime minister. To those who spent any time in Catto's company, it was never too difficult to guess the broad contours of his political outlook. His little jokes and witticisms often gave an indication of his political leanings. Oat biscuits were referred to as 'left-wing biscuits' because they were good for you but unpalatable. If a guest tried to light up a cigarette in his rooms and reached for a box of matches, Catto would sometimes warn that the box in question was filled with 'left-wing matches' (that is, they didn't work). In addition, as Sir Alan would confirm, Catto had an entire private lexicon of phrases that he would deploy to describe people of whom he approved. 'Great man on toast' meant that he generally liked someone. 'Angel fluff on toast' was used for those a level or two up. 'Rough, tough fluff', meanwhile, was reserved for only a tiny select group of people, and Margaret Thatcher was, in his estimation, firmly in that category. However, it should not be assumed that Catto was some kind of slavish follower of Thatcherism, even though it was sometimes easy to make this mistake. For some on the left in the 1980s, being a supporter of Thatcher was akin to approving of Adolf Hitler. Catto's reputation was not helped by the fact that the Oriel College library at the time held a copy of Hitler's *Mein Kampf*, on the inside cover of which the following inscription could be found: 'Thanks for the tips, Jeremy. Much love, Adolf.' Catto, naturally enough, found all of this highly amusing, but the truth is that, being naturally non-ideological, his politics were never easy to categorise and, if anything, he often enjoyed playing up to a certain stereotype by pretending that he was more right-wing than he actually was. Those, like Sir Alan, who knew him well understood that the critical distinction was that although he approved of Thatcher, he never actually described himself as a Thatcherite and was not a supporter of every aspect of her programme. Instead, what attracted Catto to Thatcher was that, if anything, she was a radical. He liked that she was an outsider and, as someone with a sense of mischief, who disliked pomposity, he enjoyed the fact that Thatcher made enemies of the party's old guard, not to mention stuffy university liberals who could not stand her. Sir Alan, who had many political discussions with Catto over the years, agrees that Catto at times, perhaps, overdid his support for Thatcher because he enjoyed teasing those he viewed as pompous, and he reveals that Catto's favourite phrase in relation to the 'Iron Lady' was that she was good at 'debunking stuffpots'. Ultimately, as Sir Alan confirms, 'Jeremy certainly supported her, but not because of economics, but because he admired her character and resolve'.

Nevertheless, his open admiration for Thatcher was unusual among Oxford dons at the time and it had a profound impact on many of his students, who sensed that he operated at the heart of an important Conservative network. Charles Bonas remembers that he was in a tutorial with Catto in 1990 when news broke of Thatcher's fall from power. 'Our tutorial had started and then Jeremy suddenly went next door, got out his little portable television, and we watched the news together. He was visibly delighted when Heseltine did not get the leadership, and I remember that there were plenty of calls from senior Tories who wanted to tell him what had happened. That's when I realised what a fixer he was.' Another example came in the run up to the 1987 general election, when the *Financial Times* published Catto's support for the Conservative Party under the heading 'Tory, Tory, Hallelujah'. He freely admitted he might not always vote Conservative, before adding a mischievous twist in the tail for Tory 'wets': 'But I will always vote for Mrs Thatcher.'[169]

When his undergraduates sat their exams, they could expect to find a personalised good-luck note from Catto in their pigeonholes. More often than not, and regardless of whether the recipient was that way inclined, the note would be in the shape of a postcard portrait of a steely-eyed Margaret Thatcher, with the inscription 'Be inspired!' in Catto's distinctive spidery hand.

It was precisely that transparency which gave many of the more Conservative-minded undergraduates the boost they needed. One of those was William Hague, now Lord Hague, and a former Foreign Secretary and leader of the Conservative Party, who was at Magdalen in the 1980s and got to know Catto through the Union. He explains that Catto, in his experience, 'was different from most dons around 1980, because he was accessible, humorous, and Tory'. Indeed, Hague adds that Catto was 'unashamedly conservative', which gave young Conservatives like himself the confidence and encouragement they needed to pursue their political goals. 'At the high point of student hostility to Thatcher, he was a reassuring and quietly strengthening influence on those of us who stuck with supporting her through everything. There weren't that many dons who were like that, and it was satisfying to know that someone with such knowledge of history could believe it would all turn out well.'[170] The historian Niall Ferguson, who was an undergraduate at Oxford in the 1980s, and also knew Catto through the Union, had a very similar experience: 'The 80s were an exciting time in Britain, the first Thatcher term was the most combative and turbulent, and they were pretty heady days to be on the side of the government when most undergraduates were not.' Looking back, Sir Niall, who saw himself as a 'Punk Tory' when he was a student, admired the disruptive element behind Thatcher's ideas, and he readily admits that he and his friends 'took pleasure in goading the CND and Labour-supporting undergraduates' at the time. As for whether Catto was a truly committed Thatcherite, Sir Niall thinks not and argues that 'he was not a doctrinaire, Hayek-reading fan of the IEA', adding that 'compared to the Peterhouse Cambridge Tories he was actually pretty "wet"'. But importantly, although there were some conservative dons at Oxford at the time, Sir Niall says that 'Catto was the most active and encouraging of them, as well as the most approachable and sympathetic'.

Although Catto's politics were broadly Conservative, he was not tribal in terms of party-political allegiance. Paul Murphy, who arrived at Oriel in 1967, was never taught by Catto, but got to know him well later in life through his involvement with the Union. After leaving Oxford, Murphy taught history for a number of years and then became a Labour MP in 1987. He was in the Labour Cabinet from 1999 to 2005 and again from 2008 to 2009, serving as Northern Irish and Welsh Secretary. Today, he is Lord Murphy and, looking back at his time at Oxford, he remembers Catto with great affection. 'He was one of the wittiest people I've ever met, but also one of the most sincere.' Murphy took part in several Union debates when he was a minister, and he remembers having many discussions with Catto over dinner after those debates. 'He was fascinated by the political process and by the business of politics, and he wanted to know how ministers operated. He was always fascinated by my red boxes.' Despite their different political views, Murphy found that they had much in common: 'He was not dogmatically conservative. When we discussed politics, there was little about which we disagreed, and we were generally on the same planet.' Indeed, on one occasion, Murphy recalls that the two men even found themselves on the same side during a Union debate on religion and politics, with both agreeing that religion and politics should be kept separate. In common with others, Murphy concludes by praising Catto for his dedication to the Union and argues that Catto was unusual among dons in that he was willing to give up much of his own time to involve himself in the lives of his students: 'He could have done nothing but teach, but he didn't do that. He was involved at the Union in a senior capacity for many years.'

Radek Sikorski was a student at Pembroke College, Oxford in the 1980s, and would go on to become a journalist and politician in his native Poland. He is the current Minister of Foreign Affairs in Donald Tusk's government, having previously served in that role between 2007 and 2014. Sikorski arrived at Oxford as a political refugee from Poland, after martial law was imposed on that country in 1981. At Oxford, he came under the wing of Zbigniew Pełczynski, a wartime émigré from Poland, who was a professor of philosophy at Pembroke and worked on bringing Polish students to British universities. When Sikorski was a student, the Cold War invariably dominated the headlines and led to many discussions at Oxford about the future of the world. With the election of Thatcher in 1979, and Ronald Reagan capturing the White House in 1980, a change in the West's approach toward the Soviet Union was marked by the rejection of détente in favour of the Reagan Doctrine policy of rollback, the stated goal of which was to dissolve Soviet influence in Soviet Bloc countries. Catto had, of course, visited Czechoslovakia in 1968, and although he was not an ideological Cold War warrior, he was nevertheless instinctively suspicious of Communism. During the course of their discussions about politics, it did not take long for Sikorski to regard Catto as very much 'an ally and a fellow anti-Communist'. Although he was not taught by him, Sikorski remembers that it was through Catto that he got involved with the Union. In 1984, following encouragement from Catto, Sikorski took part in a debate at the Union about the Soviet Union's repression, with the motion 'This House believes that the enforced stability of Poland is essential for the peace of Europe'. George Walden, a future minister in Thatcher's government, defended it, while Sikorski and Timothy Garton Ash, now a professor of European studies at Oxford, opposed it. The Union taught Sikorski the ability to make the case for both sides of the argument and to have a respectful debate, something which he describes as being 'very rare outside of England'. Over time, he came to see Catto as a mentor and friend, and he recalls that Catto had 'a great facility for talking to younger people'. In particular, he remembers that Catto's conversation was always laced with his idiosyncratic sense of humour. When discussing the political futures of the sepulchral figures of Chernenko and Andropov, Catto liked to quip that 'whilst there's death, there's hope', which was a phrase that Sikorski would himself use later in his political career. Looking back, he credits Catto with having had a significant influence on him: 'Jeremy was iconic and a really loveable English eccentric. He was the quintessential Oxford don, and he was one of the people who turned me into an Anglophile'.

Aside from networking and discussing politics, there were lighter moments too. Sir Alan Duncan remembers one particularly amusing incident involving two young men with whom he would end up in the House of Commons. One of these was Damian Green, who was elected Union President in the Michaelmas term of 1977, and would later become an MP, a Cabinet minister, and First Secretary of State during Theresa May's premiership. In the late 1970s, Union politics were loosely divided along left- and right-wing lines, and were dominated by undergraduates from Magdalen and Balliol. When the young Damian Green, who was seen to be on the left at the time, arrived at a Union dinner at Magdalen one evening, the cry from his fellow diners went up as soon as he walked in that he should go 'INTO THE RIVER... INTO THE RIVER!' Before Green knew what was happening to him, he was bundled out of the building and thrown unceremoniously into the River Cherwell that flows under Magdalen Bridge. Although he does not confirm whether Dominic Grieve, the future Conservative MP and Attorney General, was responsible for throwing his future parliamentary colleague into the river, Sir Alan chuckles and notes, tongue firmly in cheek, that 'he was certainly a close observer' of the incident. Catto, even though he was senior librarian at the time, and therefore nominally charged with being the adult in the room, saw the whole affair as hugely amusing and did not believe that anyone should be sanctioned, as it was all just a bit of harmless tomfoolery. He was 'always great fun', according to Sir Alan, and he had the ability to see the funny side of most situations. Thankfully, his river dunking did Green no harm and he did not hold the incident against Catto. In fact, what he remembers about Catto is his kindness and generosity, and he recalls with great affection a party that was held in Oriel, to which he was invited by Catto. The party was 'one of those lovely Oxford outdoor summer parties', and when Green arrived, he found to his 'complete shock and thrill' that his great hero, Bryan Ferry, was at the party too. Green was 'very much of the Roxy Music generation and owned every single one of their albums'. Not surprisingly, he remembers feeling starstruck at the time and recalls that 'to this day it feels quite surreal that the one time in my life I met Ferry was at one of Jeremy Catto's parties'. But then, in Catto's world, such overlapping connections were not so unusual.

It was not only future politicians who entered Catto's orbit at the Union. A near contemporary of Sir Alan's was Michael Crick, who was Union President in the Michaelmas term of 1979, and then went on to become a broadcaster, journalist and author, as well as a founding member of the *Channel 4 News* team in 1982. He recalls that the Union in his day was a much smaller place than it is today, with 'only about 30 per cent' of the students joining as members. It was also overtly more political then, in the sense that the majority of Union officers in Crick's day would have been interested in pursuing some kind of career in politics. As a result, the people who worked at the Union were part of quite an intimate circle. Crick remembers that Catto was 'one of the fixtures of the Union in that era', adding that he was 'always great fun and always seemed pleased to see you'. Occasionally, they would have drinks in the Union bar, and Catto was 'always keen to know what he [Crick] was doing' and 'always seemed pleased' when he got elected to something. As if to underline just how unusual it was for dons to take such a genuine interest in the extracurricular activities of their students, Crick adds that Catto was 'the only don I knew to involve himself in the Union' at that time.

Another future journalist who met Catto at the Union was Stephen Pollard, the former editor of the *Jewish Chronicle*, who is now Editor-at-

Large of the same publication, and was at Oxford in the mid-1980s. He met Catto for the first time through the Union, and then found himself sitting next to him at a John Lyons School reunion dinner at Oriel not long after. Pollard recalls enjoying 'a very convivial evening' with Catto, and that he and a few others were subsequently invited to Catto's rooms in college for drinks after dinner. Pollard remembers seeing a series of whiskies on display and venturing to Catto that he 'could not get on with whisky.' Catto then proceeded to pour him several glasses of different whiskies, before explaining every single one of them in great detail. Pollard says that it was 'the first time he had enjoyed whisky', and he recalls that the dinner was not just a most enjoyable evening, but was also typical of his host's generosity to a relative stranger. It was indeed rare for the 'river whisk' to dry up.

Finally, it is important to remember that although the Union provided Catto with the opportunity to cultivate his network, he was also genuinely committed to the institution and, as the Senior Librarian of the Union for over thirty years, he played a crucial role behind the scenes in making sure that the debating society functioned properly.

During his time at the Union, William Hague, a former President of the Society, was one of those who valued Catto's advice:

> As Senior Librarian of the Union, he would let us give our own views at the weekly library committee before weighing in on whether we should purchase a particular book. If he attended a Union debate, he would give very useful private feedback on whether and why you had made a good speech, a rare source of such advice.

Peter Jay, the economist, broadcaster and former diplomat, who was at Christ Church in the late 1950s, and would later become the British ambassador to the United States in the late 1970s, remembers Catto as 'a man of extremely wide learning and with an extremely dry sense of humour, who had a sharp eye for the irony of things, as well as a sense for human weakness'. In later life, Jay worked alongside Catto at the Union, when both men were involved in trying to provide the Union with a greater sense of stability: 'Jeremy enjoyed the process of trying to nudge them away from madness towards prudence. He liked and understood young people.'

John Stevenson also believes that Catto's role in helping to keep the Union going over the years should not be underestimated:

Jeremy played a vital role as a factotum for the Oxford Union. He got me involved quickly after I returned to Oxford in 1990 and I must have spent ten years as a senior member as a result. He also found Oriel people to take on the jobs of senior members at the Union and must have played a vital – and I stress this – part over the better part of twenty years or more in keeping the Union going with senior members who were also committed to it and seeing it through difficult times when challenges from OUSU [Oxford University Student Union], student poverty, and so on made it not inevitable that the Union could survive.

Indeed, as Stevenson points out, over the course of his thirty-year involvement with the Union, Catto contributed to that survival and enjoyed a long history of appointing the nominally elected senior librarian of the Oxford Union. In 2013, when it was time for Catto to stand down, he approached his friend Sean Power to tell him he would take the role. 'But I've never even been to the Union,' Power replied. 'Details, my dear, details.' And with that, the baton was passed on.

The Canning

Throughout Catto's time at Oxford, the Canning was a virtual breeding ground for future Tory journalists, politicians and academics. Founded in 1861 to promote and discuss Tory principles, its members to this day are a select group chosen from across the university. They meet on a regular basis to discuss both domestic and international politics over a few glasses of wine, and the atmosphere is designed to be intimate, convivial and collegiate. Catto's own politics made him a natural fit to become the club's senior member. Daniel Hannan, who was a member of the Canning in the early 1990s, describes Catto's politics in the following terms:

> He was a conservative in the mould of Leo Strauss, Michael Oakeshott or Roger Scruton – an heir, like them, to Edmund Burke, as almost every conservative intellectual is on some level. Unlike them, though, he never committed his philosophy to paper. His conservatism was lived, implicit and exemplary. He had little time for systems or doctrines, seeing conservatism as an instinct rather than an ideology. Political opinions, in his mind, ought properly to be infused with scepticism, pragmatism, irony, self-awareness and a certain wry humour.[171]

William Hague, who attended debates in the 1980s, has a similar recollection of Catto's politics:

'His political outlook was High Tory, not extreme or ideological in any way – Tory as an attitude of mind rather than a specific political programme. He didn't like fads and could easily demolish weak or illogical thinking, in good Oxford style.'

Although such views made him ideal for the Canning, Catto did not usually take part in any of the debates. Instead, his role consisted of presiding over debates and hosting post-debate drinks. The latter would usually be held in his rooms in college, and those who remember those evenings recall that Catto was always an unfailingly generous host. Over the years, he entertained the likes of George Osborne, Michael Gove, Jacob Rees-Mogg and many others who would go on to enjoy distinguished careers in the world of politics.

Another former member was the future historian Niall Ferguson. In *Always Right*, a book on Margaret Thatcher's period in office written after her death, Ferguson recalled that during his time at Oxford, 'young Thatcherites would gather at the Canning Club to drink cheap claret and listen to precocious papers'. At many of these meetings during the 1980s, the Cold War was their intellectual battleground and the Soviet Union their avowed enemy. On the domestic front, debates were often focused on the new Conservative ideas, which challenged the suffocating status quo, in particular in regards to the stale corporatism of the 1970s, and promised to transform the country along free market lines. Many of those assembled were intoxicated by these debates and saw themselves as spear carriers for those new ideas. As Ferguson recalled: 'We were insufferable but we knew we were right'. Today, Sir Niall, although he was not taught by Catto, recalls that he came to know him well through the Canning and he emphasises the impact Catto had on his education: 'The Canning played a big part in my intellectual development, and Jeremy presided over meetings with the lightest possible touch, but also kept them from veering off into frivolity.' In summing up Catto's broader influence on the generation of Tory politicians, journalists and academics who came through the Canning in the 1980s, Sir Niall stresses that Catto instilled in them the confidence they needed: 'He treated us like grownups, which universities these days discourage, and which was hugely valuable to our development.'

The Grid

The Grid was founded in 1884 and to this day remains more of a social than a political club. As with other beefsteak clubs of the eighteenth and nineteenth centuries, the traditional grilling gridiron is the club's symbol, which appears in white against Oxford blue on the club's tie. Catto was senior treasurer of the club, first with Maurice Keen and many years later with his great friend and colleague Mark Whittow. Although the club has never been especially political, Catto could not resist teasing the small number of left-wing members of the club. Alongside Whittow, he published the term card one year, reprinting a 1934 poem about the Grid that went as follows:

> *Good Communist fathers forbid*
> *Their children to dine at the Grid*
> *Conservative spies, as they justly surmise*
> *Would seduce any Marxist who did*

Radek Sikorski remembers that Catto was 'very much a presence' at the Grid in the 1980s, not least because of his distinctive sartorial style. 'You always remember people in bow ties,' Sikorski recalls with a smile. Harry Mount looks back on his time at the Grid in the 1990s with great affection, and recalls that Catto played a critical role at the club:

> He was a crucial figure as a grown-up and a senior member of the university to allow the club to maintain a prominent role in the life of the university. But he was never there to restrain its joyful activities or disapprove of your behaviour – or fill you with dread like the Oldest Member in P.G. Wodehouse's golf stories. He added to the life of the place and made you feel your frivolous life was a little less frivolous.

Mount adds that bumping into Catto at the Grid was always a pleasant experience because he was never anything other than good company: 'He was a grown-up who showed his grown-upness by knowing more than you, but not telling you that. You could work it out from talking to him. Unlike so many successful middle-aged men, he wasn't a bore or a conversation-dominator but let you say things without coming down hard on you if you got things wrong.' According to Guy Monson, a senior partner and chief market strategist at Sarasin, a leading charity fund manager, as well as treasurer to the Prince of Wales, Catto was very aware that students would come and go over time, and that a sense of continuity was, therefore, imperative for the survival of such clubs:

> He wanted the next generation to be able to enjoy these clubs, and this was especially true of the Grid which, at the time and for many years, had no actual premises. Jeremy saw himself as an anchor of the club and believed that his continuous presence would help to keep it going over time. For him, such clubs were a vital part of the broader education offered to undergraduates, and his biggest contribution to clubs like the Grid was that he almost single-handedly kept them going.

Networks

Catto was often heard to say that he liked it when his students ran the world. This was especially true if his students became diplomats, as it gave him the opportunity to stay with them when they were posted abroad. Over the course of his long diplomatic career, Sir David Manning recalls that he was visited by Catto at each of his seven overseas postings: 'He became a lifelong friend after university and came to each of my overseas postings. He always took enormous interest in what you were doing, and you never felt like the connection with him was broken.' One of Sir David's first overseas postings as a diplomat was to Warsaw. When Catto came to stay with him, he decided to take himself off in a car to tour the city. Despite being a highly distinguished diplomat, Sir David on this occasion does not mince his words and says quite firmly, but with a smile on his face, that although Catto had great facility with ancient languages, he was 'not a linguist' when it came to modern languages. The result was that Sir David was constantly having to worry that Catto might get himself into trouble by saying the wrong thing to the wrong people. More seriously, Sir David remembers that Catto also had an influence on his own career as a diplomat. He recalls that Catto advised him to go to the professional guidance people, and he thinks that Catto pushed him to see somebody who steered him towards the Foreign Office: 'Jeremy was always very encouraging about working in government, as he thought it was a very worthwhile thing to do.' Another undergraduate of Catto's who would go on to enjoy a distinguished career at the Foreign Office was Sir Richard Stagg. He remembers that Catto visited him in Sofia when he was the British ambassador to Bulgaria. Most people when asked whether they wished to visit Bulgaria tended to say, 'don't call us, we'll call you', but Catto, ever keen to find out what was happening in a former Communist Bloc country, jumped at the chance. This was in the period just before 2001, when the then King of Bulgaria was on the verge of becoming the next prime minister. Sir Richard recalls that Catto was 'very much amused by this idea, and also welcomed it as it would give a biff on the nose to the opponents of monarchy'. But in addition to that characteristically mischievous sense of humour, Sir Richard believes that Catto's approach to politics, which was marked by a sense of calmness and detachment from the political process, also had an impact on his own career as a diplomat: 'He was very good at not being swept along by current and short-term trends.' The mid-1970s were, Sir Richard says, 'quite a disturbed time and rather uncertain', and whilst most undergraduates tended to get 'hyped up by the present day, Jeremy had a calmness about him'. Looking back, Sir Richard feels that it was an approach to politics that had an influence on his own thinking as a diplomat over time.

What influence Catto did have on politics was usually indirect, oftentimes playing a significant role in forming the minds and characters of generations of future politicians. However, there was at least one occasion when he had a more direct influence on an event of international importance. Augusto Pinochet, the Chilean general and dictator who ruled Chile from 1973 to 1990, found himself at the centre of a string of extradition cases at the turn of the century, which made headlines across the world and are still considered to be of landmark importance in the field of international criminal law and human rights law. The three cases were brought before the House of Lords, which was the highest court in the land at the time, to examine whether Pinochet had the right to claim state immunity from torture allegations made by a Spanish court, thereby avoiding extradition to Spain. Pinochet enjoyed the support of some very high-profile former world leaders, including Margaret Thatcher and ex-US President George H.W. Bush. The American remembered Pinochet as a key ally in the fight against Communism during the Cold War, while Thatcher saw the general as an ideological bedfellow and remained grateful for Chile's steadfast support during the Falklands War. To sustain him during his trial, Thatcher even sent Pinochet a bottle of single malt whisky, with a note saying, 'Scotch is one British institution that will never let you down'.[172]

Despite this support, the first judgement went against Pinochet. The judges ruled that Pinochet, as a former head of state, was not entitled to immunity from prosecution for the crimes of torture, which meant that he could be extradited to Spain to face charges. However, in a subsequent judgement that was to prove controversial, not least because it led to the unprecedented setting aside of a House of Lords judgement, the ruling was overturned when revelations emerged that one of the Law Lords, Lord Hoffmann, and his wife had links to Amnesty International, a human rights organisation that had campaigned against Pinochet for many years and acted as an intervenor in the case. It was decided that this created an appearance of bias, although Hoffmann refuted these allegations and told the *Daily Telegraph*: 'The fact is I'm not biased. I am a lawyer. I do things as a judge. The fact that my wife works as a secretary for Amnesty International is, as far as I am concerned, neither here nor there.'[173] Nevertheless, the ruling stood, and a new panel of judges eventually confirmed that Pinochet was not entitled to state immunity, but that he could only be prosecuted for crimes committed after 1988, the year in which Britain introduced legislation ratifying the UN Convention Against Torture in the Criminal Justice Act 1988. In the end, however, following stories about Pinochet's failing health, medical tests were carried out, which resulted in the then Home Secretary Jack Straw deciding that the former dictator should not be extradited to Spain. When Pinochet returned to Chile, to the fury of his opponents, who had never accepted the medical tests, it was reported that the general stood up unaided from his wheelchair and waved triumphantly at the crowds assembled at Santiago de Chile's airport.[174] How was Catto involved in the case? It can be disclosed that Catto was the original source of the information that Lord Hoffmann and his wife had a connection to Amnesty. It was a detail that had not been picked up by Pinochet's legal team, but when Catto heard that Amnesty were involved, and knowing that Hoffmann's wife had worked for them, he decided to raise the matter. Although not legally trained, he understood that this fact might have a bearing on the outcome of the case. His friend Helen Whittow, an expert in international criminal law, in particular in the fields of corporate fraud, corruption and extradition, acted as counsel for Pinochet. When Catto pointed out the Amnesty link to her, she was astonished and quickly realised that this piece of information would significantly alter the nature of the case. In the end, and notwithstanding the fact that Pinochet was released due to his fragile health, the case proved to be a watershed moment in international law, with some legal scholars even arguing that it was one of the most significant moments in legal history since the Nuremberg Trials of Nazi war criminals.[175] As such, Catto's overall influence on the case was discreet but decisive. It was also a typical example of his perceptive mind and the crossover of his different networks from the world of academia and the law to politics and current affairs.

Even as he approached his own retirement at the start of the twenty-first century, Catto's appetite for reaching out to people and cultivating his network appeared undimmed. Jonathan Aitken, the former Conservative MP, who served as Chief Secretary to the Treasury in the mid-1990s under John Major and was later ordained as a Church of England priest after he had served seven months in prison for perjury, remembers meeting Catto when he returned to Oxford in the year 2000 to read theology at Wycliffe Hall, having first been an undergraduate at Christ Church, Oxford in the early 1960s. Arriving at Oxford, Aitken recalls that he was surprised to receive an 'unexpected invitation' from Catto to dine at high table at Oriel, not only because he did not know him, but also because, having just emerged from prison, he did not think that he was 'anyone's favourite dinner guest at the time'. In the end, although he was nervous about dining at high table, as he felt like 'something of a pariah' at the time, he had 'an absolutely delightful evening' as Catto's guest. Over dinner, the conversation ranged widely, and the two men discussed politics as well as religion. Aitken, who wrote an excellent biography of Richard Nixon, told Catto a story about how he had on one occasion shared a helicopter ride with the former US president. As the leader of the free world, Aitken explained that Nixon 'was able to take a route lesser mortals could not take', and as they swooped over a rather grand car park at Langley, home to the CIA headquarters, Nixon, who was famously prickly about East Coast Ivy League types, peered out of the window and, pointing at the car park below, said to Aitken: 'Just look at all those expensive cars. All of them are owned by those Ivy League guys…and yet they always get everything wrong!' As the conversation turned towards Wycliffe Hall, Aitken teased the Catholic Catto about the fact that whilst the library at Wycliffe had 'three shelves on the Protestant Reformation, it only had three books on Catholicism'. Reflecting on that evening and his meeting with Catto, Aitken still feels grateful for the invitation. 'I met him at a very low point in my life. In fact, my life was pretty much rock bottom. But I still remember his warmth and kindness, and his charm and hospitality at high table that evening.'

But Catto was not just interested in the world of politics and diplomacy. Over the years, he developed a number of friendships with artists, one of whom was the celebrated painter and illustrator Glynn Boyd Harte. In his obituary in *The Guardian*, Boyd Harte was described as 'one of the most brilliant and influential illustrators and painters to emerge in the post-pop world of London in the early 1970s'.[176] According to Gavin Stamp, the architectural historian, Boyd Harte was 'certainly a dandy and was indeed posturing, camp, arch, brittle, waspish and opinionated, but he was also kind, generous and funny, in addition to being so talented and original in many different ways'.[177] Along with his wife, Caroline Bullock, he bought a dilapidated Georgian house on Cloudesley Square in Islington, just before the gentrification of the New Labour era took hold of that part of North London. They set about restoring the house to its former glory and filled it with an astonishing collection of period pieces. The downstairs parlour and dining room, however, had no electricity supply and relied entirely on candlelight from a set of eighteenth-century Venetian and Murano glass chandeliers. 'We use the dining room strictly for formal dinners', Boyd Harte once told an interviewer.[178] When the house was complete, the Boyd Hartes would host the most magnificent parties, as Gavin Stamp recalls:

> My memories are of what was surely Glynn's happiest phase, when living in that so cleverly decorated and furnished Regency corner house in Cloudesley Square, where Glynn and Carrie held court, giving what now seems an endless succession of dinners and parties characterised, I fear, by much screaming and silliness but also by wit and music – often with Glynn himself performing on the grand piano while Carrie, ever loyal and sensible, quietly made everything work.[179]

Much in demand as a portrait painter, Boyd Harte became known for a series of striking portraits of, among others, the playwright Tom Stoppard, the musician and composer Brian Eno, the novelist Isobel Strachey, the painter Duncan Grant, and the American composer Virgil Thomson. Stoppard would later recall that Boyd Harte was dressed 'rather like TS Eliot during his Lloyds bank period',[180] when he first met him, but there was no doubting his talent as a painter. In addition to the above-mentioned portraits, Boyd Harte also painted a portrait of Catto, which can be seen on the front cover of this book. In it, he is depicted wearing his customary black-rimmed Hockney glasses, a dinner jacket, floppy black bow tie, and, rather improbably, a pair of John Wolfe's brown and white shoes with thick two-inch soles and heels. The attire and Catto's rather louche pose, with one arm languidly stretched out along the back of the sofa and the other propped up by a cane, make him look like something of a dandy which, strictly speaking, he was not. But the portrait also succeeds in capturing an element of his enigmatic persona and idiosyncratic sense of style. Sadly, Boyd Harte died of leukaemia in 2003, but the two men remained firm friends until the end and it is fair to say that Boyd Harte played a not insignificant role in helping to create the Catto mystique, as the aforementioned portrait he did of his friend would hang in Catto's rooms in Oriel for many years, thereby providing generations of undergraduates with a small insight into their tutor's more bohemian past.

Another painter friend was Diccon Swan, who met Catto through his own younger brother when the latter was a student at Durham in the 1960s. Today, Swan is a renowned and distinguished painter, who has exhibited in galleries all over the country and has painted portraits of, among others, Margaret Thatcher, John Major, and Benazir Bhutto. Over the years, he and Catto would become great friends, and they spent many holidays travelling the world together. On one occasion, Swan recalls that Catto came to stay at his house in Brixton. On a whim, he, his partner and Catto decided that they would take a day trip to the continent. 'We all got up at 5 a.m., drove on to the hovercraft at Dover, had breakfast in Calais, then drove to Bruges for lunch, and to see the van Eycks, and then on to Holland for tea, and finally back via Dover to see the *Nine O'Clock News* on television in Brixton. It was one of my favourite days ever.' Years later, Swan and Catto flew to Rome to meet with the then Italian president, Francesco Cossiga. As an honorary fellow of Oriel, Cossiga needed to get a portrait of himself done, and Catto was instrumental in securing the commission for Swan, who recalls that they 'had a hilarious time staying on dormitory-type truckle beds in the lovely Casa di Santa Brigida in the Piazza Farnese', where 'the meals the nuns prepared for them were better than in most restaurants'. When they met Cossiga, Swan remembers that he 'who was an Anglophile and who thought he knew Oxford well, mistook The Ruskin School of Art, where I had been, for Ruskin College, the trade union college, and treated me slightly suspiciously as a result!' But those suspicions were quickly overcome, as the president took both men 'with his entourage and with sirens and flashing lights, to a marvellous restaurant in the Villa Borghese'. The trip ended when Catto, thanks to some mysterious contacts, took Swan to St Peter's and to the Vatican, where the two men were escorted around the libraries, before being given a private view of the Sistine Chapel at 6 a.m. the next day. These trips provided Swan with wonderful memories. As he recalled many years later, 'Jeremy and his plans could be wonderfully life-enhancing'.

Catto's network also extended to royalty, and when members of the royal family visited Oxford, he was invariably trusted to serve as an official 'walker' to escort the royal party and to keep them entertained. According to Diccon Swan, 'Princess Margaret took a particular shine to him, partly because he could not only recite all the kings and queens, but also all the popes of Rome in order.' Her Royal Highness always said that Catto was her 'personal historian', and the two shared a fondness for drink, gossip and smoking cigarettes. He accompanied her to the theatre on a few occasions, after which they went back to Kensington Palace together to enjoy late-night suppers of salmon and scrambled eggs. A.N. Wilson recalls that Catto and Princess Margaret clearly enjoyed a strong bond: 'She especially flourished in Jeremy's company. It was a relationship which I suspect slightly echoed that of Disraeli with Queen Victoria. She played up to his Firbankian sense of humour, being by turns flirtatious and haughty. When he was showing her some medieval inscriptions in the Ashmolean, she asked him how many letters there were in the runic alphabet. "Twenty-four, ma-am". "Not enough!" she retorted.'[181]

James Howard-Johnston remembers an occasion when Princess Margaret came to stay at his house in Oxford. At the time, the Howard-Johnstons were newly married, and Her Royal Highness was on her own, so she would often spend weekends with different friends around the country. Howard-Johnston was a Labour county councillor in those days and, perhaps not surprisingly, chose to keep the identity of his weekend guest from his colleagues in the party. To keep the princess entertained throughout her stay, he and his wife asked an architect friend from London to join them for the weekend as their 'continuity man'. But he dropped out at the last moment, at which point they turned to Catto, who was only too happy to fill in. Over that weekend, Princess Margaret would ask Catto questions, and when they landed on the subject of Holy Roman Emperors, he would delight her by rattling off the names of each and every one. Later in the evening, Howard-Johnston's wife mentioned two keen equestrian friends who once *rode* along the Great Wall of China. Catto, who by now had had a few drinks, either misheard or pretended to mishear and, ever the Oriel man keen on *rowing*, said: 'I didn't know there was any water along the wall.'

In 1976, Oriel College celebrated its 650th anniversary and the Queen, as the college's visitor, was invited to mark the event. John Varley, who was one of a handful of undergraduates picked to be introduced to Her Majesty, remembers that her visit was not just a big event for the college, but also for the university as a whole, and he recalls Harold Macmillan, the Chancellor of the University, arriving 'dressed up in bright scarlet' for the day. He also remembers that he stood at one end of the line waiting for the Queen to arrive and that Catto had been placed at the other end. Even so, he was close enough to be able to observe Catto, and when the Provost arrived with the Queen in Oriel Square, Varley noticed that as the Provost introduced her to Catto, the latter quickly removed his glasses just before he was about to shake her hand. By the time the Duke of Edinburgh had moved down the line to meet Catto, however, the glasses were back on again. According to Varley, who recalls the incident with a chuckle and a shake of the head, it was clear that Catto felt that his sovereign deserved to see him without his glasses on, whereas the same element of deference was not quite accorded to the Duke. It was, Varley says, 'talismanic of Catto's sense of order'.

Finally, aside from befriending politicians and courting royalty, there were also persistent rumours over the years that Catto's extraordinary network extended to Britain's security services. In a letter to *The Times* following Catto's death in 2018, a former student of his by the name of Ben Williams seemed certain of the fact and wrote the following:

I knew Jeremy as senior librarian of the Oxford Union, and was sitting with the president in the Gridiron Club (another Jeremy institution) one lunchtime when Jeremy joined us, self-invited, and proceeded to advocate, with typical expansiveness but uncharacteristic persistence, that we 'must – must – each become policemen! Very important! You should both join the police.' This perhaps wasn't the most subtle piece of code from that subtle Oxford mind, and so I was not very surprised, sometime afterwards, to receive an invitation to a discreet townhouse in SW1 to meet a representative of one of the more interesting, but secretive, branches of government. Sadly, nothing came of it in my case, but I wonder whether we should add, to the list of Jeremy's many and varied proteges, some of those who guard us from the shadows?[182]

Clemmie Raynsford had a similar experience in the early 2000s and recalls that it began with a seemingly innocent invitation to a drinks party. Catto had slipped a note in her pigeonhole and suggested that he had an interesting guest he thought she would like to meet. Raynsford duly accepted the invitation, expecting to meet some kind of moderately famous historian. But when she arrived, she was stunned to discover the identity of Catto's guest: 'It was none other than Oleg Gordievsky. The man who escaped the Soviet Union in the boot of a car! And there were fewer than twenty of us chatting to him in the Senior Common Room like it was a fireside tutorial.' Gordievsky, a former KGB colonel and bureau chief in London, became a double agent when he spied for the British Secret Intelligence Service (MI6) from 1974 to 1985. In July of that year, he was recalled to Moscow as the Soviet authorities had come to suspect him, but thanks to a plan code-named Operation Pimlico, he was exfiltrated from the country and escaped to Britain, where he lives to this day in an undisclosed location. Following his escape, the Soviet Union sentenced him to death in absentia. According to his biographer, Ben Macintyre, Gordievsky's legacy is up there with the greatest spies in history:

> The pantheon of world-changing spies is small and select, and Oleg Gordievsky is in it: he opened up the inner workings of the KGB at a pivotal juncture in history, revealing not just what Soviet intelligence was doing (and not doing), but what the Kremlin was thinking and planning, and in so doing transformed the way the West thought about the Soviet Union. He risked his life to betray his country, and made the world a little safer.[183]

Another guest present that evening alongside Raynsford recalls that it was obvious in hindsight why Gordievsky's presence had not been properly advertised, but the talk he ended up giving to the undergraduates clearly 'fascinated' them. Gordievsky gave a standard introductory summary of his work for the UK, 'but the occasion really came alive with questions, as Oleg's anger with the brutality of the Soviet regime shone through'. His 'voice always became more emphatic as he warmed up, and his chin jutted out, punctuating enumeration of his various points', with one particular question from Jeremy prompting 'a response that visibly moved him'. Reflecting on the evening she spent in Gordievsky's company, Raynsford adds that she had not fully understood at the time just how special it was to have met him until she read up on the double agent's life in more detail after the event. 'But Catto made things like that happen, as if it was all so easy and normal.'

18

Eydon

'The heart of darkness, or the English Congo, where indigenous people do abominable things under shady trees.'
— Catto describing Northamptonshire to one of his students

'Let us be grateful to be with people who make us happy, they are the charming gardeners who make our souls blossom.'
— Marcel Proust

'Oh, where are the snows of yesteryear?'
— Francois Villon, Ballade des dames du temps jadis, 'Le petit testament'

ALTHOUGH CATTO'S NETWORK OF CONTACTS WAS EXTRAORDINARY, and as much as he was the ultimate college man, who relished involving himself in the lives of his students, there was also a paradox at play: his own private life was always kept strictly separate from his life at Oxford. A consistent theme throughout Catto's life was that he was very adept at compartmentalising his life, and although he was often quite sociable, he could also be a very private person in other ways. The result was that only a select few friends and colleagues ever saw his home life beyond Oxford, which was based around Eydon, a small village in the south-western corner of Northamptonshire. The village is one of the few remaining hill villages with a street on either side of the hill and lanes in between. The parish is bounded to the west by the River Cherwell, and to the south by a stream that is one of its tributaries. It has a church, a pub, and a tiny village green. Many of the buildings are made from a very attractive iron-rich sandstone that is a peculiarity of the area, and it is the sort of place that gives visitors the distinct impression that it has not changed very much over the centuries. It was here that Jeremy and John bought a house that would remain at the centre of their lives for the next five decades. The year was 1973 and, remarkably, the house was bought at a blind auction, with neither man ever having set foot in the property before they purchased it. But from the moment they saw it, they both knew that it was exactly what they had been looking for. Originally two cottages, one half dating back to the thirteenth century and the other half a seventeenth-century extension, it stands today in the middle of the high street and just across from the tiny village green. If Catto was not in Oxford, then he could usually be found at Eydon. Konsta Helle recalls that 'it was always nice to see him don his brown trilby and fawn overcoat when motoring in his Saab to Northamptonshire for the weekend'. Like most of his students, Helle was curious to know more about Catto's life beyond Oxford and once asked him to describe Northamptonshire. Without hesitation, Catto replied that his home county was 'the heart of darkness, or the English Congo, where indigenous people do abominable things under shady trees'.

Those who were fortunate enough to be invited to Eydon did not necessarily see a different side to Catto's life. In fact, what they saw was that Catto's home life was very much an extension of his personality: warm, comfortable, generous, unpretentious and cosy. As much as these occasions were about fun and conviviality, Catto was, by all accounts, a stickler for doing things in a certain way. According to Simon King, another friend who moved to the area to be closer to him, Catto was 'a man of strict routines'. Having been invited to Eydon, you could expect the weekend to start at the end of a stint in the Bodleian library. From there, Catto would drive you back to Eydon, usually stopping for a pint or two at a pub in Kidlington. Upon arrival, guests would sometimes be expected to sing for their supper. In some cases, this might involve chopping some wood for the fire or perhaps mowing the lawn. All of this was done in quite a subtle manner. The lawnmower would already be waiting in the courtyard, positioned conveniently near the entrance so that it could not be missed. The guest would ask whether they could make themselves useful by mowing the lawn, at which Catto would smile sweetly and say something like 'Too kind. You will get your reward in heaven, dear boy.' These tasks would often take quite a while and, in the meantime, John would be busy preparing potent cocktails and delicious food for the assembled group. After dinner, those gathered might discuss the origins of the English language, or something equally esoteric, and Catto would often be found falling asleep in his favourite armchair. The following day, John would welcome everyone to breakfast with boiled eggs and lashings of coffee. The first meal of the day, whether at home in Eydon or in the Oriel Senior Common Room, was always essential to Catto – 'Every meal should aspire to breakfast', as he was once heard to declare during a particularly pleasing breakfast at Oriel. After breakfast on Sunday, Catto would then be taken to Mass at the local Catholic church, and the group would then return to Oxford in time for chapel and Sunday formal hall dinner at Oriel.

To add to the above, a wonderful picture of Catto's domestic life is conjured up in an extract from the eulogy given at his memorial service in 2018 by Helen Whittow. It is worth quoting in full:

> If I had to think of a single word to sum Jeremy up in a domestic
> context it would be cosy. He and John bought their house in Eydon
> in 1973, and in all the years I have known it, it has never changed
> – save to have a few things added, a carpet from Morocco to place
> on top of the others (for lack of space); things picked up by John in
> a local market, about which Jeremy would then gently complain…
> Jeremy sat to the left of the fireplace, sharing gossip and academic
> insights. Unpretentious and welcoming us with a cry of 'Angel fluff'
> or 'Hello Great One' – mischievous and wicked in equal measure.
> His jerseys had large holes at the elbows. In the evenings he often
> entertained (after a bath) in pyjamas and dressing gown. In the early
> days of handheld phones, Jeremy made telephone calls from the
> bath, and it was always his ambition to catch someone else likewise
> occupied and have what he called a 'Splash to Splash' conversation.
> Always, summer and winter, a fire was lit in Eydon – Jeremy
> insisted that a fire cooled the room in summer, because it created
> a draught. John made delicious canapes from ingredients brought
> back from Morocco or France or his latest travels, or from smoked
> lobster sourced online; and Jeremy, meanwhile, called from his chair
> for refills of lethal cocktails – martinis, Manhattans and negronis
> were his favourites; and Bloody Marys, but only on a Sunday. On
> occasion, drinks would move outside. Jeremy took pride in his

garden in two particular respects. The lawn was his responsibility, as was stacking logs for the fire. The rest, the flowers and vegetables (and indeed the meals and the cottage generally), were down to John. In the summer, rugs were spread on the grass and furniture moved out – and the garden would become the setting for a similar exchange of views and gossip, on politics and on history. Gossip was high on the agenda, but never ever about people's personal lives. Only about what they had said or done. And it was tolerant gossip, never malicious. The advantage of drinks in the garden, from Jeremy's point of view, was the possibility of a visit from the neighbouring 'purr pussy'. He tolerated our dogs but was always a cat man at heart...[184]

When it came to his wider cultural preferences, Catto's private passions were eclectic but reflected a broad hinterland. He was devoted to the poetry of Betjeman and Pound. The former's 'Indoor Games Near Newbury' was a favourite of his, and he loved regaling friends and undergraduates by reciting entire passages from it. The line 'You who pressed me closely to you, Hard against your party frock' always elicited a chuckle and was delivered with extra brio. The beauty and clarity of Pound, in particular his *Cantos*, underpinned his aesthetic sensibilities and, throughout his life, he turned to Proust for the sheer depth and breadth of his insights into the human condition. He also treasured the medieval French poet Francois Villon, especially his treatment of death in 'Le petit testament'. In retirement, he re-read Virgil's *Aeneid*, having first read it when he was a boy at RGS Newcastle. Perhaps more surprisingly, Catto also had a taste for crime fiction, in particular the novels of Ian Rankin and John Buchan. Although he did not watch a lot of television, he enjoyed adaptations of Agatha Christie's Poirot as well as the classic *Carry On* films. Music was perhaps not a very significant part of his life, but he had a list of pieces he enjoyed playing. Bryan Ferry, especially his album *As Time Goes By*, could often be heard at Eydon, but Catto also enjoyed Marlene Dietrich, Noel Coward songs, especially the rather whimsical 'A Bar on the Piccola Marina', the Cuban jazz group Buena Vista Social Club, and the relatively niche 1960s band Herman's Hermits. As for sporting pursuits, Catto sometimes enjoyed giving people the impression that he was a dedicated football fan. As a result, there was, for many years, a rather improbable rumour at Oriel, no doubt spread by Catto himself, that he was a Millwall FC fan, and his students laughed at the thought of their tutor standing on the terraces at The Den shouting 'No one likes us, we don't care' at opposition fans. Even if there was ever any serious doubt about this matter, it will not surprise many to hear that Catto had no interest whatsoever in football and that physical exercise in general did not feature very prominently in his life. In fact, it was John Wolfe who was the Millwall fan, whereas Catto's only sporting talent involved standing on the terrace of the Oriel boathouse, Pimm's in hand, cheering on the college's oarsmen to yet another victory over a rival college.

The private passions he did possess he very much enjoyed sharing with his closest friends at Eydon. Over time, his friends included former undergraduates, colleagues and a variety of people he met on his travels. To be friends with Catto, or even just to spend time in his company, meant being exposed to his own private vocabulary which, in turn, felt like being initiated into an exclusive club. His language was underpinned by his idiosyncratic sense of humour and his remarks were more often than not delivered with a mischievous twinkle in his eye. Like many dons, he relished gossip, but he was never personally unpleasant or malicious about people. In addition, and perhaps most importantly, he was warm, kind, generous and loyal. What follows is a series of personal recollections from some of the many friends he made throughout his life.

Language and the use of language were central to Catto's dealings with his friends. If you had gained his approval, you would be referred to as 'great man' or 'great man on toast'; to be called 'deep fried great man on toast' you had to have done something quite exceptional. When he was in a playful mood, he would refer to you as 'you wicked old thing' or 'angel fluff'. If you made him laugh, he would say 'that was a giglet' or a 'shriekino'. At the start of the week, he might inquire about your weekend and ask whether 'giggles and squeaks' had been enjoyed. William Hague once asked him: 'Jeremy, can I be a wicked old fluff and a rough tough fluff at the same time?' To which Catto replied: 'My dear boy, how could you be anything else?'[185] Over the years and during countless dinners with friends, he must have poured thousands of gallons of 'whisk or bran', and 'the sacred river whisk' never stopped flowing.

Beyond the idiosyncratic nature of his language lay a sense of humour and a convivial sense of fun that were defining features of his friendships. James Clark recalls that Catto 'always wanted to meet at a time when you could get away with serving a pink gin', adding that whether you arrived 'despondent or elated, nothing would matter until after that first drink had been served'. Sir Alan Duncan, who was friends with Catto for many decades, recalls that there was a time when he used to speak to him every week. They frequently met for drinks and, above all, Sir Alan remembers the sheer fun of being in his company: 'He was always amusing, and you could always look forward to a giggly catch-up, during which you felt like you learned an amusing snippet.'

For Simon Kingston, Catto's humour was central to his friendships:

His instinct was always to shroud the serious in humour. Sometimes gently to deflate the vainglorious and pompous, sometimes as a way of agreeing but avoiding excess gravity, as it were. I can remember relaying the news that a Sinn Fein spokesman, who had long professed his commitment to peaceful means, had been arrested in a raid by the RUC. He was part of an IRA group intent on torturing an alleged informer, who had been hung by his heels from the ceiling for the purpose. I waxed, I fear, rather long in my furious denunciation. Jeremy was very sympathetic: 'Can you imagine,' he mused, 'the sense of relief at seeing so many upside-down policemen?'

According to Diccon Swan, Catto was 'endlessly amusing, funny and witty'. Over the years, he recalls that he and his partner at the time would often go with Catto to a Greek restaurant in Newbury, called the Riviera:

On our way back one day, in his blue Saab, he drove into St Aldate's to be confronted with the signs for the new-fangled bus route, just outside the police station. Jeremy was hesitating as to whether to drive on or not when a policeman appeared and said, 'Good evening, sir. So we think we're a bus, do we, sir?' Jeremy said 'Yes, officer', turned to Simon in the back seat, called, 'Fares please', and drove on, leaving the dumbstruck policeman in his wake.'

One former student recalls a similar episode when Catto was once stopped by the police on suspicion of drink driving. When the policeman arrived at the side of his car, Catto had to think quickly, so he wound down the window and said: 'The police have stopped me once before this evening, officer, but they told me I had not had enough.'

Beyond a taste for the silly and the absurd, Catto's sense of humour could be waspish and was often aimed at those he saw as modern-day puritans. As A.N. Wilson once recalled in an article for *The Spectator*:

We don't have Thanksgiving in Britain, but this does not stop us giving thanks and Christmas is a good time to do it. Last year, when I made a visit of farewell to the great medievalist Jeremy Catto, who was dying…John Wolfe, said that they always kept Thanksgiving. I asked Jeremy what he gave thanks for. 'I give thanks that the Pilgrim Fathers left,' was his characteristic reply. We fell to deploring the growth of modern puritanism in all its nauseating forms.[186]

He also liked to tease those whom he viewed as pompous. Robert Portass recalls one occasion at which another don questioned the need for guests to wear black tie at a particular dinner. Catto's response was typical in that it deployed gentle humour to mock his more earnest colleague: 'But black tie is the most democratic form of dress, as nobody can get it wrong.'

His humour could also be gently irreverent, but he was never nasty or unpleasant, and he enjoyed penning limericks to amuse himself and his friends. Of Robert Runcie's wife, Rosalind, he once wrote the following teasing lines:

It would be better to elope
With his Holiness the Pope
Than to cause any more pantie worry
To His Grace the Archbishop of Canterbury.

At other times, and certainly by today's standards, his humour could verge on the outrageous. The Piers Gaveston Society is a student society at Oxford which Count Gottfried von Bismarck once described as 'originally an all-gay group where the rules say members have to dress in drag and parade openly in public'.[187] When a couple of Catto's students told him that they had been invited to one of the society's parties and asked him for some advice, he chuckled and said: 'I hope you have the zips at the back, boys.' On another occasion, at the end of a long night of drinks after a meeting of the Canning, Catto spotted two students he knew to be gay and asked them what their plans were for the rest of the night. When they told him that they were off to get some late-night pizzas, he smiled innocently and said: 'Meat feast, boys?'

Sometimes, the precise meaning behind his sense of humour was hard to decipher. Many people may not have very much hanging on the walls of their bathrooms. Some might choose to hang up a series of school photos of their children; others, meanwhile, think that what their guests really want to see is a depiction of their host's illustrious family tree. But if you answered a call of nature during one of Catto's drinks parties in his set of rooms in college, you would find yourself confronted by a French poster from the 1920s by Louis Raemaekers, titled 'L'hecatombe la syphilis' ('The Mass Slaughter of Syphilis'). This poster shows a femme fatale wearing what appears to be a giant spider on her head and sporting a purple dress combined with acidic green jewellery. As she gazes out at the viewer from on top of a sea of graves, she can be seen holding the skull of one of her victims over her crotch. Raemaekers had designed the poster as a warning to men about the dangers of syphilis, after Belgian soldiers returning home from the front with the 'French pox' triggered a huge increase in STD-related deaths in the years after the First World War. What exactly Catto meant by subjecting his guests to this image can only be guessed, but it is easy to imagine him chuckling to himself as he saw the look of bafflement on their faces as they emerged from the loo.

Gossip is the lifeblood of much of academic life, and Catto certainly enjoyed sharing stories with friends and colleagues. But as many have pointed out, there was never a personal or malicious edge to the gossip he shared. According to Sir Alan Duncan, 'there was always a keen observation on current affairs from an interesting angle, and if he spoke ill of someone, it was always wittily done and never venomous'. The following anecdote from A.N. Wilson also illustrates the point:

> The historian Blair Worden, kind guardian of the flame of Hugh Trevor-Roper (1918–2003), has an annual dinner in Oxford in the great man's memory. It is something to look forward to but this year I had to miss it because of a mild mother-in-law crisis. The world of Chang's girlhood in Mao's China and Trevor-Roper's Oxford could scarcely be further apart but one thing at least links them. As a schoolgirl during the cultural revolution, Chang was made to remove the flower pots from the window ledges in her school because Chairman Mao had decreed flowers were 'bourgeois'. The last time I attended a Trevor-Roper dinner, the medieval historian Jeremy Catto amusingly recalled for us how the window boxes at Oriel College, containing some particularly suburban petunias, mysteriously disappeared one night, apparently purloined by the college's rowing hearties. Trevor-Roper's enemies in the college

knew the truth – that the masterminds behind the thefts were none other than Trevor-Roper himself and his pencil-thin aristocratic wife Alexandra, daughter of Field Marshal Haig. Much to the chagrin of the Trevor-Ropers, the window boxes were spotted in their garage at St Aldate's. Flowers have presumably been arousing passionate ideological hostility since the wars of the roses. Vita Sackville-West would, perhaps, also have agreed with Mao that flowers on window ledges were bourgeois. I am so bourgeois that it was only when I had befriended the great gardener Sir Roy Strong that I discovered hanging baskets were 'common'. Strong's war on the hanging basket in Herefordshire is as fierce as Mao's war on the flowerpot in Beijing, but less ruthlessly successful.[188]

But there was more to Catto than humour and a love of gossip. Helen Whittow, a friend of Catto's for over thirty years, sums up his gift for friendship in the following terms: 'He was himself a very private person. He somehow managed to hold the balance between being wholly welcoming of the partners and spouses of his friends – and at the same time signalling clearly that their private life was none of his business. He was that best of friends – generous and welcoming, but neither possessive nor competitive of their company.'[189] That quality of generosity was very much at the heart of Catto's friendships. Diccon Swan recalls that Catto was always immensely generous. 'He once bought me an expensive light for my painting studio. He also got me the commission from Oriel to draw his predecessor, the Oxford archivist Billy Pantin, and then, years later, to paint the honorary fellow of Oriel, Francesco Cossiga, who had been Prime Minister and President of Italy.' On another occasion, Catto believed that his friend should have a proper gentleman's suit and so took him off to be fitted out for one at his own expense. Ken Fincham also remembers his generosity: 'He was immensely generous – paying for meals, petrol when we went on historical hikes, drinks, offering hospitality, etc. He knew how "Dame Drink" relaxed people, both in and outside tutorials, and contributed to conversation. Sending a bottle of wine from high table to me and my girlfriend in my first year at Oriel was an act of kindness and singularity.'

Sir David Manning became firm friends with Catto after he left Oriel, and remembers that when he went off to Bologna to pursue some postgraduate work, Catto telephoned him from Venice and suggested that he should join him. The occasion was one of Catto's reading holidays, and he was in Venice with Michael Wheeler-Booth and a number of undergraduates. When Sir David arrived in Venice, he was delighted to find that mornings were spent reading about the sites that the group then went to visit in the afternoons. According to Sir David, 'generosity of spirit' was the key to friendship with Catto: 'He was always genuinely engaged when you spent time with him, and although his company was always amusing, he also wanted to talk seriously about the things you were doing.'

The result of this generosity was that there was no sense of pecking order to Catto's friendships. According to Simon Skinner, a colleague who also became a good friend over the years, Catto would 'never look over your shoulder at someone more important, and when you entered his world, you became important and felt enfranchised'. In that sense, there was something of a paradox in his character:

> For all his conservatism and institutionalism, there was nothing remotely hierarchical about his friendship. Many people can be very warm, and supportive, but leave you in no doubt that in terms of age or rank, you are their junior. And that's how Oxford had seemed to me – a ladder. When you entered Jeremy's world, you stepped off a vertical ladder and into a horizontal republic of letters.

Robert Portass echoes these sentiments, and suggests that Catto's obituaries made the point that 'it was easy to be sniffy about Jeremy as an old-school don, but he was in fact always very welcoming, and was very good at being inclusive in the sense that he made people feel at ease'.

In addition, it is important to note that this generous and welcoming spirit was not confined to fellow Conservatives. Simon Skinner, who came from a very different background to Catto and had very little in common politically with him, thinks that this was a vital part of his personality. When Skinner, a self-confessed atheist and certainly not a Conservative, first arrived at Oxford, he felt that he did not quite fit in. He had every confidence in his own intellectual abilities but, as a young man from a London comprehensive school, he suffered from imposter syndrome in the gilded environment of Oxford that, at that time, was still dominated by the well-heeled products of the public schools. That is until he met Catto. 'He made me feel like a senior person....and that it was appropriate for me to be in an Oxford common room.' Oxford is, by any measure, a very hierarchical place, but Skinner explains that

Catto 'trusted him entirely, and never interfered with how or what he taught.' This gave Skinner a great sense of freedom, as well as a real 'sense of belonging.' A few years later, Skinner overheard a rumour that certain colleagues had not approved of his appointment at Balliol. Understandably hurt and dismayed by this apparent slight, Skinner asked Catto what he thought about the matter. As so often, Catto found a way to defuse a potentially difficult situation: 'Never you mind, Simon. The most important thing is the quality of one's enemies.' This reply was vintage Catto. His ability to distil wisdom in a few witty words or phrases meant that Skinner's doubts were immediately assuaged, with the result that he felt once more like he belonged at Oxford after all. Robert Portass agrees that Catto's friendships transcended political divides and adds that Catto enjoyed teasing his more left-wing friends: 'He could be mischievous, but never combative, and was always keen to get on with people.' Catto was happy to put political differences to one side and what he really wanted, according to Portass, was to have 'interesting conversations with people he found interesting'. But that sense of mischief was never far from the surface. Of one particular Marxist don, with whom Catto always got on very well despite their manifest political differences, Catto liked to joke that his left-wing colleague and friend was 'very conservative, but only in the way that really committed Marxists can be'.

Over the years, some of his most important and enduring friendships were formed with colleagues at Oxford. Perhaps the most significant of those was his friendship with Hugh Trevor-Roper. Although there existed nearly a twenty-five-year age gap between them, they had much in common, and became firm friends not long after Catto arrived at Oriel in 1969. Throughout his life, Trevor-Roper was a prolific writer of letters, and in a letter to Catto only a couple of years after the latter had become a fellow at Oriel, the older don makes it clear just how much he had come to enjoy the company of his younger friend: 'I am really very sorry to miss you, as I feel in a state of profound gloom which nothing but gay, intellectual, convivial society could dissipate. The Borders have many charms, but that they cannot provide, at least out of their own resources; and I do not think that Oriel, in your absence will provide it either.'[190] Over the years, Trevor-Roper came to value Catto's sense of loyalty. In another letter, dated 15 November 1972, he thanks Catto for improving his mood following some college intrigue and describes him as a 'foul weather friend'.[191] Many years later, when Trevor-Roper was dying, Catto visited his old friend and, in an effort to lift his spirits, read passages from P.G. Wodehouse to him.

Most importantly, the pair agreed on how history should be written, and also shared the same view of the nature and purpose of Oxford University. According to Richard Davenport-Hines, who wrote Trevor-Roper's entry for the *Oxford Dictionary of National Biography*, Trevor-Roper argued that the writing of history 'must be provocative, even playful, if history was not to seem a dead subject'. Catto would certainly have agreed with that view. As for what he thought Oxford should be, Davenport-Hines notes that Trevor-Roper 'disdained irresponsible frivolity', but 'cared even less for unrelenting seriousness' and wanted the university to be saved from, as he put it, 'solemn, pompous, dreary, respectable...experts' and to be instead 'gay, irreverent, genial, unpompous'.[192] On this, as on so many other questions, the two men were of one mind.

Christopher Tyerman was an undergraduate at Oxford in the autumn of 1971, which is when he met Catto for the first time. He had been out with a friend who suggested that the two men should call on his tutor at Oriel. In those days, Catto lived in a flat on King Edward Street, 'wore round tinted glasses and was very slim', as Tyerman recalls. Ever the welcoming host, Catto invited the two young men into his flat for drinks. Several hours later, Tyerman's friend had fallen asleep on the sofa, but Tyerman and Catto continued their conversations. At around 1 a.m., the conversation moved towards the topic of Pope Gregory VII. Catto offered an opinion on the pontiff, which prompted Tyerman to exclaim: 'That's total crap!' A shriek of laughter from Catto followed and the two men were firm friends from then on. Looking back, Tyerman reflects that 'the most obvious thing was that he was enormous fun'. But that sense of fun was 'not superficial', as Catto was 'always interesting, mischievous, amusing and life-enhancing because of his mercurial character'. Laughter would always be mixed with 'an arresting or interesting point of view', and Catto was always 'enormously stimulating and thought-provoking' as a friend and companion. His personality was most clearly evident in his eyes and at the corners of his mouth, and even behind those famous glasses, Tyerman points out that 'the eyes always betrayed his quicksilver mind and personality.'

Richard Davenport-Hines liked Catto from the moment they first met. He recalls that his first encounters with Catto came via the annual Dacre Dinners, held in memory of Hugh Trevor-Roper. When the two men first met, the dinners were held at Christ Church, but migrated not long after to Oriel, where Catto 'turned them into something of a salon'. The two would often sit at opposite ends of the table, but Davenport-Hines remembers having the chance to observe Catto from across the other side of the table. He captures him in memorable terms by saying that Catto 'was always looking mischievous and saucy, like a soft living prince of the church'. When Catto died, Davenport-Hines recorded the following in his diary: 'Distressed to hear of the death yesterday morning in Oxford of Jeremy Catto...He is an ally and friend whom I will miss: gregarious & gossipy with a fund of stories still untold to me: affectionate, canny, hard to impress, very sound; this era of crowd delirium and cheap ideas was not for him.'

Sandy Hardie, who first knew Catto in a professional capacity, remembers how they became friends not long after first meeting. Above all, he stresses Catto's long-standing loyalty as a friend:

> To begin with, I lived in college, as of course did Jeremy, and so a pattern of visits to his staircase was fairly quickly established. Jeremy was naturally gregarious, a lover of good conversation, and perhaps felt a bit lonely on dark winter weeknights on his own. We enjoyed one another's company, and there was generally a good deal of banter as to how many Scotches the guest would accept. I picture him sitting on his sofa with his phone sitting beside him; and occasionally it would ring (at least once from Alan Duncan). There will have been other music, but it's Bryan Ferry's 'Miss Otis' that stands out in the aural memory. It was the start of a friendship that we kept up after I left Oriel: the occasional meal in a Greek restaurant in Summertown (with Jeremy driving happily after supper back down the Marston Ferry Road); he came to visit me in my Inverness house; and I last saw him in 2017 at my seventieth birthday at the Travellers. We all remember his pet phrases – 'Blessings', 'Blessings on toast' and 'Woaow!' I remember a man who remained a friend when others slid away.

That loyalty meant that Catto also had a wonderful gift for befriending younger generations. When asked whether he had considered himself to be a friend of Catto's over the years, John Varley replied that 'funnily enough' he thought of himself as a friend of his 'even at the age of eighteen', adding that he would be 'unable to say that of the other teachers at Oxford'. As for the nature of that friendship, Varley says that Catto had the qualities of being 'empathetic and loyal, but he would also express his opinions', which Varley found to be an invaluable asset in their friendship.

Towards the end of his time at Oxford, Catto showed that he had the ability to count some of his later students among his friends. Robert Portass 'treasured' his friendship with Catto and remembers him as being 'extremely kind'. His favourite memories are of two 'biblioteca and bodega' trips to Spain in 2009 and 2010. These trips involved driving from Oxford down to the south coast, taking the ferry to Spain, before setting off in search of manuscripts they wished to see and wineries they wanted to visit. The trips came about as Catto had encouraged Portass to go out to Spain to pursue his academic work, and also because Catto himself had an interest in Spanish history. Over lunch in Oxford one day, Catto suggested the idea, and although Portass was not married at the time, he did have a girlfriend. 'I know it may be a bit awkward on the domestic front,' Catto told his younger friend, 'but could you perhaps carve out some time so we could go and look at some manuscripts in Salamanca?' Portass needed little persuading and, not long after, the two men set off in Catto's car, with Portass noting that, with space at a premium, Catto was especially 'keen to make sure there was a slot reserved for the wine he wanted to bring back'. Arriving at the ferry port in Plymouth, Catto excused himself in the afternoon to go and have a long bath. 'Let's have dinner on board. Come and knock on my door later this evening.' When Portass did so a few hours later, he found Catto fully dressed in black tie, a sight which must have raised at least a few eyebrows among the other passengers on board the P&O ferry. Portass remembers that the first trip to Spain was 'great fun', but that he 'also learned a lot'. The second trip, he admits, 'was rather heavier on the bodegas than the bibliotecas, as Jeremy decided to bin off the scholarship'. But leaving aside all the fun that was had, Portass recalls that the trips also had a decisive impact on his future career. Spending time in cathedrals and archives examining manuscripts alongside Catto made Portass feel that he could make it as an historian. When Catto asked him his opinion of various manuscripts, he took 'great confidence' from the experience and realised that this was what he wanted to do with his life.

William Orr-Ewing, one of Catto's last undergraduates, remembers that Catto could at times be quite shy, but that they nevertheless became friends after Catto retired:

Always in awe of him at Oxford, I came to appreciate his shyness the few times I saw him after Oxford. Although he always had a witty line or observation ready, put with that irresistible mischievous smile, he was not naturally garrulous and had to be drawn out. We were both members of a lunch club in London that he confessed he was too shy to attend without a friend. It was a special joy to be able to return the encouragement he had once given me and accompany him there several times in the year before he died.

Although Catto did not have any children of his own, it is clear that he enjoyed being in the presence of young people and that he had the ability to strike up a genuine rapport with them. Emily Wilson, who is a distinguished classicist and professor of classical studies at the University of Pennsylvania, remembers Catto as her godfather. Her mother, Katherine Duncan-Jones, was one of Catto's best friends, and she and Catto were at times inseparable over the years. 'I knew him from when I was a baby, so did not know at the time how unusual he was,' she recalls with a smile, before adding that Catto was 'a lovely godfather, who always remembered birthdays and bought very thoughtful and memorable presents, including a marbling paper set and a chemistry set'.

One of Helen Whittow's sons, who left Oxford in 2017, also remembers Catto with great fondness:

He was a fascinating man and very affectionate. He and John were very kind to me as a child, feeding me good things, having a box of cars to play with and a home filled with interesting nooks and crannies to explore. I also remember him spending time with me and [my father] in the Eydon garden, probably as I attacked bramble bushes (read dragon) with a stick (read sword).

Helen Whittow, too, was similarly appreciative of Catto's ability to get on with the younger generation:

To my children George, Mary and Flossy, Jeremy has stood in the place of grandfather. Easter egg hunts in the garden; sleeping on the comfiest sofa in Eydon while Mark and I were appropriately watered and fed delicious things cooked by John; being allowed to play with the collection of antique matchbox cars, kept in the stool on which exotic Moroccan nuts always sit; Christmas Day drinks after Church; their introduction to gin (from an age that was barely legal, let alone sensible) and later their introduction to wonderful cocktails in glasses from a freezer kept exclusively for that purpose. They remember generous presents – of horsy things when desired (a headcollar, a martingale); presents of chocolate shoes or animals at Easter, but above all of being taken to Blackwell's and told they could have any book they wanted for Christmas.[193]

Finally, a testament to the strength of his many friendships is the fact that a number of those friends repaid his loyalty and friendship in turn by moving their own lives to Eydon and nearby in order to be closer to him. Helen Whittow recalls that her decision to move to Eydon was not a hard one to make:

We bought our current house as a direct result of a weekend with Jeremy. We were looking for a cottage outside London in a rather desultory fashion. The night we spent with Jeremy was without exception the most uncomfortable bed I have ever slept in. It was at an angle not unlike the north face of the Eiger. Meanwhile, Jeremy said 'you won't want this house, but it's been unoccupied for thirty years and I'd love to see inside'. One thing led to another and thirty years on, here we still are.

But even though Catto was a wonderful friend to many over the years, readers should not be left with the impression that he was somehow perfect. Like everyone else, he had his faults, and there were certain idiosyncratic and indeed eccentric facets to his personality.

For instance, it is not clear how or when (or indeed, as some have questioned, whether) Catto ever secured his driving license but, for his friends, his driving was always a source of both amusement and alarm in almost equal measure. Richard Cross chuckles when he says that Catto's driving was pretty erratic at best, and adds that he was actually better after a couple of drinks 'because it made him drive more carefully'. Matthew Bool smiles broadly when he thinks back to Catto's driving. He recalls that he was late to a tutorial in North Oxford one day, and as he was running up the High Street, Catto suddenly pulled up next to him in his Saab and offered to give him a lift. Bool was very grateful and quickly climbed into the passenger seat. To his surprise, it took Catto a good few minutes to pull away from the kerb, as he was struggling to get the car into gear. By now, Bool was growing a touch impatient and was worried that he would miss his tutorial altogether, but then Catto bent forward and started rummaging around the peddles. As he eventually reappeared from under the wheel, Catto held aloft a battered old shoe, which he had extracted from beneath one of the peddles: 'Oh look, I was wondering where I had left that.'

For others, however, climbing into the passenger seat of a car and discovering Catto at the wheel was no laughing matter. James Clark, who found himself in this unenviable position on a number of occasions, remembers that the experience of being chauffeured around by Catto was not for the faint-hearted. 'There is no two ways about it: he could not drive. It is terrifying to be driven by someone looking at the peddles!' Diccon Swan recalls a particular trip to the Bourbonnais area of France in the 1990s to look at some Bourbon tombs, during which Catto demonstrated his rather unorthodox method of staying awake on the road:

> He was an idiosyncratic driver and had a tendency at that time to get drowsy at the wheel. He used to chew his tongue and occasionally stamp on the accelerator to jerk himself awake. I found this particularly terrifying as we were driving between massive pantechnicons on the route périphérique around Paris. So when it was safe to stop, I said I would take over and that I needed to drive for the rest of the holiday!

Despite his erratic driving, Catto was rarely deterred from getting himself behind the wheel of his trusted Saab. To the amusement of many, as Alexander Morrison says, he even insisted on driving himself from Oriel to the Examination schools, which were no more than a few hundred yards from the college. His excuse was that there was a 'slight gradient' on that part of the High Street. If so, it might be noted that the residents of Oxford could count themselves lucky at this faulty design, as it probably made him drive more carefully.

Nor was he shy about providing others with advice regarding their own driving, as one of his sisters recalls:

> I remember Jeremy driving our mother and me in his super new Saab on a day's outing in Galloway. I had recently passed my driving test, and we had a lovely day visiting St Ninian's Cave, but when it came to driving home Jeremy said I would have to do it as he was going to sleep! I had never driven a car with a gear stick on

the steering wheel, and was terrified, but Jeremy insisted. His only word of advice, as he slid into unconsciousness, was to make sure I accelerated into curves. Our poor mother cowered in the back, and how we got back to Newcastle is a miracle. But I managed and eventually Jeremy woke up! Possibly it was his way of increasing my confidence in driving...

Once he had arrived at his chosen destination, Catto also showed himself to be an unusual house guest. When visiting the homes of his friends, Diccon Swan recalls that Catto had a peculiar habit involving the furniture: 'He had a curious fad when visiting some people's homes which was to rearrange the furniture to his liking. I think he was working from some principle he had absorbed, but I never gathered what it was. Most people indulged him and then put the furniture back after he had gone!' Indeed, even his own students were not immune to being subjected to this treatment. David Brierley recalls that in his second year at Oriel, Catto was in charge of allocating rooms:

Catto allocated to me a room of distinction, overlooking Third Quad, which had a separate bedroom, sitting room/study and Jack and Jill bathroom. Having just moved in, Jeremy visited my rooms and immediately turned around the design using the furniture to make separate areas for work and relaxation. It made my rooms a very pleasant place to visit, and I hosted the 'tea folk' group and other gatherings.

So pronounced was this decorating trait that some of Catto's friends even adopted it themselves. Sir Alan Duncan readily admits that he inherited the habit of rearranging rooms from Catto and even deployed his decorating skills when he visited other countries as a Foreign Office Minister: 'I moved a few things around in Tripoli and in Kathmandu, and when I left, they told me that they rather liked the changes.'

Although Catto thought nothing of rearranging other people's houses to his own taste, John Stevenson recalls that he could be amusingly touchy if someone questioned his own sense of style or taste:

As a fairly callow graduate when appointed lecturer back in 1971, I regarded his as a pretty sophisticated person and of considerable taste and sophistication – I think I only saw him once somewhat offended when he showed me his new portable radio he'd bought in the then normal stainless steel and black format. I said that it was a pity they didn't make them in a greater variety of colours – he was clearly somewhat put out that his good taste had been questioned!

All their friends agreed that Catto and John were consummate hosts and enjoyed having friends to stay with them at Eydon. However, things did not always go according to plan. Richard Cross recalls one memorable occasion when he stayed with them in Northamptonshire for a weekend. John had bought a brace of crows at the local market and had planned to turn them into a pie. Jeremy, who was familiar with the timings around John's cooking, expected dinner to be ready by 9 p.m., so took Cross off to the pub for an hour beforehand. All seemed well, but Jeremy and Cross had been 'drinking gin since about 6 p.m.', and when they returned to the cottage, they were not only slightly worse for wear, but also found that John had forgotten to skin the crows, which meant that the crow pie was even less appealing than it might otherwise have been. Cross still laughs at the memory and says that 'Jeremy arrived back home and was furious, because we'd been drinking gin all day and the pie was utterly revolting.'

In relation to matters of personal health, Catto also displayed certain amusing quirks. Although he was himself not a heavy or even a habitual smoker, he liked to encourage others to take up the vice of smoking. Leif Dixon, who was himself essentially a non-smoker, occasionally gave in to temptation whilst at Oxford. He recalls that after a few too many drinks at one of Catto's parties, he threw caution to the wind and lit a cigarette. As he stood puffing away in Catto's rooms, a nervous undergraduate approached him and asked him whether it would be alright if he too had a cigarette. At that point, and seemingly out of nowhere, Catto emerged from the throng of people and produced a cigarette case filled to the brim with all manner of cigarettes. Opening the box, he offered one to the nervous undergraduate and said: 'It's compulsory, dear boy!'

Catto was, of course, known for enjoying the odd tipple, and he usually had a pretty good level of tolerance. However, John Stevenson remembers one occasion when drink got the better of him, albeit with amusing consequences:

Jeremy could hold his drink better than most, but there was an amusing incident after a last examiners meeting for finals when

I was chairman. We all adjourned to the Eastgate Hotel next to Schools. A lengthy session resulted in Jeremy trying to catch a bus to East Oxford with a colleague who had to ask where he thought he was going – he was not at all sure!

Then, of course, there were the famous baths he so enjoyed taking. As Diccon Swan recalls:

He liked to take them often and he also liked other people to take them. He used to arrange telephone calls so that he could catch you in the bath while he was in his own bath at the time. It was always a bit worrying when he came to stay as he liked to fill the bath full and then plunge into it. The bathroom would be awash. I would sometimes wait in the kitchen below to see whether it all seeped through the ceiling.

Richard Cross also remembers Catto's fondness for taking regular baths:

Before dinner in college, Jeremy (as he often did) phoned me inviting me to have a gin in his rooms. The call was oddly echoey, and I thought I could hear the gentle splashing of water. I wondered whether he was in the bath but did not ask. It turned out he was, because while he was on the phone there was a great ruckus and then the phone went dead. I later found out that the porter, who had been unable to get through to Jeremy because he was on the phone to me, arrived to alert Jeremy of the fact that water was leaking into the room below his bathroom…which was the Provost's entry hall.

Finally, in contrast to his many intellectual gifts, Catto's relationship with physical exercise was never at the forefront of his mind. According to Helen Whittow, 'exercise and Jeremy were not words often heard in the same sentence'. When she and her family first moved to Holywell Street in Oxford, Catto would drive to their house for supper from Oriel, a journey which would have taken him no more than ten minutes on foot. So impressed were the Whittows that they signed up with Catto's GP as soon as possible, because they assumed that 'anyone who had kept Jeremy alive must be good at the job'.

19

Final Years

'Better than death…'

– Catto's description of retirement

'Nothing lasts forever
Of that I'm sure…'

– 'Same Old Scene', song by Bryan Ferry

AS HIS GOOD FRIEND BRYAN FERRY ONCE SANG 'NOTHING LASTS forever', and so it was that in the autumn of 2006, after thirty-seven years of distinguished service, Jeremy Catto retired from Oriel College. Given his distinguished record and length of service, it was only fitting that a farewell party was given in his honour, with guests including friends, colleagues and former students. One who was present recalls that Catto spoke very movingly about his life, his upbringing in the North East and his many years at Oxford, before concluding his remarks in a typically pithy and understated fashion: 'There you go…it was just one of those things.' By contrast, to those who had been taught by him, and for many who had worked alongside him, Catto's retirement seemed like the end of an era. Over the course of four decades, he had become practically synonymous with the college, and only a dwindling group of people had any kind of institutional memory of the college before he had arrived in 1969, which made it difficult for many to imagine the college without him.

Of course, times change, and people eventually move on. When Billy Pantin retired from Oriel in 1969 after thirty-three years in post, there is no doubt that many would have struggled to picture the college without him. When Catto arrived to replace him, there would have been question marks over the new man from certain quarters, and the same was true for Catto's successor when he retired in 2006. In the end, the opportunity to succeed Catto fell to a young academic by the name of Ian Forrest, who would go on to serve in the same role at Oriel for the next seventeen years. Forrest first met Catto a number of years before he retired and at a time when he was doing some work on William of Woodford who, by complete coincidence, had been the subject of Catto's own doctoral thesis. He had been advised to speak to Catto about this and subsequently spent a couple of hours discussing the subject with him. However, Forrest had not realised at the time that Catto had written his doctoral thesis on Woodford, and Catto himself never mentioned the fact during their conversation. When Forrest then followed up on his research, he was mortified to find Catto's name all over the footnotes of the articles he read. Looking back, Forrest recalls that Catto was 'terribly nice about it all', but he also admits to thinking at the time that Catto 'must have thought I was an idiot for not knowing'. When Catto retired from Oriel and the job to replace him came up, Forrest admits that he did not consider himself as a contender until he was 'accosted in the street' one day by Mark Whittow, who 'crossed the street' to tell him that he had to apply for the job. Despite Whittow's enthusiastic backing, Forrest remained unsure, not least given Oriel's reputation as a rather conservative, traditional and old-fashioned college. Succeeding Catto seemed an unusual move for someone like Forrest, who admits that, politically, they 'could not have been more different'. Indeed, in later years, he would joke to people that he was 'to the left of Jeremy…Jeremy Corbyn, that is'. But to Forrest's great surprise, Catto was very much in favour of appointing him as his successor. Although Catto was not formally involved in choosing his own successor, Forrest later discovered that Catto had decided that he was just the man for the job and had even told his students that he approved of Forrest's candidacy. Despite their political differences, Forrest reflects that they 'could not have agreed more on what students needed'. Both shared the 'core common belief that teaching came from having a relationship with your students, and that if you do not have that relationship, you can convey information, but it is difficult to teach'. Forrest also points out that Catto had friends across the political spectrum and that he believed in a pluralist history faculty, adding that Catto 'had a habit of creating a history team at Oriel with people who were very different to him'. When the time came for the handover, Catto spent a day with Forrest giving him invaluable advice about the college, but without attempting to steer him in a particular direction. Forrest recalls with gratitude that Catto 'did not hover around me or try to tell me what to do'. Although retiring from Oriel was difficult for Catto, he had no intention of being a backseat driver and he accepted that the time had come for him to move on.

But although he was prepared to give his successor the time and space to do the job as he saw fit, Catto did not relish the prospect of retirement. On the surface, and to the casual observer, he appeared cheerful enough and looked set for a comfortable retirement. Even though he was not exactly a natural sportsman, he joined the board of his local cricket club in Northamptonshire and became, for a while at least, a regular and convivial presence at matches. But those who knew him better, understood that retirement had hit him hard. For someone who was at the peak of his intellectual powers and had led such a multifaceted and intellectually stimulating life, it is difficult to imagine that he would have been able to content himself with whiling away the hours at his local cricket club. Simon Kingston remembers meeting him at a party relatively soon after he had retired, at which his wife asked him about life after Oriel. Catto responded in characteristic fashion by saying that it was at least 'better than death'. At another similar occasion, he called over to a friend and, with a wistful smile playing around his lips, said, 'Would you come and spend some time with me and my wretched life?' Making light of the situation was typical of Catto, but friends like Kingston understood that, behind the humorous remarks, Catto seemed 'very unhappy immediately after leaving Oriel'. Although some men may look forward to the idea of retiring, the reality of retirement forces most to face up to the fact that their lives are drawing to a close. It is human, and indeed unavoidable, to give in to a sense of pessimism in those circumstances and to indulge in nostalgia about the past. But even though Catto was sometimes moved by such feelings, the truth is that he was an optimist at heart. Leslie Mitchell, who knew Catto for many decades, recalls that there were several occasions when he was 'forced to accuse him of optimism'. According to Mitchell, this optimism was a typical trait of Catto's and stemmed from the fact that he was a medievalist. By this he means that medievalists have a unique sense of perspective, because 'they have seen the arrival of the barbarians, but have also then seen how civilisation eventually turns up again'.

Ultimately, that sense of optimism was fully justified, as retirement gave Catto the time he needed to work on one of his great projects, which was to edit the official history of Oriel College. In the end, it was published in November 2013, and was the first history of the college to be published for over a hundred years. It was written by a group of specialist scholars and other contributors, all of whom were hand-picked by Catto personally. The final work was very much the result of a strong collective effort, but one that was led with great authority by Catto himself. The aim of the book was not merely to write a straightforward history of the college, but to place it within the context not only of Oxford but of British and international history. To that end, the book examines the ideas which have shaped – and sometimes divided – the members of this small college in every generation since its foundation in 1326. It considers, among other areas, the Noetic era of the early nineteenth century, as well as the Oxford Movement which succeeded it, and it also takes a look at the impact of the college on national life, including sport and the government of the British Empire. It was, in other words, a remarkable undertaking, and reading it leaves one with the impression of a community that, over the centuries, developed into a very distinctive society. When the book was eventually published, the reviews were overwhelmingly positive. Writing in *The Spectator*, A.N. Wilson's review was in line with much of the commentary at the time. In a very positive piece about his friend's work, he concluded by arguing that the book 'does not have a dud chapter'.[194] Richard Davenport-Hines, who has himself written about All Souls College, Oxford, also praised Catto for his achievement in editing the history of the college. In common with others, he pointed out that Catto was 'very good at bringing together talented contributors' to produce a book of this kind, and he summed up Catto's achievement by saying that 'his arrangement of that book was simply top class'. However, praise for the book was not entirely unanimous. One drawback, according to some, was that not a single woman was chosen to contribute a chapter. Although this was not a deliberate choice, as sex was not a criteria for selection, the slightly awkward result was that when Catto and his co-contributors met for a celebratory dinner on the eve of the book's publication, the only woman present was the then Provost of the college, Moira Wallace. Even so, it would be churlish to allow such a criticism to detract from Catto's overall achievement in producing this book. Certainly, those who worked with Catto on the project thoroughly enjoyed the experience and were full of praise for their editor. Dr Alexander Morrison, who contributed a chapter on the links between Oriel and the empire in the late nineteenth and early twentieth centuries, enjoyed the collaboration with his old tutor, and recalls that Catto 'clearly really enjoyed the process and putting together the team'. Wilf Stephenson, who wrote a chapter on the buildings of the college, remembers that Catto was always 'very encouraging and supportive' of him, which was especially important to Stephenson given that he had 'not done any serious academic work since Cambridge'. Working with Catto, who always had 'constructive criticisms' to offer, and being asked to contribute to the history of the college was 'a wonderful experience' for Stephenson, and he still feels 'honoured to have been entrusted with writing a chapter'. Professor John Stevenson, who wrote a number of the more modern chapters for the book, recalls that collaborating with Catto was a pleasure because he was an exemplary editor: 'He was efficient and he had the key qualities of knowing where he wanted to get to and decisiveness. The Oriel History of 2013 was an amazingly efficiently done operation given its multi-authored character. He didn't dither at meetings, but simply got on the phone to sort things out there and then.' Matthew Bool, who wrote a chapter on the college's buildings, describes Catto as a 'ruthlessly efficient' editor. When he submitted his chapter, Catto sent him his comments within a couple of weeks, which showed what 'a very skilled hand' he was. Those who knew Catto well have argued that editing the history of the college was a real labour of love for him. He poured a huge amount of himself into the book, and it is not unreasonable to argue that the end result will not be surpassed for quite some time. In the preface, the then Provost, Sir Derek Morris, concluded his remarks by singling out Catto for praise: 'I know from undertaking a similar exercise some years ago how totally draining the role of editor can be – far more so than producing one's own work – and the college is very indebted to Dr Catto for undertaking this project.'[195]

A few years after the history of Oriel College was published, the position of Provost came up and there was further good news for Catto when, in November 2017, his good friend, former colleague, and neighbour in Eydon, Mark Whittow, was appointed to the role. Not only was Catto delighted for Whittow personally, but he was also looking forward to having a friend and an ally as the next Provost, and he felt confident that Whittow was the ideal man to lead the college into a new era. Whittow, a distinguished historian and archaeologist, who specialised in the Byzantine Empire, had been mentored by Catto as a junior research fellow in 1984. Thereafter, he became a fellow at St Peter's College, and then at Corpus Christi. Like Catto himself, Whittow was, by all accounts, a quite superb and inspirational teacher. As the author can attest, he made dedicated medievalists out of undergraduates who had never studied anything other than modern history. Apart from his quite extraordinarily broad subject knowledge, what continues to stick in the memory for those who were fortunate enough to have been taught by him was the remarkable and infectious passion he displayed for his subject. It is this, above all else, that made him such a fantastic teacher.

Like Catto, Whittow was also a popular and much-loved character. Always nattily turned out and endlessly cheerful, he was difficult to miss, especially when he drove around Oxford in a battered, rusting, double-sized Land Rover that looked as if it had been on a journey across the desert (which it probably had). By nature generous and convivial, the parties he and his wife Helen hosted at Oxford and at Eydon for students, friends and colleagues became a highlight of the social calendar. Also like Catto, he saw such gatherings as a vital part of a broad liberal education. But the joy and pride which Catto felt at his friend's elevation proved to be tragically short-lived when, only a month after his appointment, Whittow was killed in a car accident on the evening of 23 December 2017, as he was on his way back home from Oxford. He was sixty years old. There is no doubt that the sudden and tragic death of his good friend was a shattering blow for Catto in his final years, and some who knew him well have even argued that he never fully recovered from the shock. Richard Davenport-Hines, who knew both Catto and Whittow, recalls that the two men always seemed to enjoy 'an instinctive unanimity on almost everything', and he concludes that Whittow's death was 'utterly devastating' for Catto. Julian Munby agrees and argues that the news of Whittow's death hit Catto hard, because 'with Mark in place as Provost everything he had wanted for the college was finally in place', and he wonders whether 'Jeremy just gave up at that point when Mark died'. Alexander Morrison adds that the untimely death of Mark Whittow 'knocked the stuffing out of him', and he ends his remarks by saying that Catto 'was a shadow of his former self' after Whittow's death.

Aside from family and friends, one thing which sustained Catto during these difficult moments was his Roman Catholic faith. In fact, according to his obituary in *The Times*, this was an area of his life that became increasingly important to him during his last decade. Although he was always present at college chapel during his time at Oriel, he did not attend Catholic services on a regular basis. But when he retired and moved permanently to Northamptonshire, he joined his local Catholic church, the Sacred Heart and Our Lady, at Aston-le-Walls and attended its services every Sunday. As has previously been noted, Catto was very effective at compartmentalising his life, and his faith was, for the most part, a strictly private matter. But given how important religion was to him, it is worth trying to establish the exact nature of his faith, in order to gain a further insight into his character.

Although Catto spoke to very few people about his Catholicism, one in whom he did confide was Dominique Dubois, who was one of his earliest undergraduates and then one of his first postgraduates in the late 1960s and early 1970s. The two men had many discussions about their shared faith, and Dubois prefaces his remarks by pointing out that a person's faith is, for most people and to varying degrees, a very private matter. But he goes on to stress that the difference between the public and private side of Catto's life was 'huge'. He then brings up two additional points. First, as an Oriel man, Catto was very much drawn towards Cardinal Newman's example. Secondly, Dubois mentions the historic state visit to Britain of Pope Benedict XVI in September 2010 for the beatification of Newman. The event took place at Cofton Park in Birmingham, and Dubois confirms that Catto was present in the audience, as part of an Oriel delegation. He says that being there on that day was 'very important' for Catto, as it seemed that all the things that mattered to him were finally coming together at that precise moment.

Reflecting further on the many conversations they had over the years, Dubois emphasises what he regards as the essential nature of Catto's faith: 'His relationship with God was very central to his life, but also very private. He had a contemplative approach to his faith. It was private and very deep, even though it may have waxed and waned over the years.' Perhaps the best way to measure just how important his faith was to him is to consider that it was one of the few subjects about which he would rarely, if ever, make jokes. Dubois agrees and says: 'It was something he never joked about with me.' For a man who saw the funny side of most things, it is somehow especially revealing that his faith was not viewed as a suitable object of humour.

Catto's funeral was held at the Oratory in Oxford, and Dubois believes that everything about the service, which was organised by John

Wolfe, provided a series of illuminating insights into the nature of his faith. First, the choice of the Oratory was itself suggestive in that the church is very much part of the traditional wing of the Catholic Church. Secondly, the entire Mass was in Old Latin and almost all of it was sung which, once again, suggests a preference for the more traditional side of the Church. Thirdly, the choice of the hymn 'Be Thou My Vision' can also be seen as quite revealing, not least as it was chosen by Catto personally, but also in the sense that the words used in the hymn express a profound and intimate relationship with God, which appears to be consistent with the very private nature of Catto's faith. In addition, and perhaps most importantly, the choice of Newman's prayer 'May He Support' also 'says a great deal', according to Dubois. To convey its overall meaning, it is worth quoting it in full: 'May He support us all the day long, till the shades lengthen, and the evening comes, and the busy world is hushed, and the fever of life is over, and our work is done. Then in His mercy may He give us safe lodging, and a holy rest, and peace at the last'. Quite apart from the lyrical beauty of the words, which would have appealed to Catto's aesthetic sense, the message itself is important because it expresses a deep trust in God's care for an individual throughout life until the moment of death. Finally, the choice of John 17:24 is also interesting, because it is the last chapter before the Passion and is therefore considered to be among the most intimate of Jesus' sayings, in which he promises that his followers will be with him always, including in eternity.

During the last year of his life, Catto was suffering from the prostate cancer that would eventually kill him. Characteristically, he kept his personal affairs to himself, and only a few of his closest friends and family members knew that he was ill. Some only found out that he was unwell right at the end of his life. Julian Munby recalls: 'I did not realise he was unwell until the end. I had a short conversation over the phone with him and told him that I would come and see him, but he died shortly afterwards.' Other friends who visited him at this stage could see that Catto was approaching the end of his life. Sir Alan Duncan, who visited him in July of that year, and was clearly moved by what he saw, wrote the following in his diary:

I drive over to Eydon to see Jeremy Catto. He is upstairs in his dressing gown sitting in a chair beside his bed, not able to go down the stairs. He is dying. I know the look. He is sunken-faced, drifts in and out of wanting to talk, has to make every effort to concentrate,

214

and talks of his will and funeral. I don't think he will last the
summer. I stay for about forty minutes, but just know in my heart
that it's the last time I'll see him.[196]

According to Ken Fincham, however, it was also typical of him that
his sense of humour did not desert him even towards the end of his life.
'He admitted to being put on female hormone treatment so warned that
he would appear next in a skirt and heels. The last time I saw him he was
off to see Sir Michael Howard in the country and admitted there was a
competitive edge as to who was least ill.' Richard Cross also remembers
that, even in his final days, Catto liked to joke that 'the tube which took
the whiskey down into his body was working rather better than the one
for food'.

Catto was cared for at home virtually until the end, with doctors from
the local medical centre coming out to see him. But after requiring a
blood transfusion, he was taken to the John Radcliffe Hospital where,
after slipping into a coma, he died at 8.30 a.m. on 17 August 2018. By
an extraordinary coincidence, the doctor who treated him was a fellow
of Oriel College. His memorial service took place on 2 November and
was held, fittingly enough, at St Mary's the University Church, which
stands directly opposite Oriel. His ashes were buried in an urn in the
churchyard cemetery at the Catholic church in Aston-le-Walls not far
from his home in Eydon. A testament to his character, influence and
popularity can be glimpsed from the fact that the service was attended by
over 500 people. Many of those present on the day remarked that, despite
the sadness, the overall mood of the service was celebratory. His friend
A.N. Wilson summed it up perfectly in his memoirs, when he described
the service as 'an astounding event, at which politicians, actors, the
occasional rock star, men and women of letters mingled with medievalist
scholars in the packed Oratory Church in Oxford…to say goodbye to
one of the truly great university teachers of the age'.[197]

20

Legacy

'His legacy is the betterment of all those with whom he came into contact'.
                                                    – Sir Alan Duncan

'When a great man dies, for years the light he leaves behind him, lies on the paths of men.'
                                                    – Henry Wadsworth Longfellow

'He gave me England.'
                                                    – John Wolfe

---

IN THE FINAL ANALYSIS, HAVING ATTEMPTED TO PIECE TOGETHER THE many different strands of Jeremy Catto's life, how does one sum up his overall life and legacy? It is worth noting that the man himself would almost certainly have laughed at the very idea of discussing such a question. Not out of a sense of false modesty, but because he would have viewed such language in relation to himself as frightfully pompous. However, the vast majority of people interviewed for this book would take a very different view and what follows, therefore, is a series of testaments from friends, colleagues and students who knew him well over the course of many years. They have been kind enough to reflect on this question and to offer their thoughts on what his life meant to them.

Sir Alan Duncan, who knew Catto very well for several decades, has no hesitation in saying that Catto's legacy rests in the fact that he provided a 'unique and enduring example of what an enlightened don should be'. According to Sir Alan, Catto 'was an educator in the broadest sense, and that is how he would have liked to have been remembered'. But perhaps most importantly, 'his legacy is the betterment of all those with whom he came into contact'. On a more personal note, following Catto's death, Sir Alan penned the following tribute to his friend in his diary: 'Jeremy was one of the few great influences on my life. Witty, stimulating, perceptive: just one of those constant underpinnings in everything I have done or thought since I first arrived in Oxford in 1976.'[198]

Lord Hague, who met Catto at Oxford, says that the impression he made on the young is his greatest legacy.

> I liked him and greatly respected him. He combined great knowledge with a mischievous sense of humour about people, current and historic, that was never malicious but always very observant and perceptive. Even if you were discussing something serious in history or politics, he was never far away from a chuckle and an amusing interjection. He was supportive, engaging, unpretentious, sociable, individual – not a bad example for how to live when in contact with a lot of impressionable young people.

Lord Hannan describes Catto as 'a don who shaped two successive generations of undergraduates, whose connections in politics and government were matchless, and who, more than anyone else, ensured the survival of that temperate High Toryism that is peculiar to England'. In particular, he stresses the impact Catto had on 'hundreds of men and women whose minds were touched by his':

> They may not all be conscious of his influence, and they are certainly not all conservatives, but his trace can be found somewhere in their bibliographies and footnotes. Over four decades, he sent people into Whitehall, Westminster, the City and the universities who carried with them a touch of his amused, quizzical, detached approach to the great questions of life. I'd call that a magnificent legacy.[199]

Lord Sumption believes that Catto's legacy is hard to pin down, not least as the world he inhabited largely no longer exists:

Jeremy belonged to another world. He lived at a time when Oxford mattered, dons mattered, the Middle Ages mattered, and England's past mattered, all propositions which he took for granted, but have ceased to hold. As a result, he will leave little in the way of a legacy, other than the affection of the many students and scholars who crossed his path. I do not think that he would have minded.

Sir David Manning also feels that Catto's overall legacy is 'hard to encapsulate in one pithy sentence', but adds that 'it includes a fine legacy as a scholar and academic administrator; a key contributor to the renovation of Oriel's finances and buildings; a great teacher and tutor; and a loyal, generous and endlessly amusing friend'.

Sir Richard Stagg believes that the term 'legacy' is a difficult one, but in terms of the influence which Catto had on him, he refers to three specific points. First, he says that 'Catto greatly helped to develop my intellectual rigour and clarity', in particular in regards to a certain kind of 'unwillingness to be too influenced by the smoke of battle'. Secondly, 'the way he taught history made one also interested in politics, because the way he taught the medieval world made one think differently about the contemporary world'. All of this gave Sir Richard a certain intellectual confidence later in life and made him believe that he was 'always 30 love up'. Finally, and perhaps on a more personal level, Catto encouraged him to think that a career in the Foreign Office might be for him.

Professor Sir Niall Ferguson highlights three areas for Catto's overall legacy: his scholarship, his teaching and a sense of fellowship: 'As a scholar he was an exceptional figure, but one who wore his learning lightly. Although I was never taught by him, tutorials were by all accounts memorable experiences and, beyond even that, Catto gave time to our extracurricular activities which was enormously valuable, intellectually stimulating and helped to set high standards.'

John Varley believes that Catto's legacy can be seen on both an institutional and personal level. In regards to the former, Varley describes Catto as 'the standout academic figure at Oriel for decades', as well as 'a very big figure in the history faculty'. On a personal level, Varley adds that Catto had a genuinely profound impact on him – he says that he got a degree at Oxford of which he was proud, but that it was 'entirely due to Catto'. More broadly, he feels that Catto's impact on him was not only profound, but also 'entirely beneficial'. 'Quite a lot of who I am today and how I think about things, I ascribe to him,' he concludes.

Harry Mount points out that Catto provided an important lesson in how to lead one's life:

> Like Norman Stone at Worcester and Angus Macintyre at
> Magdalen, he was a glimpse into grown-up life and how to get the
> best out of it. Read lots, take pleasure in history and work hard, but
> not too hard. Life was for living, too, for conversation and pleasure.
> All three were the last fragments of an earlier age, where dons
> weren't forever turning out unreadable articles for unread periodicals
> to justify their jobs. They liked teaching and the company of the
> young and drew you out of yourself.

Professor Ken Fincham, meanwhile, thinks that Catto's legacy is based on the care and attention he put into each of his students:

> The importance of nurturing the young, encouraging rather than
> checking them; of tutorial conversations not monologues; of
> putting British history in its European context (he would now be
> embracing global history). I did a PhD on the pastoral work of
> the Jacobean episcopate, and he urged me to learn Hungarian and
> do a comparison with Hungarian bishops. Only then could I fully
> appreciate what was distinctive about James' bishops and what
> united bishops across confessional divides.

Professor James Clark stresses Catto's legacy as a scholar of a very particular kind: 'Jeremy's career spanned a period in which universities and their academic life in the UK were wholly transformed. For me, his legacy is the example of the possibility of excellence as a scholar and a teacher without careerism, earnestness, self-absorption or spite.'

Professor Jonathan Hughes feels that pinning down Catto's overall legacy is an almost impossible task, as there were so many sides to his life. In terms of Catto's contribution to the world of scholarship, Hughes cites 'his work on the Lollards and the evolution of the Church in that period, as well as the influence of Henry V on the Church'. More broadly, Hughes adds that Catto's legacy rests on 'the meaning of friendship, the joys of learning and education viewed as an all-round experience, not as a career, and the beauty of life, which was there for Jeremy to be enjoyed and sampled'. For Hughes, who came from a 'fairly bleak background' in New Zealand, this was especially important, as Catto 'taught him how rich life could be'. In summing up his thoughts, Hughes references a quote attributed to Oscar Wilde, which he feels also applied to Catto: 'He put his talent into his work, and his genius into his life.'

Professor Martin Conway mentions Catto's 'warm conviviality', adding that there were a number of things he enjoyed about being in his company, including the 'witty sparring with him, the ability to disagree with each other, and the ironic but not malicious sense of humour'. Conway remembers with great fondness that Catto enjoyed 'lampooning people who felt they had the big answer' and that this was a very significant part of his appeal. As for his overall legacy, Conway says without hesitation that it is 'a very real one', by which he means that in the world of contemporary Oxford, Catto 'encouraged us to think about history as a game to enjoy, to debate and to discuss, and that history is there to be enjoyed'.

Dr Alexander Morrison believes that Catto's legacy rests on his unique and memorable personality, which impressed itself on generations of his undergraduates. According to Morrison, Catto 'showed that you could break the mould and do things differently, so long as you backed it up intellectually'.

Dr Robert Portass undoubtedly admires Catto for his scholarship, but the question of his legacy is quite simple: 'We didn't need another book on the Wars of the Roses. Jeremy made countless people feel that their lives were a bit better after having met him.'

For David Freedman, Catto's legacy is based on his extraordinary intellect: 'Long into my business career, and still to this day, I will occasionally be asked who were the most impressive intellects I have encountered, influencing me through close association. Jeremy always sits, in this respect, alongside Kaspar Cassani – erstwhile CEO of IBM Europe and chairman of IBM World Trade Corporation, for whom I used to write speeches – at the top of that particular tree.'

Simon MacKinnon has a very vivid memory of Catto and remembers his 'enjoyment of a good tipple, his willingness to crack a smile over a drink, as the cheeks reddened, and he became different to the tutor or the Senior Dean, but with the intellectual horsepower that was then also accompanied with humour'. More significantly, he adds that 'if every decade you have an important mentor in your life, then you are lucky'. Catto, he says, was one of those people for him, who 'made possible my career' and was also 'one of those people who influenced the person I am today'.

Guy Monson believes that Catto's legacy is best summed up in his ability to encourage civilised debate. He was able 'to create an atmosphere at Oxford that was conducive to thought, discussion and, very often, laughter'. His influence 'made people think about the world in a different way and made them debate in a different way, but he did not force his ideas down your throat. He was a great listener and he was brilliant at steering you towards thinking about things in a more logical and structured manner'.

Simon Kingston agrees that Catto's legacy has several strands, and he is an optimist in regards to the lasting nature of that legacy:

> His legacy will, of course, include his scholarship: the work on Lollardism, the gifted editing of the history of Oriel, and also some of the later pieces (I especially like the one on the rise of management speak in Henry V's administration). I think, though, it will be for his way of being: a gentle, tolerant, conviction about the tradition of which he was part, that will be what people chiefly remember and wish they could emulate.

And although it has been pointed out that Catto was part of an already dying tradition when he began his academic career, Kingston is more optimistic:

> I think Jeremy inspired several generations, now well beyond Oxford, with a buoyant view of life. He was confident in this life and the next, but modest in how he expressed this. He was confident also about the Western Christian tradition and helped form the next generation to live in it. He was against the rampage of the narrow specialist, but, in that, I suspect his time is coming again. The world needs more of what I would call 'networked generalists', and he helped to make lots of them. He would have thought any such summary very pompous, but I do think it is true.

Nick Lord left the country not long after his time at Oriel came to an end in 1995, and never saw Catto again, but he is clear in his mind about Catto's legacy: 'Jeremy was an ally, a teacher, and a guide, who embodied the college more than any other don, and who was as much a part of Oriel as Front Quad. I still see him as a formative figure who changed my life, for which I will always be deeply, deeply grateful.'

Konsta Helle, one of Catto's last undergraduates, says the following on Catto's overall legacy:

I am eternally grateful to Jeremy for admitting me to Oriel and for changing my life in ways I could have never imagined. I am sure I could have got into some other college, and would have still had a great time at Oxford, but without Jeremy and Oriel as I came to know it and love it, my life then and afterwards would have been much poorer. Some men affect your life by their writings, others by what they say. In the case of Jeremy, he affected you by his personality – by being there for you. His legacy mainly lives on in the minds, memories and characters of those whose lives he so deeply affected and enriched, and who knew him and benefited from his presence and kindness and friendship in college and beyond. Perhaps the most important thing about him was the presence; that he was always and everywhere in college and took part in everything, and thereby created a strong sense of belonging to one big multi-generational family. University was then not about exams or essays but about sowing the seeds for living a good life, in all its variety and richness, which would bear fruit in years to come.

A final tribute to Jeremy Catto comes from John Wolfe:

I knew Jeremy for nearly 60 years, and his influence and legacy operated at every level. He is remembered as vividly by those whom he taught for a term as those who became his closest friends; his legacy is definitely a living one. From my biased perception, he gave me England; and cultivated a curiosity and intellectual scope that I would not have developed if I had not had his friendship over all those years. He didn't have to be physically there to be present and an influence. Our initial dispute over the value of the sociology of knowledge versus the history of ideas was quite early and easily resolved and I ultimately learned the true nature of trust and the value of companionship.

In the end, therefore, as the above testimonies suggest, it is fair to conclude that if Catto does leave behind a legacy, it is not one that can be easily measured or quantified. Catto only retired in 2006 and died in 2018, but he is remembered primarily because he represented a world that has largely vanished. As such, this book has tried to convey all the ways in which he was almost unique even in his own time. His sense of humour, although never unkind and always gentle, could be outrageous by present-day standards. His teaching style and some of his more eccentric habits during tutorials would be hard to imagine at universities today. His views on only publishing if he had something new and interesting to say would be almost impossible to reconcile with the current pressures to publish on a regular basis. His constant presence in Oriel over forty years and his active involvement in all manner of college activities, would today be viewed as an anachronism, as college life is a much more transactional affair than it was when Catto first arrived at Oxford. Finally, his quite extraordinary network of contacts, ranging across the worlds of academia, politics, diplomacy, the arts and even royalty, is no longer a feature of an Oxford don's life. In short, he was the quintessential Oxford don. Sadly, the world has moved on to quite a significant extent in a relatively short period of time, with the result that we will never see his like again.

So, if it is possible to sum up his legacy in a single sentiment, then perhaps one can say the following: Catto left his mark, as all great teachers do, on the hundreds of men and women who were fortunate enough to have been taught by him. As the American poet Henry Wadsworth Longfellow once said, 'when a great man dies, for years the light he leaves behind him, lies on the paths of men'. That is Jeremy Catto's legacy. Or, less pompously, as the man himself undoubtedly would have preferred, and as Helen Whittow put it so brilliantly in her eulogy for Catto: 'He has – in his own expression – become a stiff; but he will not be forgotten by any of us.'[200]

Acknowledgments

IN RESEARCHING THIS BOOK, I HAVE RELIED HEAVILY ON THE STORIES, memories and anecdotes of the many men and women who, over the course of nearly four decades, had the good fortune to be taught by Jeremy Catto. For this, I am especially grateful to Lord Mendoza, the Provost of Oriel College, for providing me with access to the Oriel Alumni Network.

In researching Catto's personal biographical background, I am hugely indebted to John Wolfe, as well as Jeremy's sister, Annabel Flowers, who provided much of the background to Catto's early life and upbringing.

In an effort to do at least some proper historical research, I also spent time in the archives of Balliol College, Catto's old Oxford college, to find out more about how his time at Oxford as an undergraduate in the late 1950s shaped his outlook and future life. I would also like to thank the archivist at Oriel College, who granted me access to the college files on Catto, which enabled me to research the Oxford years in greater detail. In addition, I am indebted to Professor Blair Worden and Judith Curthoys for being so kind as to grant me access to the Hugh Trevor-Roper archives at Christ Church, Oxford.

I must also thank my publisher at Unicorn, as well as my editors, for their patience and unstinting work in helping me to put together the final version of this book. Napoleon is reputed to have said that history is a set of lies agreed upon. I sincerely hope and believe that there are no lies in this book, but any errors that may have crept in are, of course, all mine.

Finally, I would like to pay tribute to my wonderful and long-suffering wife, Rosanna, who has had to learn to live with the many and varied facets of Jeremy Catto's life over the past year. She did not ask for any of this, and I am very grateful for her patience, as well as her advice, when that has been requested. Without her, this book would not have been written.

Selected Bibliography

- Annan, Noel; *The Dons* (London: Harper Perennial, 1999).

- Bracewell, Michael; *Roxy Music, 1953–1972: The Band that Invented an Era* (London: Faber & Faber, 2008).

- Catto, Jeremy (ed.); *Oriel College: A History* (Oxford: Oxford University Press, 2013).

- Davenport-Hines, Richard; *Sex, Death and Punishment* (London: HarperCollins, 1990).

- Davenport-Hines, Richard and Sisman, Adam (eds); *One Hundred Letters from Hugh Trevor-Roper* (Oxford: Oxford University Press, 2006).

- Davenport-Hines, Richard; *Universal Man: The Seven Lives of John Maynard Keynes* (London: William Collins, 2015).

- Duncan, Alan; *In the Thick of it: The Private Diaries of a Minister* (London: Harper Collins, 2021).

- Ferguson, Niall; *Always Right: How Margaret Thatcher Saved Britain* (Odyssey Editions, 2016).

- Heald, Tim; *My Dear Hugh: Letters from Richard Cobb to Hugh Trevor-Roper and others* (London: Frances Lincoln, 2011).

- Jackson, Dan; *The Northumbrians: North-East England and its People – A New History* (London: Hurst Publishers, 2019).

- Macintyre, Ben; *The Spy and the Traitor: The Greatest Espionage Story of the Cold War* (London: Penguin Random House, 2018).

- Mains, Brian and Tuck, Anthony; *The Royal Grammar School, Newcastle-upon-Tyne: A History of the School in its Community* (Hull: Oriel Press, 1986).

- Sandbrook, Dominic; *Never Had It So Good: A History of Britain from Suez to the Beatles* (London: Little Brown, 2005).

- Sisman, Adam; *Hugh Trevor-Roper: The Biography* (London: Weidenfeld & Nicolson, 2010).

- Wilson, A.N.; *Confessions: A Life of Failed Promises* (London: Bloomsbury, 2022).

Notes

Introduction

1 Noel Annan, *The Dons* (London: Harper Perennial, 1999), p.5.

2 *Ibid.*, p.6.

Early Life

3 Dan Jackson, *The Northumbrians: North-East England and its People – A New History* (London: Hurst Publishers, 2019), p.30.

4 E.H.H. Green, *Oxford Dictionary of National Biography* (Oxford: Oxford University Press, 2004), entry for Thomas Catto.

5 Record of C. Attlee's speech at Catto's retirement, Bank of England archives, G21.

6 Green, *Oxford Dictionary of National Biography.*

7 *Ibid.*

8 *Ibid.*

9 Nicholas Faith, 'Lord Catto', *The Independent*, 22 September 2001.

10 Andrew Roth, 'Lord Catto', *The Guardian*, 7 September 2001.

11 Faith, 'Lord Catto'.

12 *Ibid.*

13 *Ibid.*

14 Richard Roberts, *Oxford Dictionary of National Biography* online (Oxford: Oxford University Press, 2005), entry for Stephen Catto.

Novocastrian

15 Speech by HM The Queen, 21 April 1947.

16 'Collingwood, forgotten hero of Trafalgar', *Manchester Guardian*, 1 March 1910.

17 Brian Mains and Anthony Tuck, *The Royal Grammar School, Newcastle-upon-Tyne: A History of the School in its Community* (Hull: Oriel Press, 1986), p.292.

18 *Ibid.*, p.221.

19 *Ibid.*, p.223.

20 *Ibid.*

21 *Ibid.*, p.251.

22 *Ibid.*, p.295.

23 Catto tribute to Sidney Middlebrook in *The Novocastrian*, July 1958, p.14.

24 Balliol College archives.

25 Mains and Tuck, *The Royal Grammar School*, p.237.

26 *Ibid.*, p.239.

27 *Ibid.*

28 Mains and Tuck, *The Royal Grammar School*, p.297.

29 *Ibid.*

30 Balliol College archives.

31 Mains and Tuck, *The Royal Grammar School*, p.251.

32 *Ibid.*, p.295.

33 Jeremy Catto, *That'll be the Day! 1950s Newcastle* (Newcastle: Tyne Bridge Publishing, 2012).

34 Mains and Tuck, *The Royal Grammar School*, pp.241–2

35 Balliol College archives.

Balliol

36 Harold Macmillan, speech to Conservative party rally in Bedford, July 1957.

37 C.H. Rolph, *The Trial of Lady Chatterley* (Harmondsworth: Penguin Books, 1961).

38 Brian Harrison (ed.), *The History of the University of Oxford, Volume VIII, The Twentieth Century* (Oxford: Oxford University Press, 1994), p.209.

39 The Oxford Union archives.

40 'Oxford Letters', *The Novocastrian*, 1 April 1958.

41 Harrison (ed.), *History of the University of Oxford, Volume VIII*, p.206.

42 *Ibid.*

43 Balliol College archives.

44 Christopher Tyerman, 'Maurice Keen obituary', *The Guardian*, 26 September 2012.

45 Christopher Tyerman, *Maurice Hugh Keen 1933–2012* (London: British Academy, 2016), p.88.

46 *Ibid.*, p.75.

47 Maurice Keen, *Oxford Dictionary of National Biography* (Oxford: Oxford University Press, 2005), entry for Richard Southern.

48 'Oxford Letters', *The Novocastrian*, March 1959.

49 A.N. Wilson, *Confessions: A Life of Failed Promises* (London: Bloomsbury, 2022), p.217.

50 'Jeremy Catto, much-loved Oxford historian – obituary', *The Daily Telegraph*, 21 August 2018.

51 *Ibid.*

52 'Jeremy Catto', *The Times*, 19 September 2018.

53 Letter from R.W. Southern, 10 August 1961, Balliol College archives.

54 *Ibid.*

55 Letter from the college authorities to Catto, 16 October 1961, Balliol College archives.

56 Letter from Catto to the Master of College, 21 October 1961, Balliol College archives.

57 Letter from R.W. Southern, 10 August 1961, Balliol College archives.

John

58 Richard Davenport-Hines, *Universal Man: The Seven Lives of John Maynard Keynes* (London: William Collins, 2015).

59 'Eastern and Western Europeans Differ on Importance of Religion, Views of Minorities, and Key Social Issues', Pew Research Center, 29 October 2018, p.12.

60 Brian Lewis, *Wolfenden's Witnesses: Homosexuality in Postwar Britain* (London: Palgrave Macmillan, 2016), p.275.

61 'Homosexual Offences and Prostitution', Parliamentary Debates (Hansard), House of Lords, 4 December 1957, col. 734.

62 James Crighton Robertson, *The Hidden Cinema: British Film Censorship in Action, 1913–1975* (London/New York: Routledge, 1993), p.120.

63 Richard Davenport-Hines, *Sex, Death and Punishment* (London: HarperCollins, 1990), p.314.

64 *Ibid.*

65 *Ibid.*, p.315.

66 *Ibid.*, p.316.

67 *Ibid.*, p.326.

68 *Ibid.*, pp.326–7.

69 *Ibid.*

70 *Ibid.*, p.287.

71 *Ibid.*, p.297.

72 *Ibid.*, p.291.

73 *Ibid.*

74 Dominic Sandbrook, *Never Had It So Good: A History of Britain from Suez to the Beatles* (London: Little Brown, 2005), p.599.

75 *Ibid.*, p.600.

76 *Ibid.*

77 *Ibid.*

78 *Ibid.*, p.601.

Durham Interlude

79 Stanley Cohen, *Folk Devils and Moral Panics: The Creation of the Mods and Rockers* (Oxford: Routledge, 2002).

80 Balliol College archives.

81 *Ibid.*

82 *Ibid.*

83 *Ibid.*

84 *Ibid.*

85 *Ibid.*

86 R.W. Southern, *Smalley, Beryl, 1905–1984* (London: British Academy, 2016), p.72.

87 Balliol College archives.

88 Michael Bracewell, *Roxy Music, 1953–1972: The Band that Invented an Era* (London: Faber & Faber, 2008), p.158.

89 Dave Simpson, 'The Reader Interview', *The Guardian*, 28 April 2022.

90 *Ibid.*

91 Bracewell, *Roxy Music*, p.157.

92 *Ibid.*

93 *Ibid.*, p.158.

94 Jeremy Catto email to James Valance-White, 23 June 2014.

95 Bracewell, *Roxy Music*, p.159.

96 *Ibid.*, p.160.

97 *Ibid.*, p.159.

98 *Ibid.*

Prague Spring

99 'The Prague Spring, 1968', Library Congress [retrieved 5 January 2008].

100 'Jeremy Catto, much-loved Oxford historian – obituary', *The Daily Telegraph*, 21 August 2018.

Oriel

101 'Chancellor sees no cause for gloom', *The Times*, 21 July 1969, p.3.

102 'The investiture of the Prince of Wales', National Archives.

103 Adam Sisman, *Hugh Trevor-Roper: The Biography* (London: Weidenfeld & Nicolson, 2010), pp.299–300.

104 *Ibid.*, p.299.

105 *Ibid.*, p.300.

106 *Ibid.*, p.299.

107 Richard Davenport-Hines and Adam Sisman (eds), *One Hundred Letters from Hugh Trevor-Roper* (Oxford: Oxford University Press, 2006), p.287.

108 Jeremy Catto (ed.), *Oriel College: A History* (Oxford: Oxford University Press, 2013), p.11.

109 *Ibid.*

110 *Ibid.*, p.768.

Teaching

111 Matthew Uffindell, 'The History of the Tutorial', Greene's College, Oxford.

112 *Ibid.*

113 *Ibid.*

114 Tim Heald, *My Dear Hugh: Letters from Richard Cobb to Hugh Trevor-Roper and others* (London: Frances Lincoln, 2011), pp.9–10.

115 Alan Duncan, 'The don who embodies Oxford', *The Spectator*, June 2006.

116 *Ibid.*

117 Daniel Hannan, 'Jeremy Catto: A Tribute', *Conservative History Journal*, 2006.

Tutorials

118 Adam Sisman, *Hugh Trevor-Roper: The Biography* (London: Weidenfeld & Nicolson, 2010), p.375.

119 Giles MacDonogh, 'Jeremy Catto', blog, 17 December 2018. Available from: http://www.macdonogh.co.uk/blog_archive.htm

120 E.H.H. Green, *Oxford Dictionary of National Biography* (Oxford: Oxford University Press, 2004), entry for K.B. Macfarlane.

121 Jeremy Catto, 'Lancastrian Kings and Lollards Knights', review of a collection of posthumous lectures by K.B. McFarlane, Durham University archives, December 1972.

122 Gray et al., 2002.

123 John Watts, 'Jeremy Catto (1939-2018): A tribute by John Watts', University of Oxford, 2018. Available from: https://www.history.ox.ac.uk/jeremy-catto-a-tribute-by-john-watts

124 Sisman, *Hugh Trevor-Roper*, p.414.

125 Richard Davenport-Hines and Adam Sisman (eds), *One Hundred Letters from Hugh Trevor-Roper* (Oxford: Oxford University Press, 2006).

126 Watts, 'Jeremy Catto (1939-2018)'.

College Man

127 Jeremy Catto (ed.), *Oriel College: A History* (Oxford: Oxford University Press, 2013), p.761.

Pastoral Matters

128 Evelyn Waugh, *Brideshead Revisited* (London: Chapman and Hall, 1945), ch.1.
129 Giles MacDonogh, 'Jeremy Catto', blog, 17 December 2018. Available from: www.macdonogh.co.uk/blog_archive.htm
130 *Ibid.*
131 *Ibid.*

Admissions

132 'Admissions bias', Oriel College archives, 1999.
133 *Ibid.*
134 *Ibid.*
135 *Ibid.*
136 *Ibid.*
137 *Ibid.*
138 *Ibid.*
139 *Ibid.*
140 *Ibid.*
141 *Ibid.*
142 *Ibid.*
143 *Ibid.*
144 *Ibid.*
145 *Ibid.*
146 Brian Harrison (ed.), *The History of the University of Oxford, Volume VIII, The Twentieth Century* (Oxford: Oxford University Press, 1994), p.193.
147 *Ibid.*, p.195.
148 *Ibid.*, p.194.
149 Hugh Stratton, 'Christopher Hill: some reminiscences', in D.H. Pennington and L. Thomas (eds), *Puritans and Revolutionaries: Essays in Honour of Christopher Hill* (Oxford: Oxford University Press, 1978), pp.14–15.

Women

150 Vera Britain, *The Women at Oxford: A Fragment of History* (New York: The Macmillan Company, 1960), p.156.

151 Jane Garnett and William Whyte, 'Women Making History: The centenary', Oxford University, 2020. Available from: https://www.ox.ac.uk/about/oxford-people/women-at-oxford/centenary
152 *Ibid.*
153 *Ibid.*
154 Jeremy Catto (ed.), *Oriel College: A History* (Oxford: Oxford University Press, 2013), pp.769–70.
155 Hugh Trevor-Roper letter to Eric Vallis, 29 July 1981, Chris Church archives.
156 Hugh Trevor-Roper letter to Jeremy Catto, 30 July 1981, Christ Church archives.
157 Eric Vallis letter to Hugh Trevor-Roper, 8 September 1981, Christ Church archives.
158 Catto, *Oriel College*, p.779.
159 *Ibid.*, p.780.
160 *Ibid.*

College Finances

161 Jeremy Catto (ed.), *Oriel College: A History* (Oxford: Oxford University Press, 2013), p.586.
162 *Ibid.*
163 *Ibid.*, pp.586–7.

History Faculty

164 Reba N. Soffer, 'Ch. 14: Moden History', in *The History of the University of Oxford – Volume VII; Nineteenth-Century Oxford, Part 2* (Oxford: Oxford University Press, 2000).
165 *Ibid.*
166 *Ibid.*
167 Jeremy Catto, 'Last Impressions', 2006, Oriel College archives.

Clubs and Networks

168 Daniel Hannan, 'Jeremy Catto: A Tribute', *Conservative History Journal*, 2006.
169 'Tory, Tory, Hallelujah', *Financial Times*, 1987.
170 Hannan, 'Jeremy Catto'.
171 *Ibid.*
172 Mat Youkee, 'Thatcher sent Pinochet finest scotch during former dictator's UK house arrest', *The Guardian*, 6 October 2019.

173 'A look at Lord Hoffmann', *BBC News*, 17 December 1998.

174 Alex Bellos and Jonathan Franklin, 'Pinochet receives a hero's welcome on his return', *The Guardian*, 4 March 2000.

175 Andrea Bianchi, 'Immunity versus human rights: the Pinochet case', *European Journal of International Law* (1999), pp.237–77.

176 Patrick O'Connor, 'Glynn Boyd Harte', *The Guardian*, 18 December 2018.

177 Alan Powers, 'Glynn Boyd Harte', *The Independent*, 18 December 2018.

178 'Glynn Boyd Harte – Artist'. Available from: https://www.cloudesleyassociation. org/about-the-area/194-glynn-boyd-harte-artist

179 Powers, 'Glynn Boyd Harte'.

180 O'Connor, 'Glynn Boyd Harte'.

181 A.N. Wilson, *Confessions: A Life of Failed Promises* (London: Bloomsbury, 2022), p.175.

182 Ben Williams, 'Lives Remembered', *The Times*, 24 October 2018.

183 Ben Macintyre, *The Spy and the Traitor: The Greatest Espionage Story of the Cold War* (London: Penguin Random House, 2018), p.186.

Eydon

184 Helen Malcolm, 'Eulogy for Jeremy Catto', 2 November 2018, University Church of St Mary the Virgin, Oxford.

185 'Jeremy Catto, much-loved Oxford historian – obituary', *The Daily Telegraph*, 21 August 2018.

186 A.N. Wilson, 'A.N. Wilson: The V&A's Tristram Hunt is a modern Prince Albert', *The Spectator*, 21 December 2019.

187 Karen De Young, 'The Oxford Connection', *Washington Post*, 17 June 1986.

188 A.N. Wilson, 'The Diary', *Financial Times*, 3 February 2012.

189 Malcom, 'Eulogy for Jeremy Catto'.

190 Hugh Trevor-Roper letter to Jeremy Catto, Christ Church archives.

191 Hugh Trevor-Roper letter to Jeremy Catto, 15 November 1972, Christ Church archives.

192 Richard Davenport-Hines, *Oxford Dictionary of National Biography* (Oxford: Oxford University Press, 2007), entry for Hugh Trevor-Roper.

193 Malcom, 'Eulogy for Jeremy Catto'.

Final Years

194 A.N. Wilson, 'Oriel: The college that shaped the spiritual heart of 19th century Britain', *The Spectator*, 5 April 2014.

195 Jeremy Catto (ed.), *Oriel College: A History* (Oxford: Oxford University Press, 2013), p. vi.

196 Alan Duncan, *In the Thick of it: The Private Diaries of a Minister* (London: Harper Collins, 2021), p.319.

197 A.N. Wilson, *Confessions: A Life of Failed Promises* (London: Bloomsbury, 2022), p.216.

Legacy

198 Alan Duncan, *In the Thick of it: The Private Diaries of a Minister* (London: Harper Collins, 2021), p.323.

199 Daniel Hannan, 'Jeremy Catto: A Tribute', *Conservative History Journal*, 2006.

200 Helen Malcolm, 'Eulogy for Jeremy Catto', 2 November 2018, University Church of St Mary the Virgin, Oxford.

Index